MAKING EASY LISTENING

Commerce and Mass Culture Series
JUSTIN WYATT, SERIES EDITOR

Making Easy Listening: Material Culture and Postwar American Recording
Tim J. Anderson

Citizen Spy: Television, Espionage, and Cold War Culture
Michael Kackman

Hollywood Outsiders: The Adaptation of the Film Industry, 1913–1934
Anne Morey

Robert Altman's Subliminal Reality
Robert T. Self

Sex and Money: Feminism and Political Economy in the Media
Eileen R. Meehan and Ellen Riordan, Editors

Directed by Allen Smithee
Jeremy Braddock and Stephen Hock, Editors

Sure Seaters: The Emergence of Art House Cinema
Barbara Wilinsky

Walter Wanger, Hollywood Independent
Matthew Bernstein

Hollywood Goes Shopping
David Desser and Garth S. Jowett, Editors

Screen Style: Fashion and Femininity in 1930s Hollywood
Sarah Berry

Active Radio: Pacifica's Brash Experiment
Jeff Land

MAKING

Easy
Listening

Material

Culture and

Postwar American

Recording

Tim J. Anderson

Commerce and Mass Culture Series

UNIVERSITY OF MINNESOTA PRESS
MINNEAPOLIS • LONDON

Lyrics from "There's a New Sound" (BMI Work #1489069) as coauthored by Tony Burrello and Tom Murray are reprinted courtesy of DBA Omnibus Music Co.

Portions of chapters 1 and 2 were originally published as "Buried under the Fecundity of His Own Creations: Rethinking the Stockpile, the Standing Reserve, and the Recording Bans of the American Federation of Musicians, 1942 to 1944 and 1948," *American Music,* Summer 2004.

Portions of chapters 3 and 4 were originally published as "Which Voice Best Becomes the Property? Tie-Ups, Intertexts, and Versioning in the Production of *My Fair Lady,*" *Spectator: The University of California Journal of Film and Television Criticism* 17, no. 2 (Spring/Summer 1997).

Published by the University of Minnesota Press
111 Third Avenue South, Suite 290
Minneapolis, MN 55401-2520
http://www.upress.umn.edu

LIBRARY OF CONGRESS CATALOGING-IN-PUBLICATION DATA
Anderson, Tim J.
    Making easy listening : material culture and postwar American recording / Tim J. Anderson.
        p.   cm. — (Commerce and mass culture series)
    Includes bibliographical references (p.   ) and index.
    ISBN 13: 978-0-8166-4517-6 (hc) — ISBN 13: 978-0-8166-4518-3 (pb)
    ISBN 10: 0-8166-4517-5 (hc : alk. paper) — ISBN 10: 0-8166-4518-3 (pb : alk. paper)
    1. Sound recording industry—United States—History.   2. Sound recordings—Production and direction—United States.   3. Popular culture—United States—History—20th century.   I. Title.   II. Series.
    ML3790.A63 2006
    781.490973—dc22
                                                                                    2005035679

Printed in the United States of America on acid-free paper

The University of Minnesota is an equal-opportunity educator and employer.

12 11 10 09 08 07 06   10 9 8 7 6 5 4 3 2 1

Is it so wrong, wanting to be at home with your record collection? It's not like collecting records is like collecting stamps, or beer-mats, or antique thimbles. There's a whole world in here, a nicer, dirtier, more violent, more peaceful, more colorful, sleazier, more dangerous, more loving world than the world I live in; there is history, and geography, and poetry, and countless other things I should have studied in school, including music.

—NICK HORNBY, *High Fidelity*

CONTENTS

ACKNOWLEDGMENTS

IN MANY WAYS THIS BOOK BEGINS IN THE RECORD STORES OF Arizona, particularly Circles, Roads to Moscow, Zias, Zips, Locos, Eastside Records, PDQs, and Dab Nabbit's. Some of these have folded, others grown, but my research began in the aisles and beside the counters of these stores. Like all good record stores, they provided me with a new way to imagine what the world was. Through imports, novelties, rarities, used catalogues, healthy debates, and heartfelt laughter, the people I met and worked with in these stores—people like Mike Cejka, Mike Pawlicki, Ned Simonson, Bruce Williams, Anne Cavness, and Jon Lauer—laid the foundation for this book. Even though I have lost touch with some of them, I consider them among my first serious teachers of why popular music matters.

My intellectual preparation for this work began when I was an undergraduate at the University of Arizona under the tutelage of Mary Beth Haralovich and Eileen Meehan. Each challenged me to think through media history and theory in a manner that kept audiences, artists, art, and social context in a vibrant dialogue where—while everything mattered—the writing should be focused on one specific problem at a time. They also encouraged me to ask the same questions at the graduate level and supported me as I often stumbled through my midtwenties, wondering whether I should be spending a significant chunk of my life in a city as cold as Chicago trying to answer questions few seemed to care about.

Luckily, I received gracious support from Northwestern University's Department of Radio/Television/Film, a department whose intellectual engagement was matched only by enthusiasm for study and the challenges of research. Here I learned how to become a scholar whose intensity would at least begin to match the demands of the objects and artists

I studied. This project began as a dissertation, and I am grateful for the guidance offered by Tom Gunning, Mimi White, and James Schwoch. Each provided honest, thoughtful criticisms and extended both intellectual and personal support throughout. This is particularly true of Jim, a fine scholar and a good friend whose advice helped nurture the core of this study. No doubt, without his influence this study would be dramatically different.

Writing, I have learned, never begins or ends: it is more of an ongoing conversation where those who listen with twice the effort of those speaking receive little of the credit but produce much of the clarity. The editorial work of Justin Wyatt and Andrea Kleinhuber has been of immeasurable influence on this project; every writer should have editors as attentive and as collaborative as Justin and Andrea. In the academy, where intelligence is abundant, grace is that quality that so many of us need yet few of us practice. Each of these editors possesses and practices grace, and without their insights and suggestions this collection of thoughts would be little more than that.

Along the way support for my research and encouragement to pursue the questions I examine throughout the study came in many forms. My friends and peers have been immensely important to this work and deserve recognition. Many thanks to Noah Lopez, Susan White, Anahid Khassabian, Keir Keightley, Rebecca Leydon, Randall Doane, Tony Grajeda, Rick Altman, Jay Beck, Amanda Lotz, Daniel Goldmark, Suzanne Condray, Steve Waksman, Lisbeth Lipari, Dave Gilbert, Lonelle Yoder, Heather Pristash, Levi Stahl, Deborah Singer, Rhonda Morgan, Deron "Mookie" Overpeck, Dave Hammargren, Jess Walker, Julie Lindstrom, Priya Jaikimur, Mark Kligerman, Richard Leider, Bill Bush, Patti Matheny, Edmund Chibeau, Barbara Willinksy-Selznick, Anna McCarthy, Laurel Kennedy, Cathy Coppolillo, Stacey Bailey, Saylor Breckenridge, Bob Fanning, Angie Record, Nina Martin, Bonnie Keene, Anne Chase, Marc Giordano, Laura Pierce, Chris Hayden, Deborah White, Tim Porges, Jennifer Blackwood, Nicole Gonzalez, Ingrid Cardon-Downey, Laura Hensel, Renay Wilson, Sandra Collins, Donna Dudgeon, Susanne Block and Yves Deval-Block, Laura Kissel, Peter Sarram, Larra Clark, and Derek and Sally Kompare. I cannot say enough to express how much each person has assisted me during this research. Their affection and intellectual curiosities have kept me in clover throughout a long and trying part of my life, and these efforts cannot go forgotten.

This book is dedicated to *mi familia*: Ken and Carmen Anderson, Monica, Cristina, Annette, Nana and Tata, Grandma and Grandpa. Their support has been the most spiritual and miraculous of all. Whenever I found myself in a bind, whether it be spiritual, emotional, or intellectual, family members would do all they could to bolster my spirit and strengthen my hand. I thank them, knowing full well that I am lucky: not every family is as supportive as mine. For this reason, my book is dedicated to the Andersons, the Pereydas, the Guzmans, and the Wilburns. With a sense of wonder I acknowledge how the people who have come before me and left, the very people who will never read this book, have ultimately had the greatest influence on its composition. I love you all.

Introduction

Opening Tracks

There's a new sound
The newest sound around
The strangest sound that you have ever heard
Not like a wild boar or a jungle lion's roar
It isn't like the cry of any bird
But there's a new sound
And it's deep down in the ground
And everyone who listens to it squirms
Because this new sound, so deep down in the ground
Is the sound that's made by worms

IN 1952 SONGWRITER AND JAZZ PIANIST TONY BURELLO AND
his colleague Tom Murray found themselves in an interesting dilemma.
Although their collaborative efforts had yielded a small catalogue of
what they considered to be attractive, if not excellent, songs, they had
been unable to persuade any prominent artists to record their material.
Particularly annoyed by the situation the two concluded, "We are in an
era where good is bad and bad is good" (quoted in Demento 1995, 7).
And, as the story goes, "with that they set out to write the worst song
they could imagine." Half of what the duo composed is the above set of

lyrics. The other half is a less-than-impressive arrangement. On its face, there really isn't much to "There's a New Sound." With a flat melody, the lyrics are spoken, not sung, in an emphatic monotone over and over while accompanied by a repetitive, fast-paced "looping" phrase. With each repetition the passage is raised a half-step until the song ends, an exercise that, even effected by an initiate songwriter, betrays a simplicity bordering on the disgusting. To emphasize this point the team released a recording of the song on their very own "Horrible" record label. With its slogan printed on every record, the Horrible label proclaimed, "If It's Really a Horrible Record—It's Bound to Be a Hit." Adding one-half tongue-in-cheek sales pitch to one-half prescient understanding of the revolution-in-sound-to-come, the record was a hit, "selling well into six figures by spring 1953" (Demento 1995, 7). Yet despite its initial popularity, the song has for the most part receded from the memory of the general public: "There's a New Sound" is rarely heard, almost never performed live, and it would be hard to imagine any self-respecting music educator ever mentioning it. If anything, one can attribute the song's obscurity to the fact that it is, aesthetically if not technically, unperformable. Still the song continues to live on, albeit if only with a popularity limited to personal record collections and the occasional inclusion on novelty record compilations.

Yet its occasional appearance on these anthologies is puzzling: one would suppose the record's actual "novelty" would have worn thin by now. But I think there is a simple explanation: while Burello and Murray wrote an insufferable song, they produced a wonderful record. Opening the record is an unidentifiable noise that resembles a gurgling/whining/coughing voice that for close to ten seconds repeatedly enunciates "WHEEZ-A WACK, WHEEZ-A WACK." Buried under layers upon layers of electric reverberation effects, the voice leads into the beginning of the song and quickly disappears as the singer proclaims, "There's a new sound/the newest sound around." Reciting these words (one could hardly call them lyrics), our orator reminds us, over and over, that the sound is neither that of a "jungle lion's roar" nor "the cry of any bird." Rather the record provides the listener with a sound that ostensibly represents a "lion's roar" in addition to the "honk" of a bicycle horn. And the sounds, they keep on coming. Throughout, the narrator is supported and his audiences barraged by what sounds like a small pipe organ that pumps out another, even more annoying, duo of notes. And once our narrator notes that this new sound "is the sound that's made by worms," we once again hear the "WHEEZ-A WACK, WHEEZ-A WACK" sound, which is, of course, worms.

Of course the "sound of worms" really isn't the "sound" of worms. The sound, which supposedly comes from "deep down in the ground," is actually an effect-laden recording of a human voice, most likely produced by a recording made at a slower than usual tape speed. The result of such a tape manipulation is that playback at its standard speed creates a higher-pitched sound that exaggerates any effect placed on the initial track. This particular tape technique continued for close to forty years as a common, almost elementary procedure in novelty records, with its most famous appearance in the Alvin and the Chipmunks record series for children. But in "There's a New Sound" the technique has a dual purpose. The first is simply aesthetic commentary: the new sound as abject noise, a nonsensical reverberation whose appeal is partially a fantastic discovery, a monstrous technological find unearthed as a less-than-praiseworthy sonic treasure. The second objective of the technique is to act as self-reflective comic relief and provide an emphatic observation that these new recording processes are the primary material, the source of the record's novelty. For the principal element of "There's a New Sound," of this "Horrible" record, is not the song but the recording process. With the record's foundation purchased on the recording gimmicks it exploits, the subsequent popularity of the record is something of a testament to a tacit understanding, however minimal, that recorded sound was the source of novel pleasures and frustrations.

For the songwriting duo of Burello and Murray, no doubt, the record must have been an entertaining moment to comment on the circumstances in which they found themselves working. No longer were the ears of the nation turning from the middlebrow machinations of Tin Pan Alley and ASCAP to the more rough-hewn and, seemingly, gimmick-laden fads of rhythm and blues, rock, and country. Instead, these musicians, trained in a time when lyricist/composer arrangements were a, if not *the*, primary source of popular music (as well as celebrity), were caught in a cultural shift that they may not have appreciated but certainly could mock. So while this three-minute wall of sound may no longer sound "novel" today, "There's a New Sound" is still a compelling *record.*

Just listen, and as sounds gush, skip, and pipe out of the speakers you will be left with little choice but to ask, "Why on earth would anyone create this, let alone find it amusing?"

This shift from song to sound was not limited to one aesthetic oddity but was felt throughout the entire music industry. As early as a year before "There's a New Sound" was released, the May 31, 1952, edition of *Billboard* magazine announced, "the prevalence of so-called 'noise and sound' disks are riling some of the publishers who claim they can't get a look-in with 'legitimate material.'" While the article is a relatively minor item placed on page 18, it continues by noting, "With regard to the frantic search by diskeries for new sounds, there is much speculation as to the true effect of this on sheet music. Some old line publishers feel that a more stable sheet music sale will return when the diskers revert to more orthodox arrangements" ("Sheet Slump Blamed on Gimmick Disks, Floods" 1952). Following up one week later, *Billboard* noticed that RCA Victor was promoting its latest Perry Como release, a single release of "Black Moonlight" from his *TV Favorites* album, with a card from Famous Music sent to disc jockeys across the country. While the single presents a more or less "orthodox" arrangement, the article states that the release was promoted primarily for what it was not. What the Como single offered, according to the card's heading, was "No Gimmick! No Echo Chamber! No One Playing 'Hot Triangle'!!!" ("Serve Platter, Sans Gimmick" 1952). In other words, disc jockeys could rest assured that throughout this period of noisy gimmicks and cacophonous records they could still remain within the confines of "good taste" with the latest Perry Como offering.

As marginal as these notices are and as trivial as "There's a New Sound" is in American popular music history, their appearance signals an interesting aesthetic anxiety: the concern that a faddish prevalence of noisy contrivances and cacophonous records was proliferating across America's popular cultural landscape. Of course, this concern over new musical sounds, whether it is viewed as fashionable or part of an avant-garde movement (or both), was nothing new then and it is still with us today in the form of genre debates and the ongoing debates over music technologies. Whether they come from fans, critics, or musicians themselves, the music world cultivates and harbors numerous stories wherein the palatability of new sounds is discussed and debated. But unlike many of those stories about what kind of guitar/keyboard/drum sound works in what kind of genre, what is interesting about the above two examples is that they reflect an aesthetic anxiety focused solidly on recordings. In each case, it is the modern-day record, not the "song," not a musician's ability or inability to perform, that channels forth a then-fashionable yet contemptible sound of popular music.

It is at this historical schism between the record and the performer that I want to place this study. It is a rupture that has long been ignored by popular music histories that privilege artists and genre over material culture. For example, the above focus on the record by the music industry and musicians is not without a specific context. Only a few months earlier, in March 1952, *Billboard* introduced a new sales chart. For the first time *Billboard* would plot the sales of an important industrial product: the record. According to the periodical, the "Music Publisher's Record Scoreboard" would be "designed to supply carefully compiled facts concerning the single sphere of activity most vital to successful music operations today—record activity." *Billboard* continued to explain and justify why the record had earned its status as a product worthy of measurement and publicity:

> For the past several years it has become increasingly clear that the sole medium for creating a hit tune is a phonograph record. Large, medium and small publishers have, for some time, concentrated a major portion of their time, money and manpower on securing and exploiting disks of their tunes. With all due recognition to the income derived from performances thru [sic] the American Society of Composers, Authors and Publishers, Broadcast Music, Inc. and minor licensing agencies it is an acknowledged trade fact that with the exception of standard works (controlled for the most part by a handful of publishing firms) a publisher's business builds or declines in direct ratio to his ability or inability to secure recordings.

As if to reassert the importance of the record, *Billboard* further noted that the "exploitation of tunes, via live radio, films, television or in-person plugging has long been regarded as insignificant in the creation of big sheet music sellers and big performance tunes" ("New Music-Record Feature" 1952).

For the modern-day reader, it probably comes as something of a surprise to realize that a periodical so closely associated with charting record sales did not have a chart devoted solely to the sale of the nation's most popular records for the first fifty-eight years of its publication. Yet even more surprising are the explanations that this report would include information such as "how many records a publisher has gotten, [and] by whom . . . whether he got a Patti Page or a Joe Nobody platter." The new *Billboard* column would also harbor a quantitative section that would merely indicate "how many records each publisher [had] received from the arbitrary starting date of January 1, 1952 thru to the present" ("New Music-Record Feature" 1952, 15). In a world where charts and top-ten lists are a major part of mass media discourse, this explanation holds something of a nostalgic charm when one compares it to the everyday cynicism that permeates our understanding of the modern music industry.

Indeed, in this book I want to request that the reader *suspend* some of his or her cynicism and distrust of the music industry. This book has no interest in forging the kind of criticism wherein the recording industry is portrayed, once again and always, as a less-than-necessary evil. If anything, I would like to alter our understanding of this period as one that holds many of the keys to understanding the many pleasures that have since arisen. These include, but are not limited to, the rise of numerous popular genres and aesthetic and economic debates that center on questions concerning the production, distribution, and consumption of recordings rather than performances. Throughout this study I argue that we need to reevaluate our understanding of the recording industry not only as it existed then but as a far more complex machine that creates, harbors, and possesses particularly productive capacities. So, rather than clutching at an understanding of the music industry as simply something that limits artistic and consumer visions, desires, and choices, we need to better understand how industrial forces help produce our need to invest in a culture of recordings and playback technology. By focusing on a few topics in what is roughly the period from after World War II to the rise of rock music as the dominant genre of the day, I hope to illustrate how rich and relatively underresearched this period is in terms of material culture. In this context, all three of the above-mentioned phenomena—the "gimmick" record, the fad, and the record chart—are prominent parts of popular music past. And while the anxiety, excitement, and the seeming necessity of the times may have diminished, they nevertheless were prominent. As a scholar, I consider our inability to explain how and why these marginal moments made sense to mainstream music audiences and industrial actors a severe analytical, historical, and theoretical blind spot. Furthermore, this blind spot cannot be sufficiently addressed without a willful challenge to our conventional understanding of this period. In essence, this study argues and engages the thesis that after World War II the concerns of the recorded music object began, for the first time in the history of popular American music, to overshadow the previous terms of aesthetic and industrial production. This is the period in which the musical recording became a distinctly different product from what it had been before. The recording, in effect, replaced sheet music as the dominant material unit of exchange and musical distribution. While the industry adapted many of the methods and jargon of the music publisher and applied them to the sale of the recording, methods of musical enjoyment once familiar to so many families faded away. As the family piano became less and less a common sight, in its stead the hi-fi system became the dominant space for musical audition. And as Americans lost their collective touch across the black and white ivories, they developed a greater interest in listening and record collecting.

Of course, this was not an overnight paradigm change. The postwar period includes a past when the song became a hit because of a combination of record and sheet music sales. Unlike today, when "the song" and "the record" are virtually synonymous, it was a transitional period wherein recording materials gained a cultural and industrial significance palpable to almost all who listened. As in any historical shift (or shift in historical understanding), there exists both significant opposition and sponsorship. But the consequences of this particular shift went far beyond any simple affirmation or dissent. The rise of the musical recording begat multiple effects, forces that rippled throughout the homes, stages, radio studios, and film productions of the United States. Indeed, no single history or historian could do justice to this change, for its impact was so widespread and so fundamental that the record would overtake the importance of live performance in terms of its industrial, aesthetic, and, eventually, cultural influence.

Reorienting the Record of American Popular Music History

The shift from performance to playback surely has as many stories and influences as it does participants. For example, a study concerned with the rise of the postwar-recorded music object could simply focus on the emergence of those musical performers and celebrities who negotiated the tensions created by their sometimes conflicting onstage and studio reputations. Additional research investigations could examine the growth of a record industry that must market, distribute, and develop a catalogue of artists and recordings in a postwar environment. And others still could scrutinize how newly developed recording technologies affected an artist's oeuvre or a specific popular music genre. To the disappointment of some, this study deals very little with purview of these examples. Rather, I have organized my research around three distinct issues that I believe are critical to understanding the general aesthetic and industrial popular music economies of post–World War II America: the issue of reproduction and production, the aesthetic repercussions of the recorded version and the processes of rendition, and the aesthetic problems and fantasies of realistic sonic representations. Throughout this study I underline that an emphasis on variety, rather than a sense of comprehensiveness, is key. Like the periodical of the same name, variety acts as a principle for modern media economies. Entailing various media modes, genres, actors, musicians, and forms, variety is a primary conceptual force through which this study expects to shed light on the multitude of effects that this shift exacted on that heterogeneous machine known as the "mass media."

Much in the same way that modern film and mass media studies generate and demand that artists and producers acquire and build a significant historical purchase that assists them in understanding past and present-day industrial formations, operations, and decision making, I hold that there would be immense benefits if popular musicians and producers gained a similar historical understanding of their own field. I am under no illusions that my one small contribution is sufficient to constitute a base understanding of this distinctly decentralized field. In terms of the recorded music object, there are a number of adequate histories that cover its development in American history. Yet these studies provide little if any theoretical purchase through which we can consider larger cultural issues.[1] For some, advocating that musicians and musical actors should better understand the history of how and why their industry is arranged the way that it is may sound like the most anesthetic, asocial form of analysis possible for any history of popular music.

Indeed, the fear that this kind of popular music history could consist of nothing more than accounts of media programming (i.e., genres, playlists, etc.), industrial development, and technological advancements (or failures) is justifiable. But we must understand that such a reaction is precisely what has motivated many of the concerns of social and cultural historians dedicated to providing alternative accounts of film, television, and radio. Thus the study of these mass media in the past twenty years has generated detailed accounts of media audiences, activist organizations, social clubs, independent media producers, and so on. Perhaps the most important point that these historians argue is that mass media histories should consist of accounts far richer and complex than histories that view the mass media as nothing more than a simple straight line of textual and technical events.[2] This study takes a cue from these histories, particularly the manner in which they recount the widespread negotiation of social processes necessary to create, distribute, and champion popular mass media formations and products. Indeed, the significant question throughout this book is, "What *makes* popular music popular?" The answer I advance is that after World War II it is a complex social technology known as *recording.* In this sense, the technology of recorded music is always engaged in specific social processes. These processes include cultural strategies that continually address and assemble organizations, frame concepts of democracy, and cultivate potential pleasures and aesthetic sensibilities.

If this sounds oblique, that is because this type of history documents what Félix Guattari calls "aesthetic machinery," assemblages that result from and emerge from forms of social, cultural, and aesthetic engineering. This machinery is not and can never consist of simple, top-down arrangements led by industrial moguls who simply "produce," or audiences who simply "consume." As a technocratic assemblage, our simple conception of the record as a passive "object" that is simply controlled by the listener/musician "subject" can no longer be maintained. In each case, the record, the listener, and the musician are involved in these political formations, economic strategies, social programs, moments of history, aesthetic movements, and desires.[3] These technological assemblages are never static. Instead, they can break down, become damaged, need updates, be involved in reformatory movements, or simply be discarded for new formations. Most important, I view these assemblages as part of and interactive with cultural formations in general. In this framework culture is understood as it connects etymologically to the Latin *cultura,* meaning a tending, care, cultivation. Culture is never a static entity but rather a generative process that can be altered, is never universal, and must always deal in contingencies. Culture does not emanate out of these fabrications as an epiphenomenalistic entity; rather *it comprises* the processes that keep aesthetic machinery performing and operational.[4]

Many of the problems that this concept poses to cultural media historians concern issues of method. I do not want to avoid those questions. They are important, for they demand an understanding of what should constitute history, how it is written, and where the line between the historical actor and historian needs to be drawn (or if it even needs to be drawn at all). This is particularly relevant to this study. Long-forgotten strikes, actively forgotten LP versions of a musical, and recordings of "stereo gimmickry" don't command much in the manner of cultural capital. And I, personally, am not convinced that this history makes a convincing case that Enoch Light or Esquivel records should be accepted as part of any "canon" per se, but the fact is that subjecting marginalia such as demonstration records and various renditions of a specific musical property to analysis allows us to ask the question, "Why, exactly, did these things make sense?" In fact, it forces us to ask, "What exactly made this music and musical issues popular?" When past popular issues have faded, often the competing concerns of New Criticism and New Historicism conveniently dovetail: as the existence of many of these texts fades so does any claim that a text can make on autonomy; as what was once "popular" is pushed into positions of marginal obscurity, the need to resuscitate our understanding of historical contexts breathes life back into these texts and makes them, once again, inspired and inspirational. To be sure, this does not resolve the basic tension between these competing understandings of our aesthetic past, but it illustrates one of the most basic tenets of history and historiography: one can study a text only if it exists and people save only those texts they value.[5]

Beginning in the early 1980s and throughout the 1990s, some of these once-forgotten texts, namely, Martin Denny, Three Suns, and "Stereo Demonstration" records, began to wind up in my collection. I was hardly alone. Punks, post-punks, reformed new-wavers, and various other hipsters found these records too interesting, too defiant to pass up as they scrounged through the used record bins and thrift stores of America. By 1993 this interest reached a critical mass of sorts with the release of the first of two volumes of *Incredibly Strange Music,* books of interviews accompanied by CD compilations of some of the selections documented in these volumes. As V. Vale and Andrea Juno note in their introduction, "many amazing recordings seem to have escaped critical attention" (1993, 2). Furthermore, many of these recordings, produced on vinyl between 1950 and 1980 but the most interesting coming in the "golden years" of high fidelity between 1955 and 1965, allowed listeners "to explore the frontiers of sound effects, percussion and 'foreign' music toward the goal of providing amazing entertainment." Still, as omnipresent as these LPs seemed during these buying years, many of us listeners had no operational theory to explain why they existed in such numbers or what could have made them appealing at any point in time other than their novelty in relationship to our own ears. These LPs seemed beyond any understandable genre. Instead, this gathering of vinyl transients seemingly confirmed, if nothing else, that a greater misunderstanding of this period of popular musical history existed: "Most of this ephemeral music that never had a defined place in musical 'history' existed in a shadowy area between categories" (3).

I argue that this "shadowy area," this blind spot, is the direct result of inadequately theorizing and methodically researching and writing about this historical arena. Of course, a lack of historical theorization is not uncommon. As Jackson Lears points out, "It is no secret that Anglo-American historiography has shown a persistent hostility to theory. At every turn, writers hear the constant refrain: do not 'impose your own framework' on the past, let the historical actors speak for themselves, understand them through the categories and idioms they created for themselves." While Lears believes that "this is a good idea up to a point," one of these problems for historians of post–World War II America is that they "can be badly misled if they turn to the social thought of the 1940s and 1950s—the thought generated by the historical actors themselves—as a guide to understanding American culture and society in the postwar era" (1989, 38). To be sure, it is simply imprudent to apply any preconceived understanding of postwar mass media to an understanding of popular music. Popular conceptions of television and film, concepts such as mass consumption or aesthetic and cultural homogeneity, run the risk of blinding us to how rapidly growing and multifaceted the industry and culture of recorded music and sound were and remain to this day. This kind of blind spot cultivates general assumptions that mass culture is "undifferentiated." Furthermore, it obscures the many cultural conjunctions that affected many postwar Americans. Whether these conjunctions include the world of stereo experimentation, cross-genre explorations of musicals, or the combined labor issues of jazzmen and chamber players, we continue to nurture the belief that musical production and consumption remained relatively similar in structure to their prewar modes. Without a rethinking of this period, one might see the extraordinary growth of the music industry in the postwar years as little more than a matter of magnitude, wherein popular music becomes *more* popular, the classics gain a *wider* availability, and recordings become *more* pervasive and ubiquitous than ever before.

The most cursory examination of recorded sound history reveals that it is by no means unified. We need to excavate the many paths of recorded sound history. Some of them buried, some of them forgotten, the ambitions of sound recordings have carved out numerous social and technical passages. Simply because the recording industry has become much more oriented to the goal of producing musical products does not mean that we adequately understand how and why this occurred.[6] Finding a record such as "There's a New Sound" may be a novel discovery, but more than that it indicates not only a path taken but also one forgotten, ready to be unearthed and investigated. Indeed, no matter how trashy one might find these recordings and issues, we should never forget that trash is some of our best evidence of an "everyday" popular past.

As primary indicators of popularity, trash, rubbish, and linings of thrift stores all have one thing in common: they don't lie. In fact, this junk, whether it comes in the forms of shredded mounds of sheet music or abused Mantovani LPs, is literally the neglected materials that have made music popular. I have no desire to argue for the canonization of easy listening albums, but I do argue that we should pay closer attention to what we have ignored. One of the primary contributors to this neglect has been the aforementioned disregard of the basic materiality of music in favor of a more standard vision of music as a transcendental artform. One form of this neglect is what John Corbett recognizes as an eloquent "disavowal" of the recording as a musical material that has had a profound cultural influence:

Against traditional music history, which is constructed around the abstraction and idealization of music as art (or entertainment) and consists of musical periods, genres, movements, and styles, it is possible to elaborate another set of histories. These would focus attention on the material objects deliberately overlooked in the production of standard musical history. As a blatant instance of such "overlooking" we might invoke a scenario familiar to anyone who has studied music: imagine several partitioned cubicles, each of which contains a headphoned student who faces an amplifier and a turntable; on each platter spins a record of Beethoven's Ninth Symphony. One student lifts his needle to run to the bathroom; another listens twenty times to a difficult passage; a third is frustrated by a skip in the record and proceeds directly to the next movement of the symphony; at the same time another finds it difficult to concentrate due to the volume of her neighbor's headphones. Even as they do these things that are made possible only by the technology of recording, these students are required to develop a historico-theoretical interpretation as if the technical means through which the music is accessed—right there, staring them right in the face—are of no significance whatsoever. This is disavowal, as in the Land of Oz: "Pay no attention to the man behind the curtain."

Corbett notes further that "such idealization is not limited to classical musicology" and, in fact, is part and parcel of how popular music criticism is perpetuated by academics and journalists.

The characterization of music as an abstract, autonomous entity is extremely pervasive, appearing as historical assertion in the popular music press from *Rolling Stone* to

> *Option,* as categorization in music guidebooks from the *Illustrated Encyclopedia of Rock* to the *Da Capo Guide to Contemporary African Music,* and in the form of "music cultures and subcultures" in academic music criticism by George Lipsitz and Larry Grossberg. All these sources base their analyses on *recorded music, thereby accurately recognizing recording as the primary contemporary mode of musical exchange. Nevertheless, the question of the nature of the recorded music object remains relatively untheorized, its elements not yet sufficiently teased out.* (Corbett 1994, 36–37; emphasis added)

This overlook, this disavowal, has two immediate and discernible impacts on music criticism in general. The first effect is that the material cultural aspects of the recording and the recording processes are re-moved, in many cases simply thrown away, and culture is defined as something that can exist beyond these materials. Music, conceptually adrift and unanchored to the recording, becomes the privileged site of any cultural concern or investigation. The record and recording culture continually exists beyond investigation, one step away, as something that can almost always be addressed later. And, of course, "later" all too often means never. By positioning the recording outside the investiga-tional premises of any cultural and aesthetic critique, we foster an ex-tremely naïve realist aesthetic that positions these objects as secondary, background objects. In this vision, the record, at best, *reflects* music and circulates it within a specific musical culture; at its worst, the record ex-udes an artifice that contaminates a somehow purer music culture. This latter issue of aesthetic corruption is best ascertained in those critiques of records that are somehow "overproduced" and are aimed at making music too popular, too mainstream, too palatable. Within this discourse, to produce a record that radiates such an obvious affinity for artifice is to be out of step with "folk"-oriented traditions of musical production and enter into a modern industrial aesthetic where the recording and its processes exert an obvious, self-reflexive (and often pernicious) effect on musical decisions.

Furthermore, this disavowal is not a simple act but an ongoing pro-cess that obscures how a number of industrial arrangements affect the production of the recording. These include, but are not limited to, issues of copyright, labor agreements, and contract details. It also masks issues of exhibition and distribution, thereby couching them as *natural* forma-tions that need not be questioned or investigated in their own right. As modern music is further disengaged from the record, these issues recede, their importance to be questioned only when one is inconvenienced by material arrangements of the system. In other words, it is only when one cannot listen to music, or, more specifically, the musical recordings one wants, that the material contingencies of the recording are invoked or de-liberated by most listeners and critics. This is most evident when record collectors and fans trade and circulate rare recordings or solicit record companies to rerelease recordings from their out-of-print catalogues. In each case the demand for "music" is almost *always* discussed in terms of available recordings, forgotten catalogues, and in-print productions. In this sense, music is never autonomous. Instead, musical appreciation, enjoyment, and criticism are contingent on the material demand and cu-ratorial efforts of fans, musicians, historians, and the industry itself.

And for many fans, musicians, historians, and industrial agents the recorded object is, quite literally, instrumental in both its musical and technical influence. Thus this study is designed to act as a small reminder of a larger point: our vast material culture has always intertwined tech-nological, economic, and artistic ambitions. From Pythagoras to Kepler, from the latest "techno" disk jockey to the most elaborate nightclub, the thematic link between music and the physical sciences has always been viewed as a conspicuous force for production.[7] The debates surrounding this link are various: some are concerned with the transcendental con-nections that music forges with earthly terrains, while others contain more base formations. In many ways each of the topics I present em-braces the latter, more materialist perspective. Thus this study is cut from the same methodological cloth as those investigations offered by Jacques Attali (1985), Simon Frith (1981, 1988a, 1988b, 1993, 1996), Theodore Gracyk (1996), Steve Jones (1992), and Michael Chanan (1994, 1995). Each of these scholars has a fundamental commitment to bringing to the forefront spe-cific material forces and the organizations that operate to produce music and musical culture.

It is important to note that this scholarship is interesting because it stands as a countervailing force to the more traditional manner of study-ing music. In the introduction to *Musica Practica*, Michael Chanan argues that hiding the material organization of music preserves a keystone of romantic ideology: that musical contact is a transcendental moment be-tween the soul of the composer and the audience. For Chanan, this par-ticular fantasy is produced by a number of ideological institutions that are partially dedicated to reinforcing this belief in a pure, unhindered music. Within these institutions, music could be understood as a form of pure communication by providing an *immediate*, transcendent form con-tact that bridges and eliminates, if only temporarily, all class and cultural differences. In contrast each of the scholars mentioned above advances an analytical interest in music as a highly *mediated* form of communi-cation. Whether this mediation occurs through the concert hall or the recording booth, these scholars never allow music to slip away as some autonomous force that stands independent of its media. Drawing from the work of Richard Leppert and Susan McClary, Chanan attaches great importance to how the ideological position of romantic transcendence particularly affects how scholars both understand musical processes and comprehend the self as a musical subject:

> as long as music is regarded as a purely autonomous activity, then the apparatus, including the technologies and institutions, which determine what is performed, published, recorded and broadcast, remain in crucial ways invisible (or inaudible). They are merely the channels through which the composer's subjectivity comes into contact with that of the listener, and the mystical union of composer and listener admits no actual mediation. However, once the processes of mediation become matters for discussion, they believe, the components of that mystical union fall apart, adding that perhaps the most disturbing loss that then occurs is the dissolution of the traditional construct of subjectivity itself. (1994, 7)

It is important to understand just how seductive it is to develop and maintain a belief that music somehow exists as an ideal, transcendental art form. For many, it is our daily contact with music that often frees us by allowing us to sense "a form of expression purged of the temporal and contingent concerns of daily life." Nevertheless, it is a seduction that carries with it significant risks. Most important, when we adopt this stance we often lose a more refined, material understanding of what it means to be a musical (or artistic) subject, such as a listener or composer, in any social or historical sense (1994, 8). To better develop and claim our sense of musical history, we need to take better account of many of the material factors involved in modern musical production and mediation. I maintain that because the primary material factor in today's musical culture and industry is the recorded object, it makes sense that we need to begin to comprehend how this product is produced, distributed, and mediated.[8]

I would like to reiterate just how much I am interested in the creation of music. Understanding music making is primary to understanding how communities make sense of themselves, and this is why I find popular music so enticing. It *is* a fundamental force in day-to-day communal gatherings, whether they be concerts, carnivals, ballrooms, or even simple picnics. While many of these occasions involve live musicians, when "live music" is not available, records and a favorite radio station often fill these gatherings with comfort and joy. As banal as this statement may be, it is true that, with rare exception, we have scant scholarship that deals with the cultural ubiquity of music and how music's industrialization, no matter how much we may resist, has been *the* primary agent of this apparent omnipresence. Simon Frith points out, "The contrast between music-as-expression and music-as-commodity defines twentieth-century pop experience." But it is this very tension, this contrast between the visions of industry and romantic artistry that, as Frith argues,

> means that however much we may use and enjoy its products, we retain a sense that the music industry is a bad thing—bad for music, bad for us. Read any pop history and you will find it outline the same sorry tale. However the story starts, and whatever the author's politics, the industrialization of music means a shift from active musical production to passive pop consumption, the decline of the folk or community or subcultural traditions, and a general loss of musical skill. (1988, 11)

Frith's understanding of this issue goes far beyond any simple explanation that our collective mistrust of the media industry is the result of any critical disavowal of the music industry. Instead, Frith suggests that our resistance to the "music industry" reflects a deep, collective shame. For too many of us, the products we enjoy so much seemingly eat at and rot our common musical core. Frith argues that this shame is continually recirculated as a trope throughout popular music history and journalism, but let me be very clear: I have no interest in perpetuating this cycle of critical shame. Rather, I begin with the dominance of the music industry and its products in our life as a kind of "conditional given." That is, I accept the fact that the products of a fully developed music industry dominate much of our lives, but I believe they do so only through specific sets of contingencies, potentials that can only be successfully articulated if they respect the social and cultural needs of any given moment.

The given moment I want to turn to is America's postwar period, with a specific focus on developments between 1948 and 1964. Like all investigational limits, these reflect my own analytical aims more so than they do any preexisting borders or borderlike phenomena. Yet there is some precedence set by other popular music scholars who argue that this period of American music history involves a profusion of industrial, social, and aesthetic changes. After the war it became evident that the recording industry was growing as an important facet of the overall music industry. Russell Sanjek points out that 1947 was a key year for the record industry. After surpassing its 1921 peak for retail sales, the American record industry finally felt that there would be no other way "but up" (1988, 229). Richard Peterson and David Berger argue that, for three reasons, 1948 is the most significant year in the establishment of the record industry's corporate concentration: "by [1948] the material shortages caused by the war and pent-up consumer demand had been eliminated; the protracted and stormy labor negotiations with the American Federation of Musicians' President Petrillo had been successfully completed, making possible the uninterrupted production of records; and finally, the 45 and 33⅓ rpm record formats had been established" (1990, 140–41). Peterson and Berger's final reason is interesting, for it underlines at least a specific technological development as a reason for industrial expansion. Andre Millard echoes this line of thought and contends that the development of new technologies was a substantial strategic initiative that helped advance both electronic and recorded music into the music entertainment market. According to Millard, although 1947 was a "peak year," "record sales were disappointingly flat after the war." The preceding year continued the recession by producing a 20 percent decline of retail sales in terms of constant dollars. The industry reacted by making a marked investment in "new and improved technology, based on 'the legacy of war research'" already performed by many of the major labels. This, as Millard remarks, "was to be the weapon of the industry as it struggled to regain the mass market for recorded sound" (1995, 201).

The social effects of extensive, postwar technological change are alluded to by several scholars as important developments in the day-by-day operations of the modern music industry. Of the many ballyhooed and revered developments of the postwar era, high fidelity recordings and playback devices stand unequaled in the minds of many of today's record collectors and musicians as the period's representative technologies. Still, as Rick Wojcik notes, "The rise of high fidelity, stereo, the long play (LP) record, and their effects on listening practice have been long neglected as a subject for rigorous analysis." For Wojcik,

> It is important to note that [many musical developments throughout the postwar period] were part of a recognition in the record industry of the advances that were being made in audio tech-

nology. By the end of the fifties, sales of records had reached an unprecedented high [by 1960]—an increase of 202% over the past decade. This success was attributed to the phenomenal rise of the LP, and to the inroads made in high fidelity and stereo recording. (1994, 18)

Similarly, Keir Keightley argues that the success of high fidelity and the LP is sorely underresearched and undertheorized. Because of the cultural distinction that separated them from prewar music technologies, Keightley argues that these technologies need to be seen in contradistinction to the rise of television. Drawing from Lynn Spigel's work on television (1992), Keightley asserts that while television in North America developed in a "feminine" domestic context, "home audio sound reproduction equipment [was] hardened into masculinist technologies *par excellence*" as a kind of cultural reaction-formation. According to Keightley, before the war this type of technological gendering of home electronics equipment had not been enunciated (1996, 150).

While Keightley's argument is interesting, I simply want to mention it and go forth without an in-depth exposition. This is no slight. Rather, I feel that scholars such as Keightley and Wocjik are indicative of an intricate and diverse set of interests in this period. Indeed, this period has held an interest for popular music scholars for some time. For example, both Phillip Ennis and Simon Frith provide more systemic, organizational accounts of the record industry's technologies of production and distribution in relation to postwar American musical culture. Ennis claims that in the twenty years after the war, "rocknroll" emerged in the wake of a new set of technological and industrial arrangements including the rise of the disc jockey, the prominence of the record, and the collision of pop, country, and rhythm and blues genres caused by recordings and greater social mobility (1992, 131–255). While Frith has an avid interest in rock and roll, his interest in the music industry's postwar developments is more fundamental to the production of popular musical commodities rather than to one specific popular music genre. As a result, Frith asserts that 1945 is the year in which "the basic structure of the modern music industry was [finally] in place." Although Frith frames this structure as the "technological roots of rock," it is evident that his interest in this structure relates to its ability to produce a new type of popular music culture that stretches beyond genre:

Pop music meant pop records, commodities, a technological and commercial process under the control of a small number of large companies. Such control depended on the ownership of the means of record production and distribution, and was organized around the marketing of stars and star performances (just as the music publishing business had been organized around the manufacture and distribution of songs). Live music-making was still important but its organization and profits were increasingly dependent on the exigencies of record-making. The most important way of publicizing pop now—the way most people heard most music—was on the radio, and records were made with radio formats and radio audiences in mind. (1988, 19–20)

This study is greatly indebted to these scholars and their interest in popular music and technology. Specifically, I find their attempt to nuance our perception of the postwar context and construct a complex cultural understanding inspirational. The result of their influence is a study that hopes to frame recording technologies as items and logics that exert specific aesthetic and cultural influences on our musical experiences. Because of my focus, I find Frith's ambivalence between popular music and rock extremely interesting and productive. While general critical memories of the postwar period regard rock and roll (or "rocknroll"), rhythm and blues, country, and Tin Pan Alley tunes and jazz as primary popular music focal points for studies and analysis, the most novel and most *direct* popular musical experiences of the public throughout this period were provided not by any one set of genres but by *recordings*. Through an expanding postwar record industry, the recording offered musicians, producers, critics, and the general public novel aesthetic liberties and potentials *because* of its specific materiality. In other words, popular music *belonged* to the public in a materially distinct and different manner than before. This new and improved record industry provided consumers not only with a popular commodity but also with a different mode of industrial-aesthetic potentials. By emphasizing the cultural-material processes involved in the production, distribution, and exhibition of the musical recording, this study hopes to pose and evoke new sets of questions and investigations regarding our possible understanding of popular music and popular music history. To be sure, the central question emanating from these sets of questions is that of how publics cultivate, circulate, and work with recordings. This question could never be addressed by a single study. Cultural-material analyses demand a respect for specific cultural and historical contingencies. Any approach that frames communication as a set of cultural-material processes must be flexible enough to accept that various cultural-material arrangements are specific expressions of cultural difference.

I firmly believe that this accent on multiplicity and difference opens up various cultural, industrial, and artistic avenues for scholarly researchers and popular investigators to explore and forge. With regard to my work, these include, but are not limited to, the study of recording aesthetics; the consumption of the recorded object; the display, production, and distribution of the recording; the consideration of the recording as evidence, as illusion, as both; the political economy of the recording; the critical expectations of a recording; and so on. More than anything else, by highlighting the recording, its affiliated technologies, and the terms through which they operate, the study of popular music can make a comfortable and profitable shift toward communication studies. The major reason for this is that it is within this terrain that the questions of how mass communication texts and technologies are arranged tend to be posed and examined.

Nevertheless, despite Frith's statement that the basic material and industry elements were in place for a new popular music culture in 1945, a statement made over a decade ago, we still know relatively little about how these assemblages developed throughout the postwar period. Indeed, the primary reason for this study is to begin to tease out a few of the multiple issues that popular music scholarship has, in my opinion, not yet sufficiently addressed and in some cases not even acknowledged. By stitching together a number of historical topics that identify issues surrounding the recorded and repeated performance, "the copy," "the version," and the "staging" of realistic and fantastic audio, I want to describe a portion of our musical past that is far from well understood, a past wherein a particular aesthetic culture is involved in recording, reproducing, repeating, and representing immediate "pasts," specific events, on a widespread and unprecedented basis. This past is one where large portions of the music industry that are not necessarily fully engaged with recordings encounter a set of unforeseen aesthetic possibilities and problems, hold them up for inspection, and negotiate what is acceptable on a case by case basis. The differences between the cases I profile here, Frith's vision of pop music, and Ennis's vision of "rocknroll" are fundamental: the two latter visions emerge and result from a music culture based on recordings, while this book forefronts the assemblage and confrontation of traditions that predate a musical culture where recordings stand as the primary element produced by the music industry.

Of course, the history of any artistic movement's development is non-teleological. One of the arguments I make throughout is that industrial movements such as the widespread interest in stereo and Broadway musical properties intersect with and presage other modern-day, popular music developments. In many cases, these developments may have no clear-cut connection in terms of musical style. Yet when one examines the cultural affinities between the "rock" cultures that began to emerge in the mid-1960s and pre-rock culture of the 1950s, these connections begin to become evident and materialize in manners that demand further investigation. To be sure, the reason I end this study at 1964 is that this date acts as a general mark for the emergence of rock artists such as Bob Dylan, the Beatles, the Rolling Stones, the Byrds, and the Beach Boys. Starting in 1964 rock begins to become, for much of North America, a dominant, an almost hegemonic system of popular music consumption production, and it remains so until the late 1980s and early 1990s. Brandishing a romantic ideology of "serious" artistic creation, rock flourished with accounts of authentic self-expression despite the genre's obvious (and sometimes overt) reliance on technological artifice (Frith 1988, 22). In short, rock and roll went from being a genre of pop music to the more "mature" popular form known as rock. Before this period, rock and roll was a genre that existed among a variety of other popular music genres including doo wop, rhythm and blues, country, hillbilly, and rock-a-billy. In fact, it is fair to state that rock was *heard* as a fad among a number of other musical fads. Once rock begins to dominate the popular musical scene, many of the industrial-aesthetic concerns of its preceding period become principal to the genre of rock itself. By investigating ore-rock industrial-aesthetic concerns, we gain an insight into why rock and subsequent American-based popular music cultures developed in the manner they did.

The Scheme of This Book

This book does not present a linear history of events and facts. Rather it is organized around a nexus of topics. I keep these topics distinct and separate not because they do not share common themes but rather as an act that conveniently focuses on the specific analytical topics that are in play. What brings these cases together is that each is concerned with the material-cultural position of the recorded music object. But whereas these topics are distinct, throughout these chapters the industrial and aesthetic issues that affect the presentation and construction of the recorded sound object are intertwined. There is a simple reason for this: in popular culture both aesthetic and economic issues have decided influences on our understanding of any given product or movement that cannot be easily distinguished from one another. Each chapter attempts to tease out the ambiguous nature of this relationship between industrial and aesthetic decisions.

The first chapter gives an account of the recording strikes of 1942–44 and 1948, the preconditional struggle between labor and industry that established recordings as the primary means through which Americans would experience music in the postwar period. Led by the American Federation of Musicians, the strikes were an effort to claim control over the methods of musical production and reproduction and reduce the potential harm to a standing labor force of musicians. Key to my rethinking and researching these events are concepts developed in Jacques Attali's *Noise: The Political Economy of Music* (1985): the "stockpile" and "repetitive society." As a result, I argue that the strikes are essentially a conflict between musicians, who are invested in an entertainment economy based on performances, and an advanced mass media economy, which is based on the production, reproduction, stockpiling, and repetitive playback of entertainment "molds." The mold is the key, for it allows, according to Attali, the "mass reproduction of an original." The result is that "the necessary labor for production [is] no longer intrinsic in the nature of the object, but a function of the number of objects produced" (1985, 128). Thus the appraisal of success for musicians and musical composers within repetitive society is no longer primarily measured by referring to the number of one's performances; rather, success is measured in one's ability to facilitate the production, distribution, promotion, and sale of mass-produced objects. But unlike a publication of a specific composition, these objects' performance and reproduction are *intrinsically* removed from the musicians and composers who produce the initial master recording, or mold. The postwar era is distinguished from the prewar music industry, a period where publishing firms who produced and sold sheet music to amateur and professional musicians for performance constituted and stood as the dominant economic structures. Within this period the songwriter was positioned as the intellectual sparkplug that fired the industry's engines. Thus within this framework something like *Lady Be Good*'s fictional account of a successful songwriting duo whose song succeeds within a number of cultural arenas can be seen as the representative portrayal of big-time, prewar music industry success (McLeod 1941).

After the strikes it is clear that the postwar music industry is no longer primarily oriented around selling sheet music but rather the production and sale of recorded objects whose consumption takes precedence over live musical performances. This changes not only the direction and aims of the music industry but our vision of the artist as well. While the songwriter and performer remain important, no longer were they the only celebrated musical entities. Indeed, the network and promoters needed to circulate and champion these objects became heroes in their own right. To draw on another vision from American cinema, the promotional nodes of this network are best represented and celebrated by Alan Freed of *Mister Rock and Roll* (Dubin 1957) and *Go, Johnny, Go!* (Landres 1958), and Wolfman Jack with his role in *American Graffiti* (Lucas 1973). In each case, the disc jockey, not simply the musician, is revered as the promoter and distributor who brings together diverse audiences and exhibits an assembly of recordings and recording artists. The vision of the heroic DJ is part of a specific industrial-aesthetic dynamic, a dynamic that demands an operator who can effectively place recordings into a dialogue with a listening audience.

Chapter 2 asserts a more fundamental point: the recording strikes resulted in a long-fought-for technological reformation, wherein both the economic and cultural position of musicians and the basic mode of musical consumption were and remain deeply affected and altered. I do not argue that musicians became second-class economic or artistic citizens and that audiences no longer took great pleasure in live performances. Rather, I argue that the strikes were actually a struggle over whether or not American audiences and musicians should accept recordings as the *primary* means through which they experience music. As a result, I focus on these events as their participants attempted to frame issues of labor, reception, and dissemination of culture for what many of the participants foresaw as a specific technological destiny that foreshadows a general repetitive economy of molds that rearranges the status of laborers and their relationship to the production of products.

As noted above, essential to my understanding of these strikes as "prophetic" is the work of Jacques Attali. Attali argues that one of the paradoxes regarding the proliferation of molds and their stockpiling is that molds can exist everywhere:

> Molds . . . are everywhere: computer programs, car designs, medicine formulas, apartment floor plans, etc. The same mutation also transforms the usage of things. The usage to which representative labor was put disappears with mass production. The object replaces it, but loses its personalized, differentiated meaning. A paradox: the object's utility is exchanged for accessibility. *Considerable labor* must then be expended to give it a meaning, to produce a demand for its repetition. (1985, 128; emphasis added)

Producing something of a variation on Benjamin's concern that art in the age of mechanical reproduction has lost its aura (Benjamin 1968), Attali locates aura, the element essential to an object's status as a singular and unique entity, in the representative labor of musical production. In other words, the distinctive agents of musical production, musicians, are no longer necessary for continual musical rendition and/or the production of "musical objects." As a result, the project for the music industry is to make its objects "unique" by generating and attaching "auratic" significance to its commodities. In most cases, although not always, this involves the systematic establishment of star systems that publicize and bring significance to these recorded objects. In all cases, the recorded object needs to be cultivated in order to endow it with a distinct exchange value in order to make certain that its consumption can become somehow meaningful. The result is, ideally, the generation of desire for these distinctive differences within a system of objects that would otherwise be perceived as somehow more similar than different. Of course, because it would be inefficient to make every single recorded object unique, the record industry produces an interesting tension. Indeed, it is something of a contradiction that results from the desire to gain the greatest profit margin possible from a mass product that simultaneously aspires to be ubiquitous and distinct.

Chapters 3 and 4 focus on one case where the music industry directly confronts the contradictory problems that arise in the creation of simultaneously ubiquitous and distinct commodities. Through the example of *My Fair Lady*, I point out that this is a specific case wherein Columbia Records acquired a property and then systematically fashioned multiple recordings of the Broadway musical to meet a variety of different musical and industrial desires. It should be noted that although the musical score exhibits a number of textual elements that relate to sound and music as they incorporate issues of gender, nationality, and pedagogy, these particular chapters are primarily a study in an industrial production process. My specific interest is to use *My Fair Lady* as an example of a text that illustrates both the industrial and aesthetic practice of "versioning." Hence these chapters have two goals. First, they aim to make a particular industrial point. Supported by the fact that capitalist media industries hope to exploit their properties for the maximum profits possible, I argue that versioning is one manner through which the repetitive practice of standardized production can create and accent significant differences, whatever they may be. In this sense, versioning is *not* a static practice that initiates similar products. Rather, versioning is a means of producing *marked difference(s)*. I specifically illustrate this point by detailing the development of the *My Fair Lady* property from 1956 to 1964. By focusing on one of the most important musical properties of the initial postwar period, I draw on a continuum of textual realizations that span from the musical's initial Broadway stage version to its fabrication into a Hollywood spectacular in 1964. Throughout these chapters I focus a good amount of my critical attention on the various musical sound track records that sought to promote and capitalize on the success of *My Fair Lady* as a sort of perpetually presold property.

The second theme of these chapters addresses how the proliferation of versions produces sites for contrast and comparison. The production of "sites of difference" is an important concept. After these sites are constructed, they are able to produce an interest in properties that generate a set of synergistic relationships through which audiences are encouraged to engage (or be engaged by) a variety of texts for the purpose of evaluation. In the case of *My Fair Lady* this "economy of comparison" was best expressed by the debate over the selection of Audrey Hepburn to play Eliza Doolittle in the Warner Brothers film version over Julie Andrews, who had starred in the original Broadway musical. My contention throughout is that this debate should not be viewed as a mere casting controversy. Rather, this was a specifically "intertextual" controversy between an audience that was well acquainted with both Julie Andrews's and Audrey Hepburn's recorded voices. Furthermore, I argue that the debate about this debate was not simply one of appropriate star image but primarily an audio-oriented debate about the sound track. Indeed, it was well known (and publicized) at the time that Hepburn's singing voice was a source of substantial concern for the producers and was "dubbed over" by Marni Nixon in the postproduction process. Though I do not argue that this controversy was deliberately cultivated by major record or film industries, I do claim that this site was, nonetheless, the result of these media industries' recording activities. In short, the debate was a specifically intertextual site of controversy that concentrated on the recorded objects of the music industry, Hollywood's penchant for spectacular use of recorded audio, and their mutual relationship. By no means do I assert that this was the only site for intertextual pleasures.[9] Yet this convergence of concerns and judgments regarding sonic and musical abilities suggests that at least some film audiences held a rich understanding of Hollywood's aesthetic techniques as well as the materiality of the film- and music-making processes. And, of course, we should not ignore that this was another forum through which significantly different versions of the *My Fair Lady* text were debated.

These chapters are also attached to another critical engagement: a contemporary understanding of pre–rock and roll popular music texts. Despite the importance and influence that stage and film musical recordings held (and continue to hold in some cases) for audiences and the record industry, these recordings tend to be left unattended by the academics with an interest in popular music. Thus this large terrain of popular texts has remained largely uncharted by critical scholars, thereby creating the kind of analytical blind spot that mars even the most basic understanding of North American popular music standards and practices.

The final case this study considers focuses on a decidedly different set of technological concerns. Whereas *My Fair Lady* illustrated the problem of multiple recordings, chapters 5 and 6 address the pronounced exhibition of audio space in recorded music. It is clear that scholars interested in sound and music technologies require a diverse set of methods and questions through which we can discern many of the aesthetic issues and cultural contexts that affect recorded music and sound. Indeed, these methods should be developed through an ongoing project of collective research and criticism, rather than a single case of historical examination or theoretical offering. To be sure, this focus on heterogeneity is pertinent for even the most conservative of musical genres. For example, we should not forget that "Western classical music" has always been exhibited and performed within and through a heterogeneous set of spaces. In many situations these spaces anticipated modern mass mediums such as FM radio and high-fidelity theaters. In other cases, as Michael Chanan reminds us in his work on the social practice of Western music, composers such as Berlioz and Giovanni Gabrieli created works explicitly designed to take advantage of the spatial signatures provided by the individual architectural frameworks of specific churches and cathedrals (1994, 48–49). In other words, as the site of exhibition has always figured prominently in the process of musical rendition, it has also markedly influenced, consciously or not, the compositional process. Given this fact, it is curious to note that popular musicology has often ignored these spatial and historical contingencies and the influences they may have exerted on audience receptions. It is only recently that musicologists have begun to examine how different audiences may understand similar pieces in differing fashions. For example, in his essay "Adequate Modes of Listening," Ola Stockfelt argues that "it is clear that, during its 200-year history, Mozart's g-minor symphony has not been *one* work but rather a series of different works with different meanings in different contexts." More importantly, Stockfelt points out, "It is unclear whether the symphony may be said to have existed at all as a 'living' work during the fifteen years following its composition insofar as it may not have been performed at all during this time" (1993, 154). For Stockfelt, a specific piece can only exist within a specific listening context, a context that audience actively assists in generating. The audience, of course, does not exist outside its own specific historical context. I have argued elsewhere that the performative parameters of popular musical interpretation and performance must negotiate and be constructed through specific situational contexts (Anderson 1997). Of course, ethnomusicology has always maintained an interest in the cross-cultural contexts of musical expression and reception. More so, ethnomusicology has much to offer any scholar interested in the cultural issues that affect the reception of sound and music (see Chernoff 1979; Feld 1982; Feld and Keil 1994). In other cases, when the cross-cultural concerns of ethnomusicology are mixed with more sociological analyses, the results have been especially fertile for popular music scholarship (see Malm and Wallis 1984; Marre and Charlton 1985; Frith 1989; Slobin 1993). By working with these insights, I hope future popular music scholars can better contextualize modern listening experiences.

Indeed, one of the main thrusts of this study is to encourage scholars to continually study and reevaluate how listening contexts are fabricated and how they influence musical experiences. Moreover, I believe that this focus on the listening context and the listener should become a primary focal point for popular music scholarship. Throughout this work it is the context of the recording as a composed and performative object that provides a specific set of challenges. Part of the challenge rests in creating an appropriate analytical lexicon for recorded sound. As Rick Altman argues, this lexicon should be developed in a manner that actively engages an adequate understanding of the techniques and materials involved in the constitution and formation of recorded objects (1992). This is an important objective for popular music scholarship simply because the production and encounter of modern music revolves around issues of recorded sound. As a result, popular music scholars are left with very few formal options through which we can address recorded music objects. Unlike scholars in film studies, a discipline that has a healthy lexicon of terms and theoretical means of addressing the recorded materials of cinema, popular music scholars have no comparable grasp on many of their own objects of analysis.

This is not simply an "academic" matter. Rather, it is clear to even the most casual observer that a clear-cut division between music and recorded sound is one that many musicians, let alone listeners, do not make. To be sure, in casual parlance "to play music" is heard as synonymous with "playing a recording." Driving this point further in his work on popular music and technology, Steve Jones explains that most popular musicians do not "read" standard Western musical notation; instead, they gain their training from both *listening to* and *mimicking* the sounds they hear on radio and records. In many cases these records are assembled from a collection of *other* recordings, electronic effects, and mixed amplification. Quite simply, as Jones puts it, "popular music is primarily mediated via electronics, via sound, and not written notes" (1992, 53). Still, as the Chicago Recorded Music Workgroup argues, "music, indeed all sound, historically has been conceived as separable from the recording medium, which may explain why music scholarship lacks a general theoretical vocabulary for talking about recording" (1993, 172). To be sure, this places many modern music scholars at a severe disadvantage since, as the group further argues, "Recordings are the principal means by which music circulates in global mass culture. Even live instances of music are arguably now bound to the medium of recording. All music—perhaps all sound—has lost its fabled ontological and psychological autonomy" (171). Indeed, this book works with the premise in hand that a principal question for popular music scholars is no longer how does an autonomous set of musical practices negotiate the terrain of recorded sound but how the advent of specific recorded sound technologies has transformed what we consider to be musical or essential to the production of music.[10]

In an attempt to establish at least one theoretical structure on which we can fasten an understanding of the aesthetic principles of the recording, chapters 5 and 6 delineate a few of the major discursive formations through which the postwar phenomenon of stereo recordings was produced. As such this section exists as an account that ties the specific aesthetic interests of high-fidelity and stereo sound to measured, progressive visions of the technoscientific developments of sound playback and recording. As mentioned earlier, while there has been some recent work on the relationship of high fidelity and long-play records and their gendered positioning as masculine technologies, little scholarship has been devoted to the thought that these technologies ushered in an era of "new" sounds that expanded both the musician's and the listener's sonic palette. This final section of the book is the most theoretically involved as it draws from similar discussions concerning the field of photography and details issues of representational integrity.

Acting as an unarticulated influence throughout this section is Michel Chion's concept of "rendered sound" echoing in the background. Chion argues that, although portrayed as seemingly intangible, the arena of cinematic sound effects has yielded an expanded field of possible "materializing sound indices" (1994, 109–20). Drawing from Chion's work, I position stereo as not only a part of a high-fidelity movement that is invested in designing an intricate recorded sound architecture but another form of "cinematic sound."[11] One of the reasons for connecting in-home stereo systems with Chion's interest in cinematic sound is that both theatrical and in-home systems are interested in designing and reproducing acoustic spaces. For both the in-home and film listener, these systems bring the audience closer to specific aesthetic details that create the material sound indices, which, according to Chion, make us "'feel' the material conditions of the sound source," whatever they may be. Although Chion argues that "in many musical traditions perfection is defined by an absence of m.s.i.s [material sounds indices]" (114), I argue that the multiple ambitions of high fidelity act as a specific challenge to this vision. As a result, high fidelity and stereo aim to reveal "sound signatures" that betray a number of spaces or performers through "non-musical" means. Hence, whether these include the brittle brilliance of Henry Kaiser's Aluminum Dome, the frenzied, aural distances of Southern California's open-air Hollywood Bowl, any specific cities or natural landscapes, or the accompanying breathy mumbles of Glenn Gould, Thelonious Monk, or Keith Jarrett, listeners engage these material sources through once inaudible acoustic inscriptions.

Yet chapters 5 and 6 argue that stereo and high-fidelity technologies should not be viewed as simply positivist ambitions that aim to reproduce and represent "realistic sound." Instead, one of the aims of high-fidelity technology and culture, despite their realist connotations, severely alters our perception of sound and musical objects. As a result, the section also constructs the very real vision that stereo technologies held for many as systems that provided "fantastic acoustic spaces." Throughout, I read "fantastic" as a term that keeps its connotations of the wonderful and the imaginative firmly intact. The search for new sounds in the high-fidelity movement of the postwar period included not only the gimmicky manipulations of "There's a New Sound" but the fantastic creation of spaces "once-inaudible" to the average listener. I argue that the tension exerted between fantastic and realistic sound does not create divisions; rather this tension works to create an aesthetic binding. As such, the searches for fantastic and realistic audio are complementary explorations that utilize similar aesthetic techniques and instruments that aim to represent and create illusions of acoustic space. Throughout these sonic experiments, the terrain of electronic sound materials is continually refined to the point that it can repeatedly generate "new sounds."

Most important, this desire for acoustic illusions is the result of an aesthetic movement that is listener-oriented rather than music-oriented. In other words, I argue that the aesthetic innovations of stereo and hi-fi technologies correspond not so much with traditional musical pleasures but with the newer, modern pleasures of listening. The reason for this is simple: the high-fidelity movement was a movement dedicated not simply to listening to the musical terrain but to a wider terrain of listening possibilities. Some of these possibilities demanded exact representations, others required audio novelties including the novelty of exact representations, and in other cases a sound producer would be challenged to take nonmusical sound objects and make them "musical." Indeed, to this day fans of high-fidelity equipment and production privilege the rights and liberties of the listener rather than one singular vision of aesthetic representation.

The convenient satisfaction of the individual listener through recordings, rather than the edification of a collective public, is arguably the most important change in postwar music culture. Accentuated by a postwar culture of mass consumption wherein "everyman" could purchase recordings and hi-fi systems, the shift in American music culture, however unacknowledged today, was quite profound. In no way does this study explain (or even attempt to explain) every facet of this alteration. This work attempts to fashion a new terrain for future scholarly attention by tilling a field that many recognize but do not fully understand. Throughout I place the recording in the foreground, demand we give it our utmost attention, and request that we closely listen to its rustles, whispers, scratches, repetitions, and stirrings. These are the marks of the recording. They exist as both abject and revered reminders of the object's potentials. Whether they are desired or loathed, we need to amplify the recorded object, bring it out of the background, and make it an audible portion of modern music history. No matter how much we may aspire, the recording will never be completely silenced. At best it is quieted, hushed under cultured reverberations designed to beget melodies and rhythms. This study aims to give the recording and its construction a voice through which its historical presence can be expressed, so that it is no longer lost in sound.

PART I

Managing the Recording Process and Rethinking the Recording Bans

Buried under the Fecundity of His Own Creations

The First Strike of the American Federation of Musicians

COMMERCIAL MASS ENTERTAINMENT ECONOMIES ARE STRANGE and impressive technologies that, despite their scale, must adhere to that most basic tenet of capitalism: they do not have the luxury of stasis. These machines suffer the wills of style, and without regular tune-ups they fall apart, rust. There are no other options. As an example, take one of the most famous technological assemblages of American tourism, luxury, and amusement. For many Americans, Las Vegas is a uniform fantasy consisting of unrestricted gambling, music, and sex. Yet despite this image Las Vegas is no longer completely "Las Vegas." Within the past fifteen years, through gestures of demolition and the forces of fashion, metamorphoses of sorts have taken place. Several of the city's most fabled works of architecture, so-called landmarks such as the MGM Grand and the Sands, have been flattened, smoothed over, and redesigned. A refuge of "masculine" varieties, the "legitimate good time" best represented by the Rat Pack of famous and infamous musical entertainers such as Dean Martin, Frank Sinatra, Joey Bishop, Sammy Davis Jr., and Peter Lawford, was obscured by a new decor, a haven of family-oriented amusements. To attract vacationing families, the grand hotels of Las Vegas no longer promoted only promises of the burlesque and ribald. In the 1990s, when the age of information reigned, a new mob of multinational capital guaranteed its clientele protection, as well as passage, into the unpolluted, the efficient, and the tamed, yet still spectacular and, if one looked for it, still quite sexual. With this change a two-pronged promotional campaign began. The first campaign is overt: the official campaign of tourist boards and chambers of commerce. Throughout the 1990s this included pictures and stories of a present and future Las Vegas where "clean," "safe," and "family" have become operative words for a new venture. For almost twelve years, Las Vegas marketed a new kind of "protected risk" where Lady Luck still reigned but in a somehow more "ladylike" way than before. And in the twenty-first century, Vegas is marketed again as if it has returned to its sinful roots. This time Mafia money is gone; corporate capital leads the way in an attempt to attract both the family and the under-thirty crowd that longs for poker tournaments and exhibitionism.

The second promotional campaign is less overt, though apparently very effective. This one promises that only memories of the insurgent, dispersed corruption that built the city remain. Of course, the degenerate is never leveled. Rather, the Mafia, prostitution, and drunkenness continue to be celebrated and longed for in films such as *Bugsy* (Levinson 1991), *Casino* (Scorsese 1995), and *Leaving Las Vegas* (Figgis 1995). These portrayals manifest themselves not only in network television and mainstream feature films but in the seemingly disengaged realm of independent music as well. Take the two CD volumes of *Las Vegas Grind Part 1* and *Las Vegas Grind Part 2* as a particularly obscure example. Including no production dates or address for correspondence, an American expatriate residing in Hamburg produced these discs. Each compilation is as generic as the unknown artists and forgotten players it includes. Still, the bawdy, humorous rhythm and blues–based instrumentals on these discs hold a unique allure. If you are unaware of these records, don't worry: none were hits in their initial release or subsequent reissue. What distinguishes these discs is the odd, quasi-burlesque performance style they have preserved. With a wink and a nod, each CD exists as a kind of history preserve. Once lost singles, tapes, and albums, these records, exhumed from the garages, storage spaces, and warehouses of the nation now have a new life as a vision of musical burlesque.[1] Each volume is adorned with pictures of strip performances and forefronts the adjectives "sleazy, cheesy, bad," each word imparting a decidedly nostalgic tone. Not despite but because of the humor and the campy positioning

BURIED UNDER THE FECUNDITY OF HIS OWN CREATIONS

of the product, each album is a complex wish for a sort of homecoming, a reprieve from the exile from a technocratic and less ribald present. No matter how firmly one's tongue is planted in cheek, this is a wish to resuscitate remnants of a specific culture of live, burlesque performance. Within these intimate settings, musicians would accent a dancer's movement, highlight titillating moments, please the crowd with an on-the-spot rendition of a popular song or two, be blasé, or worse, simply awful. Yet, as fleeting as these performances were, as "unknowable" as these musicians may seem to be, it is through a myriad of household turntables, cassette decks, and college/underground radio programs that these records render and repeat a genre from the culture of Las Vegas's "good old days."

"Every performance a risk": this is the primary maxim informing both the performance of live music and games of chance. It is risking loss that injects the thrill of life into these activities and spaces. But the desire to minimize risk is too great a gamble to resist. Because investors prefer predictable, sober profits to larger-than-life winnings, one form of Las Vegas's "good old days" no longer remains. Reporting in 1989 that "the good old days began to die this summer," the *Chicago Tribune* noted that the carnivalesque varieties of Vegas revues were now possessions of history (Schmich 1989). Always threatening to move to the forefront were the musicians, a fundamental element to Las Vegas's entertainment economy as early as when Bugsy Siegel opened the Flamingo. An ignored cultural isle, Las Vegas was treasured as one of the few American cities where performing musicians could carve out a comfortable life. This oasis existed well after most other public spaces in the United States were employing recordings for their musical pleasures. Blossoming in the late 1950s and early 1960s, many professional musicians cut from the payrolls of major Hollywood film studios sought and found Las Vegas's expanding economy as an ideal place to relocate. With a low cost of living, negligible taxation, and available work opportunities, the professional musician of reputable skill could maintain a comfortable home base and avoid the road.

But in Las Vegas's late-1980s reformation, many entrepreneurs viewed the elimination of musicians, a staple of the city's entertainment labor force, as a financial necessity. "We're not doing this because we hate musicians," stated a spokesman for the Ballys Corporation. Rather the decision to discontinue these jobs was merely the result of cost cutting.

The prospect of eliminating these positions in exchange for an improved bottom line could no longer be ignored. With some hotels claiming that this new practice would save close to one million dollars a year for one show alone, hotel and casino management commissioned a few engineers and programmers to operate a system of synthesizers and tapes to replace their corps of musicians. As one of the many cogs in an industry that is seemingly synonymous with excess, Las Vegas musicians were simply entertainment laborers too costly to be retained. The result was a solution derived from the logic of capital investment: utilize a new means of efficiency to replace these employees, free up capital, and use the new resources for further corporate expansion and development. As one report noted, "Just as video poker is replacing the old-fashioned slot machine, the beat of the live band is being supplanted by the beat of the recorded tape, digitally mastered, reel-to-reel, as improvisational as a stone" (Schmich 1989). Despite their aesthetic advantages, musicians were too much of an economic hazard, too much of a gamble. And as everyone knows, the most important law of gambling is that the house will, in time, always win.

Responding with picket lines, the local chapter of the American Federation of Musicians (AFM) asked, "Why don't they just videotape the dancers and jugglers and show it all on a screen?" Other entertainers noted that the need for live musicians was not simply limited to the audience's desire to witness a unique event. Indeed, musicians' ability to milk a routine for all it has, quickly end a song that is bombing, or accent the performer's delivery makes them treasured comrades. As stage allies they are invaluable. Marquee performers such as Dean Martin, Rodney Dangerfield, Burt Bacharach, and Dionne Warwick refused to cross the picket lines. Other names such as Robert Goulet, Sammy Davis Jr., Jerry Lewis, Tony Orlando, and Shecky Green held a press conference to express their concerns for the welfare of the friends and colleagues who were losing these jobs. The AFM also received temporary support from other unions such as the International Brotherhood of Painters and Allied Trades and the National Treasury Employees Union, each of which canceled or moved their annual Las Vegas conventions.

Although this resistance resulted in some nationwide attention, the expressions of goodwill and concern were not enough to sway the public from attending Las Vegas's new attractions (did anyone think they would be?). Soon thereafter, the city's many major hotels and resorts quickly refined and standardized the practice of using recordings for musical accompaniment. Of course, these recordings could not be made without musicians. Mark Massagli, then-president of the local Las Vegas AFM chapter, noted the bitter irony involved in the manufacturing of these recordings that those who were necessary to their creation were the very ones whose jobs are no longer needed. As stockpiled reserves of their labors, the musicians' own recorded creations became the very source of their own displacement. In Massagli's words, "If tape is used, the musicians get stabbed with their own knife" (Schmich 1989).

Mr. Massagli must have understood that his organization was involved in a sort of backward skip into the annals of his union's history. Beginning in the late 1920s, the AFM organized a good portion of its members around issues of technological displacement. Although the union focused on a number of technologies including radio and television networks, recorded film soundtracks, and international broadcasting, the AFM's most pointed interest was in the production and use of recorded music. This interest culminated in two national recording strikes in 1942–44 and 1948 that, though still relatively uninvestigated by media scholars, are now part of American music industry folklore.

I argue that these two strikes should not be viewed simply as a set of resistances to new technologies. Rather, it would serve us to consider these struggles as organized moments of crisis and protest in the construction of a new economy of recorded musical production. In other words, if the AFM "resisted," it was not against a specific technology or machine, but rather a particular techno-cultural assemblage. In other words, these strikes were involved in a struggle over the terms, forms, and goals of popular musical production in the United States. The significant distinction between musical production in the pre- and postwar period is the result of an industry aimed at constructing repeatable-use values. The basis of the prewar music industry was live performance of music by amateurs and professionals. Whether it involved the purchase of to-be-performed sheet music, ticket sales, or using musicians as attractions for the sponsored broadcasts, the live performance was the major method through which music was appreciated, danced to, consumed, listened to, and anticipated. After the war, the music industry systematically altered itself around recordings, all of which are vital to our modern-day conception of how we conceive of popular music. Certainly the transformation of production modes was by no means absolute: there are still artists and musicians who make their living primarily from live performances. But the two nationwide recording bans, their resolution, and the loss of power by the AFM pointed to a new mode of musical production that affected not only the music industry but also mass media in general. In short, this chapter suggests that the strikes signal the end of a music industry based on performances and the beginning of one in which the production of recordings creates a standing reserve of music. By way of evidence culled from *Variety, International Musician,* and an assortment of general newspapers and journals, the importance of these events will become clearer.

Although my argument might be met with a healthy amount of skepticism, this skepticism may derive chiefly from earlier scholarly framings of these events. This is not to say that there is anything close to a unified stance on the topic of the AFM strikes. The typical account of the strikes in mass media histories is, to say the least, limited.[2] Still, there exists some interest in the study of the AFM strikes in other, less broadcast-oriented forums. The four scholars who have generated the most significant amount of research regarding the strikes are Robert Leiter (1953), Mary Austin (1978, 1980), George Seltzer (1989), and James Kraft (1996). Leiter, Austin, and Seltzer present these events as a specific struggle between the entertainment industry and the AFM as led by the eccentric James Caesar Petrillo. Furthermore, the research by Leiter, Austin, and Seltzer emphasizes the 1942–44 strike. Though Austin, Leiter, and Seltzer correctly identify Petrillo as the major source of fuel for the conflict, their respective accounts fail to offer a broader cultural understanding of the strikes. By overemphasizing the situational and individual motives, their accounts fail to recognize the more widespread and collective anxieties many musicians held regarding the vast technological reformations they witnessed. By simply highlighting Petrillo, no matter how tyrannical or charismatic he may have been, these historians tend to pin the responsibility for the bans on him, ignoring the many members of the AFM who shared his concerns. Their position inclines readers to view the strikes as the actions of a conservative trade union, a union whose desires were void of any agenda beyond the procurement of a larger share of profits in the form of wages, benefits, and more. To be sure, the AFM was never a bastion of left-wing politics: unlike other labor organizations, it had few socialist ambitions. In fact, in many ways Petrillo's AFM exhibited all the worst tendencies of American trade unions: undemocratic structures, despotic labor leadership, the systematic expulsion of "communist" and "socialist" members, markedly jingoistic policies in the name of national allegiance, and so forth. Certainly the AFM was never a revolutionary force, nor am I proposing that we need to reconsider the union as conservative or insurgent. Rather, I believe we need to look closely at this trade union and its activities because the AFM's critical responses to recordings were attempts to negotiate a much larger economic reordering for a specific entertainment workforce and their labors.

Among the above scholars, Kraft's work stands out. Kraft systematically constructs a historical account that offers a greater cultural understanding of the strikes and their context and import. Researching the period of techno-cultural rearrangement from the 1890s to 1950, Kraft frames the strikes as the culmination of a social and economic restructuring of the music industry from "diffused, labor-intensive job markets and workplaces into more centralized and mechanized ones" (1996, 193). Although many musicians' jobs "fell by the wayside" to recordings, Kraft claims that ultimately it wasn't simply efficiency that recordings offered the industry. Rather, the success of recordings was the result overall of consumer demand:

> The triumph of recorded music was possible, in the final analysis, only because the consumers came to prefer, and then to demand, the superior product it made available to them at an almost nominal cost. Like movie-goers who lined up for talkies, radio audiences tuned in to the music of big-city bands, regardless of whether it was transcribed or live. Consumers were indifferent to the concerns of musicians, and even hostile to them when they threatened the supply of recorded and broadcast music. The issue, then, was largely decided by marketplace forces. (198)

In some fashion Kraft is correct: the market embraced recordings and the consumption of music severely constrained job opportunities for musicians. But Kraft, despite his research, does not recognize the struggle for what it was: not simply a struggle over not only how music would be consumed but an across-the-board reformation of how music would be *produced*. This reformation was not only affected by expanding postwar entertainment industries but demanded by them. The reason for this demand is simple: as the mass media ventures of radio, television, and film grew, so did their respective programming needs. This growth created the need for an easily accessible and reproducible archive of musical labors, a need which begat the more centralized and rational production of records. As a result of diminishing opportunities for live musical jobs, the need for recordings as a more *decentralized* and *flexible* means of musical production grew. This growth, I contend, is what the hotly debated marketplace of recordings and playback technologies both helped generate and satisfied.

Oddly enough, in some ways one can trace this reformation back to radio's rise and the collapse of the recorded music industry in the late 1920s and early 1930s. Before radio's emergence as a dominant media technology, much of the record industry's growth was built on the booming economy of the twenties and the new forms of leisure this fashioned. Consumers found much of what they desired in the form of recorded music.[3] However, with the Great Depression audiences were forced to find more inexpensive means of musical entertainment and the sale of recordings greatly dwindled. For the most part, this meant more public rather than private forms of listening. Yet as Russell Sanjek points out, the need for public forms of listening was conveniently satisfied by a recorded music industry that seized on the Depression as an opportunity to rearrange where it would distribute its commodities (1988, 117–83). The results were varied but important: (1) Recording industries became more dynamic in fostering their young but spirited relationship with Hollywood that resulted in the development of synch-sound films. (2) A number of technological developments, programmers, and legal decisions made it possible for recordings, particularly recorded music, to find more radio airtime than ever before. (3) The evolution of coin-operated record players, that is, jukeboxes, rapidly found success in a number of public spaces such as taverns, cafes, restaurants, and lobbies.

Of course, this use of recorded music in public spaces did not occur without a significant amount of antagonism between those displaced laborers and the managers who embraced new methods of procuring profits. Organized and much-publicized conflicts between organized musicians and the implementation of these new technologies developed as early as 1927 with Warner Brothers' introduction of the Vitaphone sound picture system. As a merger of disk and film that relied on their precise synchronization, it became apparent that, despite the numerous errors involved in exhibition, audiences would accept this combination. Faced with the fact that either the Vitaphone or some other form of mechanical reproduction would replace a large number of filmhouse orchestras, the AFM launched a publicity campaign designed to deter audiences from attending these films by ridiculing the generally inferior visual and musical aesthetics of talkies. Purchasing advertisements in a number of newspapers, the AFM contended that the use of "canned music" made the movies nothing more than "dehumanized entertainment" (Leiter 1953, 53). Though it is not clear why the AFM espoused an aesthetic argument instead of arguing that musicians were being mechanically displaced, one should not misidentify which of the two issues the AFM found to be most pressing. With their day-to-day stability and freedom from the road, these theater positions were viewed as among the best, if not *the* best, jobs that an average professional musician could hold. Although no one knows exactly how many positions these sound systems eliminated, some estimates put the number at close to 22,000 (Seltzer 1989, 24).

Additional job losses followed as the jukebox grew in popularity. Throughout the thirties, many hotel, restaurant, and bar managers found coin-operated record machines to be much more efficient, less demanding employees than unionized musicians. Although many managers vowed to rehire musicians at the end of the Depression, by and large these were little more than empty promises. Especially brutal was the all but permanent loss of those jobs directly related to the sale of liquor, given the American experiment of prohibition. Unfortunately for musicians, the popularity of the jukebox in many public spaces of drink and camaraderie nullified any chance at regaining these positions after the enactment of the Twenty-First Amendment (Seltzer 1989, 23). One *New Republic* article estimated that 350,000 jukeboxes had eliminated the need for live musicians in a variety of spaces (Smith 1945). Of course, the potential loss of jobs could have been anywhere from two to three times this count given that most establishments employing musicians hired duos or trios for the purpose of public dancing and pleasurable backgrounds.[4] But if the massive change of music in social spaces was exciting for the recorded music industry, these new markets provided the industry with profits that added up to little more than a small portion of its collective peak, $106.5 million, established in 1921 (Sanjek 1988, 62).

As various forms of recorded music became established in more and more public arenas, it would only be a matter of time before the AFM would begin to openly protest this transition to a general use of recordings. The earliest actions taken against a specific use of recorded music by organized musicians occurred on behalf of the Chicago Federation of Musicians (CFM Local 10) throughout the 1930s. Led by Petrillo, the CFM threatened to call a strike of all radio musicians beginning New Year's Eve 1931. Insisting that all commercial records be barred from radio airplay, the local gained a small victory when Chicago area broadcasters agreed to reduce the working hours of broadcast musicians. Six years later in 1937, Petrillo and the CFM followed through on a threat to strike, which, this time, involved every musician in the local. While the 1931 threats were primarily concerned with broadcasters, the 1937 strike did not permit members of the local to make recordings of any kind. The 1937 strike claimed a much more antagonistic tone with this action designed ostensibly to eliminate "for all time the menacing threat of recorded music" ("A Resolution Authorizing an Investigation" 1943, 16).

Petrillo's sweeping, almost melodramatic sentiments regarding the threat of records, a sentiment he would voice repeatedly throughout the next ten years of his career as a sort of personal motto, resonated strongly with a large number of musicians across the AFM's nationwide local chapters. The sentiment of these musicians began to become evident in 1936 when the AFM filed a number of lawsuits attempting to establish the right of musicians to restrict the employment of commercial recordings to in-home use only. Although the courts never granted this right,[5] the AFM's suits elevated their concerns to a national level. Combined with the activities of the CFM these legal actions curried enough favor among unionized musicians to bring the issue of recorded music to the floor for debate at the AFM's national convention in 1937. Spreading the conviction that recordings were problems for the majority of musicians was not as demanding as one might think. As Russell Sanjek notes, "throughout the 1930s the [AFM] was adamant in its opposition to radio's use of recorded music on the air, correctly anticipating that 'canned' music would lead to the displacement of live musicians" (1983, 35). Because of the concerns expressed at the 1937 convention, Joseph Weber, then-president of the AFM, requested a number of meetings with representatives of the recording and broadcast industries. According to at least one author, the list of demands was accompanied by a threat to halt not only the production of recorded music but also "all work by musicians." After fourteen weeks of conferences and negotiations, the two sides agreed on a quota system that would involve the hiring of musicians and acceleration of their wages until 1940. In return, Weber and the AFM withdrew the union's objection to the use of recordings in broadcasting (Leiter 1953, 69).

Although this success occurred on Weber's clock, his tenure as the AFM president ended in 1940. A combination of age and bad health were significant factors in ending his governorship, but a strident, well-organized Petrillo was certainly as important. Petrillo's fame was the result of his almost militant ability to organize. His reputation fated to be forever tarred with the brush of organized corruption so often associated with the city of Chicago, Petrillo never distanced himself from the brusque manners of his hometown and its residents. Armed with the same blunt and effective rhetoric wielded by many famous Chicagoans, Petrillo brandished enough political savvy to mobilize large numbers of working musicians on both local and national bases. A one-time saloon proprietor who began his business career as a cigar-stand owner after giving up the trumpet in his teens, Petrillo never strayed far from the streets, and one could certainly make the case that the rough-and-tumble space of the street is where he learned his most important lessons of strong-willed negotiation and salesmanship. To say the least, Petrillo, who needed nine years to get through the fourth grade, was not a man of "book knowledge" (Austin 1978, 11). Still, this union boss could exercise an uncanny, if oblique, logic that often cloaked itself as unscrutinized wit. One of the more famous examples of Petrillo's opinions was his refusal to recognize any significant differences among musical laborers. When questioned as to whether it was fair that the famed violinist Jascha Heifetz should suffer under policies developed to protect musicians of lesser skill, Petrillo replied with both a question and answer of his own: "Since when is there any difference between Heifetz and the fiddler in the tavern? They're both musicians" (Leiter 1953, 114).

No matter how odd that statement may appear, it epitomizes the logic that underpinned and mobilized the actions of the AFM under Petrillo's administration. Beginning in 1940 the AFM conducted an aggressive strategy to enlist nonunionized competition as well as to stave off competing unions. By pressuring the American Guild of Musical Artists (AGMA), a union dedicated to organizing theatrical and variety performers, with a set of hardball tactics, the AFM was able to annex and incorporate a majority of instrumentalists from the guild. But certainly the most celebrated annexation for the union occurred when the AFM organized and enrolled the Boston Symphony, the only major nonunionized symphony at that time in the United States. Because of these organizations, by 1941 Petrillo and the AFM were able to make a much more forceful claim that the AFM could provide a substantially more unified front needed to operate in a war against recorded music (Seltzer 1989, 33–39).

With the significant advancements in membership came a palpable boost in confidence. At both the 1941 and 1942 national conventions the AFM researched the possibility of enforcing a national recording ban and examined how they could increase the number of job opportunities for live music performances. In the summer of 1942, the annual AFM convention gave Petrillo the authorization needed to begin the ban. Working swiftly, by June 1942, Petrillo had sent a letter to every recording company in the United States announcing that, as of August 1, 1942, those musicians affiliated with the AFM would no longer render their services to the recorded music industry (Seltzer 1989, 39). Printed in the July edition of the AFM's in-house organ, *The International Musician*, the letter stated,

> Gentlemen:
>
> Your license from the American Federation of Musicians for the employment of its members in the making of musical recordings will expire on July 31, 1942, and will not be renewed. From and after August 1, 1942, the American Federation of Musicians will not play or contract for any other forms of mechanical reproductions of music.
>
> Very truly yours,
> James C. Petrillo,
> President, American Federation of Musicians
> ("A.F. of M. Prohibits Making Recordings" 1942)

As one might suspect, such a letter spurred a number of retaliations by the radio and recording industries, but none were more vocal or important than those of the federal government: in an attempt to block the implementation of the ban the Department of Justice filed an antitrust suit ("Music Union Cornered" 1942). Although dismissed by both a federal district court and the Supreme Court, the lawsuit had at least one success: it brought the union under the spotlight of public scrutiny. The lawsuits were not the only actions taken by the government to publicize what it and the industry believed was an egregious and dangerous act. One month after the implementation of the strike in September 1942, a subcommittee of the Committee on Interstate Commerce in the U.S. Senate held three days of hearings on the "use of mechanical reproduction of music" (Resolution Authorizing an Investigation 1943). With testimony given by Elmer Davis, head of the Office of War Information; Lawrence Fly, Chairman of the Federal Communications Commission and of the Board of War Communications; and Thurman W. Arnold, Assistant Attorney General of the United States, the hearings addressed the need for recorded music during a time at which the nation was at war. Lawrence Fly asserted that there was an economic imperative as broadcasters relied heavily on recorded music. According to a FCC survey of the nation's 890 stations (796 replying), Fly noted that 58.2 percent of these stations claimed to operate without the employment of any musicians. Furthering the importance of recordings to the demise of the in-studio band and orchestra, another 15.6 percent of these stations claimed to employ only one player at a time (Resolution Authorizing an Investigation 1943, 18). On the other hand, Elmer Davis argued that, though his department held no official concern for individual broadcasters or proprietors, the industry's dependence on recorded music made this crisis pertinent as it had the possibility of harming the nation's morale. According to Davis, given that most American broadcasters needed musical recordings to profitably operate, a void of new musical recordings would endanger the ability of the Office of War Information to communicate to the nation about wartime goings-on (6).

If Davis and Fly were in some way or another concerned with the effects on radio and mass communication in general, other government voices noted that this, too, was an issue central to America's industrial output. On the final day of testimony, Thurman Arnold asserted that

> the A.F.M. is attempting to coerce their immediate employees to use unnecessary and useless labor. It is attempting to destroy independent businesses which do not employ musicians, such as small independent radio stations, small restaurants and hotels,

juke box operators and manufacturers, as well as manufacturers of phonograph records and electrical transcriptions, because they have adopted inventions for the rendition of music.

While Arnold viewed the issues of production and labor in question to be unique to broadcasting, the Department of Justice held the issues contested as a more general concern. In this regard the Department of Justice's opinion regarding these activities could not be clearer: "We regard a handicap on industrial progress by preventing the use of improved mechanical equipment in an industry as an attack upon industrial production ("Charges Petrillo Attacks Freedom" 1942).

Dovetailing with both the National War Labor Board and President Roosevelt's inabilities to end the ban through executive declarations or appeals to authority, these hearings helped to forge public opinion about Petrillo and the AFM as less than positive entities. But these governmental bodies were not alone in informing the public that Petrillo's actions should be seen as a major threat. As one *New York Times* editorial noted, "[Mr. Petrillo] is grossly mistaken, for example, when he assumes that if he forbids radio stations and restaurants from using records they will have to use orchestras and bands." Rather, the editorial asserted, the net result of the strike would be, simply, less music ("Petrillo as a Case Study" 1942, 18). And the progressive voice of *The Nation* opined that "chances are that [audiences] will continue to choose first-rate recordings in preference to second or third-rate 'live' music." Given the rise of technology, no matter what measures the AFM could take, "[these] would not restore the musician to his pre-jukebox position. Small-time musicians have become as obsolete as the Indian. James Caesar Petrillo, for all of his confident toughness, will not be able to erase that fact." Although the AFM's 1942 war on recorded music would achieve a limited success, *The Nation* regarded its ultimate goal as "hopeless" from the beginning and tended to frame Petrillo's resistance to recordings as a form of vain ludditism ("Mr. Petrillo's Hopeless War" 1942). Echoing this sentiment, the *Chicago Daily Tribune* asserted that Petrillo's aims were attempts at putting "the United States back to the days before Thomas A. Edison" (Editorial 1942). And while this progressive fantasy of technology was upheld, other opinions perceived Petrillo as a sort of modern autocrat. One of the few letters to the editor printed in the *New York Times* regarding the AFM's ban observed that "the unpleasant situation in which radio stations and musicians find themselves under the dictatorship [of Petrillo] is most timely. . . . Steps should be taken forthwith to change the [law] so that labor dictators can be dealt with as we deal with dictators in other fields" (Gehman 1942).

Certainly, this rhetoric had a number of aims, at least one of which was strictly associational. By equating union leadership with the fascist and imperialist forces that the United States was fighting, many editorials suggested that the strike was not a collective action but a dictate forced onto its rank and file membership. The depiction of Petrillo as the "Boss of Music" who forced the nation to "play his tune" was a popular one, as seen in political cartoons of the day ("Petrillo Cartoons" 1944). To be sure, a good portion of this characterization was on the mark. Perhaps "Slim" Gaillard put it best in his 1951 song, "Federation Blues." According to Gaillard, musicians, no matter how skilled they were, would "go nowhere, til' they seen James C. Petrillo." This sentiment may have been widespread, but like this song, which was not released from the Verve vaults until 1994, it was typically left unexpressed for economic and political reasons (Gaillard 1994).[6]

However, to claim that the national strike was forced onto the union by the despotic will of one leader is simply mistaken. As mentioned earlier, the strike emanated out of a collective concern for the status of musicians as employable, productive laborers. And this was a concern that other labor organizations viewed as legitimate. Perhaps the most significant statement of solidarity came from the executive council of the American Federation of Labor. Meeting at their annual convention in Toronto, the 1942 executive council unanimously endorsed the strike with a resolution that recognized the collective struggle of unionized musicians ("A.F. of L. Convention Unanimously Endorses Federation's Record Fight" 1942). And in 1943 *The International Musician* printed a letter that had been sent from Petrillo to the "Musician's Union" in Britain. According to Petrillo, the British union expressed a "great interest" in the strike, since British musicians "were faced with many difficulties related to recording and re-recording, both for films and subsequent public use in theatres, and for other forms of public entertainment" ("British Musicians Back A.F. of M. Recording Ban" 1943). With support from both international and national forums, both the strikers and the union as a whole must have formed a much stronger sense of purpose and alliance.

Despite this support, the length of the strike (almost two years) suggested the economic stamina of record companies. Although record companies felt the initial effects of the ban, it is not clear if these were conclusively positive or negative. To be sure, there was a sharp decline in the number of records released to the public, but there is also evidence that record collectors generally had such enthusiasm for new releases that, according to one *Newsweek* article, "a flop [was] almost unheard of" (quoted in Austin 1980, 39). This enthusiasm was the result of scarcity caused by not only the strike but also a very real deficit of the main material component needed to make records: shellac. Given the rationing of shellac, along with other materials needed for recordings and record players, many record companies viewed the dearth of materials and the strike as an opportune time to clear out their warehouses and unearth much of their catalogue.[7] As it stood, most of these catalogues were classified as "classical" rather than popular material (Seltzer 1989, 41).[8]

Affected most severely was the supply of "pop" recordings. Unlike the classical catalogue, the demand for pop artists and records is far more contingent on cycles of musical fashion that can be neither predicted nor controlled by the music industry. Though record companies continued to release popular music, these records were the products of numerous maneuvers and production tricks. These techniques, which ranged from using categories of instrumentalists not represented by the AFM to the use of vocal beds in lieu of strings, have become legendary among record collectors and music writers (see Ward, Stokes, and Tucker 1986, 32; Lanza 1994, 115; Chanan 1995, 86).[9] Oddly enough, despite the variety of restrictions placed on consumers and manufacturers, record companies were able to earn unexpected profits during the initial bans.

Of course, reports of music industry successes should be taken with a large grain of salt. Despite their profits, the AFM's ban had significant consequences on the record industry, if only by reason of its longevity. At close to twenty-four months, the strike forced major record companies such as Columbia and RCA-Victor into an awkward situation as smaller, more upstart, independent labels used the strike as an opportunity to become more competitive (Chanan 1995, 86). In his history of country music, Bill Malone points out that the Los Angeles–based Capitol Records was able to effectively benefit from the ban. Because the label was organized shortly before the beginning of the strike, Capitol was able to grow much more quickly and acquire a much stronger position than they may have gained "had the strike not been in progress" (1985, 180). The most important independent company to take advantage of the strike was Decca, which effectively catalyzed the string of events that led to the end of the ban. After signing Jascha Heifetz, one of RCA's premium classical instrumentalists (as well as one of the world's leading violinists), Decca agreed to a list of AFM demands, the most significant of which resulted in the institution of a fixed royalty to be administered and received by the AFM for each recording and transcription manufactured and sold.

This royalty system was central to the formation of the Recording and Transcription trust fund, arguably the most important result of the ban. Founded on the principle of gaining monies to employ jobless musicians, the fund's mechanism of redistribution was seen as an apex for the musician's union. In lauding the AFM's triumph over the recording industry, Petrillo claimed that this event was "the greatest victory ever achieved by a labor organization" and an achievement for labor in general (Petrillo 1944a). By gaining a means through which organized musicians could profit from the sale of musical recordings, Petrillo's AFM secured significant gains. To be sure, this was truly the greatest triumph for the union. Still, one should not ignore the AFM's accomplishments with Hollywood film studios during the same period. In May 1944, *The International Musician* reported that the international executive board of the AFM had met with representatives from MGM, RKO, Columbia, Paramount, Twentieth Century-Fox, Warner Brothers, Universal, Republic, Technicolor, and the Producer's Committee and Association in New York City to discuss the terms for a new set of contracts ("Meetings with Film Industry" 1944). Through these negotiations the federation had, by September, procured an unprecedented written contract with the film industry. Among the many requirements of the contract were quotas for the full-time employment of musicians on a studio-by-studio basis, wage scales, and union representation. Perhaps most significant was a provision relating to the practice of "dubbing." According to a column by Petrillo,

> Those of our members who are employed in this phase of the
> industry know that dubbing has always been a curse to the music
> profession. Dubbing is the re-recording of film music. This film

music is commonly known in the profession as "sound track."
After the utilization of sound tracks in the picture for which they
were originally made, the studios accumulated over a period
of years a tremendously large and comprehensive sound track
library on their shelves. It was a common practice for the studios
to take these sound tracks from their shelves and dub them on
to newly made moving pictures, thereby saving the expense of
employing live musicians. This, of course, curtailed tremendously
the amount of employment our members were rightfully entitled
to. (Petrillo 1944a)

One major accomplishment of this contract was that it countered another threat: it made the dubbing of musical soundtracks "a thing of the past." Under the terms of the general contract, if dubbing soundtracks were to occur, a studio would have to gain permission from the international executive board (Petrillo 1944a).

It was this library, this stockpile of recorded soundtracks, that, for the AFM, posed a great threat to the musician. This issue of stockpiling, whether involving a radio station or a Hollywood studio's record library, is absolutely fundamental to understanding the debate involved in the 1942–44 and 1948 strikes. Although American media historians and theorists have not invested much thought or research in the recording/media stockpile, Jacques Attali's theoretical work on the political economy of music provides us with an analytical purchase on this issue. According to Attali, "stockpiling" is an essential element for what he terms "repetitive society." For Attali, the repetitive society is a technocracy involved in the massive creation of time-objects that are able to perpetuate the unfolding of labors performed across time beyond their initial usage;[10] these time-objects are musical use values that can be repeatedly employed beyond the desires of the musician:

In repetition, the entire production process of music is very
different from that of representation, in which the musician
remained the relative master of what he proposed for the listener.
He alone decided what to do. Of course, as soon as sound technology started to play an important role in representation, the
musician was already no longer alone. But today, under repetition, the sound engineer determines the quality of recording,
and a large number of technicians construct fashion the product
delivered to the people. (1985, 105).

In short, "Music escapes from musicians." As a unit in the mass production of objects within repetitive society, musicians find their role reduced to guiding "the unpredictable unfolding of sound production." In
other words, "One produces what technology makes possible, instead of
creating technology for what one wishes to produce" (115).

The stockpile, then, is the accumulation of use-times in objects whose
possession and preservation is the social expression of its service (Attali
1985, 124). Central to this logic is the archived catalogue. Through the accumulation of recordings, or as Attali would more generally term them,
molds, entertainment economies involved in mass reproduction no longer
subscribe to a logic that prioritizes the labor necessary to the creation of
the object. In fact, labor (in this case the musical performance) is no longer
intrinsic to the production of these objects once the mold is cast. In essence, "the information included and transmitted thus plays the role of
a stockpile of past labor, of capital" (128), hence the almost immeasurable value that accrues to the possession of all types of entertainment
archives and catalogues in today's economies.[11]

Since the creation of demand and the distribution of products are
the most important labors in an economy of mass production, the economic importance of the "mold makers"—musicians, producers, and
engineers—is no longer primary. Instead, the molder finds herself in an
economic triangulation wherein the organized promotion and dissemination of recorded wares find equal, if not superior, standing. Therefore,
the economic status of the molder can vary immensely. For example, if
musicians or producers are accorded any kind of authorial status, then
there is a possibility of residuals as well as a payment for performance.[12]
If not, in most cases musicians and technicians receive a one-time payment for duties rendered. In worst-case scenarios, their labors are recorded without payment for performance or the promise of residuals,
which is often the practice in many kinds of media institutions.[13] But in
every case the stockpile grows. With each recorded performance, with
each object that contains the potential of being repackaged in multiple
fashions across time, control of the stockpile leaves the musician. And
in many cases, musicians have little to no "say" about the reproductive
status of the time-object mold they helped cast.

As noted above, most media historians have framed the AFM strike
within the strict context of broadcast history, thereby failing to recognize
the numerous industries that it affected. Most importantly, the focus on

broadcasting has blinded media historians to the AFM's greater challenge, the challenge to a large-scale industrial paradigm that placed a premium on the flexible stockpiling and packaging of "use times." The AFM correctly recognized that the stockpile's governance and preservation was key to creating a recording-based media economy. The construction of the library (and the time objects therein) is essential in allowing media economies to efficiently unlock, on command, the energies that the object contains. The most useful understanding of the stockpile lies in Martin Heidegger's use of the term "standing-reserve" in his essay "The Question Concerning Technology." For Heidegger, what distinguishes modern from premodern technologies is how the modern forms unlock, transform, store, distribute, and switch natural energies in processes that reveal particular "standing-forths":

> Everything everywhere is ordered to stand by, to be immediately at hand, indeed to stand there just so that it may be on call for a further ordering. Whatever is ordered about in this way has its own standing. We call it the standing-reserve [bestand]. The word expresses here something more, and something more essential, than mere "stock." The name "standing-reserve" assumes the rank of an inclusive rubric. It designates nothing less than the way in which everything presences that is wrought upon by the challenging revealing. Whatever stands by in the sense of standing-reserve no longer stands over against us as object.

Heidegger continues,

> Yet an airliner that stands on the runway is surely an object. Certainly. We can represent the machine so. But then it conceals itself as to what and how it is. Revealed, it stands on the taxi strip only as standing reserve, inasmuchas it is ordered to ensure the possibility of transportation. (1977, 17).

One of the more interesting concepts in Heidegger's thoughts regarding modern technology is the *manner* in which the "modern" organizes energies to be harnessed, stored, and employed at command. In terms of modern mass media, the assembly and organization of recorded performances is absolutely necessary to ensure the possibility of easily stored, deployed, and repeatable programming. It is in this manner that we can see why the stockpile of musical labors in the form of recordings has been so coveted by all forms of modern American mass media. In essence, the modern mass media archive allows programming decisions to be made in an efficient and flexible manner. For broadcasters, recordings render both the issues of assembling musicians and the need for multiple rehearsal performances moot. To be sure, mass media libraries allow for a number of industrial logics and practices of production and leisure to unravel in interesting manners, of which programming is only one.

This is an important point. Despite making an ostensive attempt to eliminate the extensive record libraries owned by radio, television, and Hollywood, the AFM accepted terms that only somewhat limited their use. As mentioned earlier, while the AFM was able to restrict the use of catalogued recordings in films, the celebration was tempered by the fact that one of the main objectives of the strike—the elimination of recorded music from the airwaves—had been compromised in the bargaining process (Leiter 1953, 142–43). Indeed, the radio industry went relatively unscathed, despite the fact that Chairman Fly of the FCC insisted that the effects of the strike would be traumatic for small radio stations. At worst, many of these stations received only minor abrasions.[14] Given that the AFM always claimed that radio's abusive use of recordings was a major impetus for their strike, it is interesting that the union decided that, at least for the moment, it would tolerate the practice of utilizing recordings instead of musicians. Indeed, despite the union's initial protests, the AFM accepted the use of recordings on the air in exchange for an enforced limitation rather than the strict elimination of recording stockpiles. In this sense, the objections to dubbing and the construction of the recording fund were limits that allowed musicians to profit from the stockpile and/or remain as an employed reserve army of labor. On the other hand, mass media entities could, within the limits established at the end of the strike, continue to benefit from the ease provided by recordings.

The primary reason for this tolerance was that the union considered the recording fund as sufficient enough to forward their cause in this modern music economy. The rationale for this was simple: the fund acted as the device through which organized labor could benefit from the unique abilities of the recording. Presented to all record labels, the AFM's contract demanded a mandatory royalty "from 1/4 cent to five cents for records selling up to two dollars." As Seltzer details, "for all records selling above two dollars the fee was two and a half percent of the sale price. No fee was charged for commercial transcriptions for single broadcasts, but the fee for library transcriptions was three percent of their gross revenues" (1989, 44). The AFM never disguised the fact that the fund was established as means for the redistribution of profits made on recorded music to support musical performances. In fact, the union praised the fund as a solution to the problems musical recordings posed to musicians. As noted in the editorial statement from a 1945 article in *The International Musician,* a recording's ability to not only be reproduced without the aid of the musician but also to displace musicians from their jobs rendered this commodity unlike any other previously known to laborers. This point was repeatedly made before and during the strike. Yet the article noted that a distinction needed to be made since the royalty acted toward "a partial balancing of accounts. It is a case of a solution fitting itself to the abuse, of payment extending to the whole body of musicians, since it is the whole body that has been made to suffer" ("No Parallel in Other Crafts" 1945).

Of course the fund was not publicized simply as a means of amelioration for musicians. By underwriting free concerts and performances, the union explained, the fund would benefit communities across the United States. Although the terms of the fund stated that it would be kept "separate and apart from all other funds of the Federation and *that no part of the Fund would be used for the payment of the salaries of any officer of the Federation*" ("Truth Crushed to Earth" 1944), it is unclear, given that we know relatively little about the internal workings of the organization, how strictly the letter of the contract was upheld. Nevertheless, the fund remained central to the AFM, and in the three years that the contracts were valid the fund had accumulated over $4.5 million (Austin 1980, 60). In February 1947, over two years after the signing ended the first strike, the AFM published their "First Plan for the Expenditure of the Recording and Transcription Fund," with a detailed set of rules for eligibility as well as a sample chart for the allocation of funds, which eventually yielded nineteen thousand free music concerts in schools, parks, and other public places (ibid.).

All the same, the importance of the fund to the AFM cannot be underestimated. In short, the AFM viewed the fund as a distinctly modern answer to a distinctly modern problem. As one 1947 editorial published in the *International Musician* claimed, the fund was the solution to "the invention of sound amplifying machines—the phonograph, the radio, the synchronized film—with their illusion of 'free' music":

> Discs—those culprits that were in the course of convincing an all-too-acquiescent public that music can be divorced from musicians embarrassingly possessed of stomachs to feed and fingers to warm—are put to work collecting this revenue to be turned back to the source of all music—the "live" musician. Thus this fund system, as a sort of alchemy of modern human relationships, transforms records from potential destroyers of living musicians into their partial sustainers. ("Editorial Comment" 1947)

The allusion to the transformative powers of alchemy, that ancient dream of converting base materials into the luxurious splendor of gold, should not be overlooked. In this case, the fund embodied one of the basic dictums of liberal social sciences: the fund was created as the reasonable, democratic solution to a discrepancy between the powers of labor and capital. Through the development and effective administration of a bureaucracy of percentages and contracts, the AFM strove to make mechanical means of production and reproduction the partner of musician, rather than "his most dangerous competitor." Most important, the fund was viewed as strictly "modern" in its formation ("Editorial Comment" 1947). The solution's "modernity" rested on the fact that, rather than eliminating the stockpile, the fund identified and attempted to work with and profit from the standing reserve of musical labors. It is this kind of optimism concerning technology that many modern-day labor historians and critics all too often leave forgotten.

Indeed, the AFM did not simply harbor a negative critique of recordings. For the union, their primary objections were not about the record but the manner in which it allowed for the unlicensed duplication of artistic labors. Again, the AFM was not simply concerned with the workings of radio and the music industry. Instead, the union found many mass media practices objectionable. For example, the AFM, Petrillo in particular, was just as concerned with the prospects of television and FM radio. As it became clear that the war would end and the Allies would triumph, labor in the United States salivated over the prospects of well-earned luxuries and the conclusion of self-imposed rationing. Anticipating the new media fields where musicians could prosper or from which they could be excluded, the union needed a strategy to deal with them. As a result, Petrillo's administration prohibited AFM musicians from working on either television or FM in 1945 until the proper contracts between the union and the broadcasters were signed (L. White 1947, 52). In this sense, the AFM challenged the conditions of how modern production and distribution of entertainment products should be constituted, rather than the recording's existence. We should not be too surprised to learn that broadcasters, networks, and film studios were just as interested as, if not more than, the record industry in breaking the union's power and influence over how one should manage and profit from recordings.

Counterreform and Resignation

The Second Strike of the American Federation of Musicians

PRESIDENT NIXON: Frankly, I don't want to have in the record [that is, the tapes] discussions we've had in this room on Watergate. You know, we've discussed a lot of that stuff.

H. R. (BOB) HALDEMAN: That's right.

— Quoted in Stanley Kutler, *Abuse of Power*

IF THERE IS ONE FASCINATION I HAVE WITH RECORDINGS AND their relationship to history that outstrips all others, it would have to be the manner in which recordings are able to re-present the past. Recordings not only lend significance to the presentation of moments captured but also present the absence of others. As a small child who grew up mindful of something called Watergate, I knew that taping someone could muster trouble for even the most powerful people. The fact that one's own voice could be used against oneself, a concept I somehow found patently unfair if not simply frightening, was the issue of the day. It turns out that the struggle over whether or not an investigator could access the president's tapes, a primary plotline of Watergate that is so well known it needs no repeating, is what took President Nixon aback. His puzzlement over his own voice and how he "lost it" has become mythical. While Oliver Stone's *Nixon* is as tormented and moved by voices from the past as any spiritualist (*Nixon*, 1995), Nixon the bungler, in *Dick* (1999, dir. Fleming) is befuddled by the infamous eighteen and a half minutes of silence. But unlike the popular theory of coverup, this Nixon creates the silence because he is embarrassed to find that a pubescent girl has left an eighteen-and-a-half-minute-long testimony of devotion and love on his reel-to-reel machine.

We can speculate in any fashion and with any fantasy we want, but we do have Nixon's voice and it tells its own tales. The documents show that Nixon understood the power of recording as early as 1947. In his interrogation of James Petrillo before the Special Subcommittee of the Committee on Education and Labor in the House of Representatives, Nixon flaunted his position of power by explicitly recording his dialogue with AFM's president:

> Mr. Nixon. One point before you get away, Mr. Petrillo. You indicated that the American Federation of Musicians, and particularly you, have the control of the last word on the making of recordings. I assume that wherever a member of the American Federation of Musicians appears on the program, or in public, that you want to see that no recordings are made unless you have given permission. I think we would like to know whether or not you gave permission for the recordings to be made of these hearings today.
>
> Mr. Petrillo. I didn't know there were any recordings.
>
> Mr. Nixon. Are you going to call the Congress unfair, then?
>
> ("First Session pursuant to House Resolution 111" 1947, 225)

Certainly this is something of a cheap swipe at Petrillo, but as cheap swipes go, this one had quite a vicious fee, a fee paid back in the form of history's future shame. The release of the Watergate tapes and the publication of their contents, most prominently in Stanley Kutler's edited volume *Abuse of Power* in the late 1990s, were given significant attention by the political press. Yet it is clear from his memoirs, first published in 1978, that Nixon found listening to his own conversations simultaneously assuring and strenuous. Nixon notes that on June 4, 1973, he encountered his own voice for the first time:

> Monday, June 4, was the first time I listened to a tape. Steve Bull [presidential aide] brought a tape machine to my EOB office and

cued the first one for me. I put on the earphones and pressed the "play" button. The reel began unwinding. Sounds drifted in and out; voices overrode each other. Gradually, as my ears became accustomed, I could pick up more and more. I listened to conversation after conversation with [John] Dean [Counsel to the President] in February and March, all before March 21.[1] At the end of the day I was both exhausted and relieved. (Nixon 1990, 874)

As Nixon would soon learn, however uncanny it was to hear one's own voice speak without his intentions in the first place, the ensuing struggle to control the tapes would become the coverup that would end his presidency. Nixon knew this and in an August 22, 1973, press conference claimed,

What is involved is not only the tapes, what is involved, as you ladies and gentlemen well know, is the request on the Senate committee and the special prosecutor as well, that we turn over Presidential papers, in other words, the record of conversations with the President made by his associates. Those papers and the tapes as well cannot be turned over without breaching the principle of confidentiality. Whether it is a paper or whether it's tape, what we have to bear in mind is that for a President to conduct the affairs of this office and conduct effectively, he must be able to do so with confidentiality intact. (*Watergate* 1975, 288)

On the one hand, one can see an issue of privacy. The ability and right to keep what has been spoken, what was performed to one's own person whether it was taped or not, is certainly a matter of confidentiality. But also at stake was Nixon's desire to retain his power of self-representation. Nixon and his administration understood that these recordings not only documented the past but had the power to effectively undermine his right *not* to have his own voice testify against himself. The Nixon tapes are not only among the most memorable pieces of evidence in American history; they are among the most salient examples of the recording's challenge to self-representation. To underline the power of the record as a representational force, I want to return to Jacques Atalli in *Noise:* "Right from the beginning, machines invented to counteract temporal erosion, to constitute a *speech* that would be indefinitely *reproducible,* to overcome the ravages of time by means of the construction of mechanical devices, were moving in the direction of a death blow to representation" (1985, 85–86). From this perspective, recording processes and their products then cannot be seen as simply a neutral technology with little purchase on public management:

> Recording has always been a means of social control, a stake in politics, regardless of the available technologies. Power is no longer content to enact its legitimacy: it records and reproduces the societies it rules. Stockpiling memory, retaining history or time, distributing speech, and manipulating information has always been an attribute of civil priestly power, beginning with the Tables of Law. But before the industrial age, this attribute did not occupy center stage: Moses stuttered and it was Aaron who spoke. But there was already no mistaking: the reality of power belonged to he who was able to reproduce the divine word, not he who gave it voice on a daily basis. Possessing the means of recording allows one to monitor noises, to maintain them, and to control their repetition within a determined code. In the final analysis, it allows one to impose one's own noise and to silence others: "Without the loudspeaker, we would never have con-quered Germany," wrote Hitler in 1938 in the *Manual of German Radio.* (87)

The ability to represent one's self-will and the ability to control one's own labors and energies are the most contentious topics of struggle in liberal democracies. These struggles are ongoing: we need only take a cursory look, for example, at the court cases and general debates sur-rounding online file sharing. At the heart of these debates lies the knowledge that recordings exist beyond the reach of those who make them. The special faculty of the record is that it contains and is able to reproduce one's own labors, however ephemeral these labors may have been. That these labors could be used again and/or against oneself through their uncanny and efficient retrieval is both a significant con-cern and a tempting promise.

It is within this set of political concerns that we need to recognize that the anxieties of the 1942–44 ban were manifest. We should never forget that these concerns were those of not simply the working mu-sician but the businessmen and their political representatives, each of whom hoped to exploit the modern potentials of recordings to their full-est extent. Both groups from the public and private sector concerned by

COUNTERREFORM AND RESIGNATION

the power of the AFM were united in at least one manner: even though recorded music is neither a sufficient nor necessary element for broadcasting, both entrepreneurial forces and the U.S. government viewed the ban as a distinct threat to the productive capacities of the nation's broadcasters. The state-sanctioned expressions of concern in the hearings of 1942 are indicative of how dependent the radio industry was, and still is, on stockpiles of recordings. Of course, part of this reliance has to do with the nature of program syndication, distribution, and scheduling, but it also points to another, more decentralized mode of production and reproduction. It is a mode that emphasizes and develops the ability to propagate and move significant amounts of information across large portions of geography in smaller and smaller amounts of time. In this manner the recorded music industries are, as noted before, part and parcel of the modern methods of information condensation and distribution. Within these industries the labors of the musician are posited into specific codes, which, through standardized systems of distribution and interpretation, are easily reproduced. That there is not an adequate understanding of the historical importance of recording technologies with regard to the history of broadcasting reflects an immense assumption concerning both the nature and the history of the recording in mass media, one that is by no means self-evident.

This assumption of "self-evidence" is most apparent in the present absence of research regarding the second AFM recording ban in 1948. The 1948 ban was not simply a strike brought on by an impasse in contract negotiations. Instead it can be seen as an attempt by the AFM to deal with an across-the-board counterreformation, a movement wherein private capital rolled back some of the more important gains of labor in order to reclaim power once lost. In other words, the events leading up to and being addressed by the 1948 ban were actually quite distinct from those in the first national work stoppage.

Still, despite its significance in popular music history, the 1948 ban suffers from obscurity. While the research on the 1942–44 strikes may appear incomplete, the writing about the 1948 strike is scant in comparison. Certainly, the general perception of the recording ban as both a bluff and an inevitable failure has functioned as a particularly limiting framework. Let us consider George Seltzer's account of the 1948 ban. According to Seltzer, the primary motivation for the strike stemmed from the criminalization of the Recording and Transcription Fund through passage of the Taft-Hartley Labor Relations Act. In light of this legislation, the proclamations made by the AFM that the organization would "permanently and completely abandon" the making of records were viewed as empty threats. Indeed, by 1948 the U.S. media industry had heard the AFM make the same assertion many times, and this time record companies prepared themselves for a walkout. Receiving close to a three-month warning, record companies pushed studios into overtime schedules and developed a sizable stock of records and transcriptions they could use through the strike. Seltzer characterizes the 1948 recording strike more or less as a "waiting game." Giving way in October, the strike ended with negotiations forging new provisions that would become the Music Performance Trust Fund. The result was a compromise that made the new fund lawful under the Taft-Hartley Act (Seltzer 1989, 52). But other accounts leave us with little understanding of this second strike. Sterling and Kittross mention the AFM's status in the immediate postwar period only briefly to highlight the issue of AM-FM duplication of programming, ignoring the 1948 strike altogether (1990, 306). And, even more unfortunate, Mary Austin leaves us with no insights into the issues at stake in the 1948 ban. Through numerous omissions, the above scholars offer us very little as to how and why the industry's counterreformation operated to weaken the AFM. Worse yet, by leaving the developments of broadcasting operations unquestioned, such analyses tend to frame the outcome of the strike and its reformation of labor's relationship with technology as an inevitable and only logical result of the needs of broadcasting in general.

While the first recording ban generated a large amount of criticism regarding what many viewed as Petrillo's and the AFM's less than progressive vision of technology, the negative public opinion of the AFM did not wane after the first ban ended. Harsh feelings abounded not simply because of the AFM's work stoppage but also because of other acts of AFM defiance that functioned as less than popular public relations measures. In addition to the recording ban was the infamous "Interlochen affair." In 1943 the union barred their musicians from teaching at the Michigan music camp for young people because NBC broadcast an annual student concert. Petrillo argued that this concert was another lost performance opportunity for union musicians, in this case unpaid child musicians. Furthermore, in 1944 the AFM marshaled a national campaign to force radio stations to employ musicians as "platter turners" who flipped and spun discs at scale. Both of these well-publicized actions angered broadcasters and the public significantly enough to all but ensure some form of legislative reaction. Three years after the end of the initial strike, a newly elected Republican Congress erected a national forum for this debate when the first session of the Eightieth Congress held an investigation of Petrillo and the AFM before the House Special Subcommittee of the Committee on Education and Labor. Although the Federation and Petrillo had been the subject of congressional hearings in 1942, the 1947 hearings were much more extensive. According to George Seltzer, that these hearings were officially labeled as an investigation made them the first formal congressional investigation of a labor union in United States history (1989, 33–53).

Although the investigation considered every influence that the Federation had exerted on musical organizations (i.e., education, theatrical employment, etc.), the Subcommittee focused a large portion of its investigation on the Federation's criticism and rejection of a variety of recording and broadcasting technologies. Representative Richard Nixon of California perhaps best articulated the disposition of the Subcommittee. After almost a hundred pages of testimony given by Petrillo and the Federation's counsel, Joseph Padway, on the plight of the modern musician, Congressman Nixon voiced his lack of conviction:

> I do not believe a case has been made that all of these new developments are going to have the effect of putting musicians out of work, since they have not done it yet—but assuming that your argument is correct, I believe that the musicians' union and the federation generally could well take a more forward-looking attitude in attempting to solve this problem rather than simply the arbitrary attitude that "we will fight television, we will fight FM radio, we will fight the making of records, we will not allow the importation of foreign broadcasts, we will not allow transcontinental broadcasts because it is going to put musicians out of work."
>
> It seems to me, and I say this from a constructive standpoint, that the solutions and suggestions which have been made by Mr. Petrillo today have not at all been constructive in attempting to find a solution to this problem. ("First Session Pursuant to House Resolution 111" 1947, 225)

Not surprisingly, the Republican congressman offered nothing but stiff opposition to the AFM's "solution" of the Recording Fund. The fund would become a prime target of the Republican congressional majority, and Nixon's continual criticism is indicative of the attitude that media industries held for the program. The fund itself would become outlawed through a clause in the Taft-Hartley Labor Relations Act later in 1947.

As a whole, the Taft-Hartley Act aimed at restraining and countering the rank and file unrest, militancy, and Marxist rhetoric of class warfare that was evident in the large wave of general strikes that were staged in 1946 (Lipsitz 1994). But the immediate effects that Taft-Hartley had on the AFM arose from Section 302. This specific clause, in the words of George Seltzer, "made the Recording and Transcription Fund criminally unlawful by forbidding a union to '. . . cause or attempt to cause an employer to pay or deliver or agree to pay or deliver any money or other thing of value, in the nature of an extraction for services which are not performed or not to be performed'" (1989, 51). In short, the clause singled out the redistributive function of the fund for prohibition. And once this function was outlawed, the Recording and Transcription Fund was effectively disabled.

Taft-Hartley followed on the heels of another legislative blow to the AFM, delivered in 1946 by a then-Democratic majority in Congress. To guarantee that broadcast employers would remain in control of the basic terms of production, Congress produced the Lea Act in April 1946. Sponsored by a Democratic congressman from California, Clarence F. Lea, the act was a direct response to the AFM's attempts to salvage musicians' jobs in the face of new and rapidly changing broadcast technologies. In essence, the act primarily empowered broadcasters to employ whomever they desired, relieving them from the pressure of unions. As it read, the Lea Act "made it unlawful to force a broadcast licensee to, among other things, hire unneeded personnel, pay salaries in lieu of those unneeded personnel, pay more than once for a single service, or pay for services which were not performed." Although the AFM filed a number of appeals questioning the constitutionality of the act, the United States Supreme Court upheld the act in June 1947 (Sterling and Kittross 1990, 306). Despite this defeat, Joseph Padway made it clear that, while the Lea Act and the Supreme Court provided prohibitions regarding what the Federation could exercise to get an employer to comply with union demands, "the Supreme Court did not decide that the American

Federation of Musicians or any of its affiliates cannot strike or picket to force a licensee to hire more musicians than are needed" (Padway 1947). Given that both the Lea Act and Taft-Hartley greatly diminished the power of the union by eliminating its ability to alter the contingencies of both their employment and the "unlicensed" duplication of their labors, the AFM was left with little choice: either strike and attempt to regain power, or have members accept their newfound marginal status in the postwar mass media industries. In October 1947 the organization's executives voted unanimously to take the former option and sent a letter to all recording and transcription companies informing them that with the expiration of contracts to make musical recordings on December 31, 1947, there would be no renewal of these contracts. Including an oft-repeated threat, Petrillo's letter claimed, "This notice carries with it our declared intention, permanently and completely, to abandon that type of employment" ("For the Information of the Members" 1947).

For an American industry that had finally surpassed its all-time sales high in 1947, a mark established almost twenty-six years earlier (Sanjek 1988, 229),[2] this notice must have come as quite a disappointment. Having risen from its own dramatic downfall and stagnation during the Great Depression, the industry gained new confidence from the quick and intense postwar growth of record manufacturers. With major recording companies feeling significant growth, many began to reevaluate ways of continuing their market expansion. According to *Variety*, some labels contemplated sponsoring an "association with the primary view of bankrolling an institutional campaign to sell the public on the oft-repeated idea of record ownership as a hobby [with] ad copy [that] would center around the theme: it's fun to collect and play records at home" ("Diskers Mull Assn. to Hammer Buying Theme" 1947). The record industry's confidence that it would continue to expand grew as it received even more encouraging news. In 1948, during the second recording ban, *Variety* reported that "while the phonograph record field doesn't even show any signs of leveling off, music publishers are complaining that sheet sales have taken a sharp dip" ("Music Puzzler" 1948). With 3.4 million record players produced in 1947, it became apparent that the listening habits surrounding popular music were shifting increasingly to electronically rendered recordings of compositions, which were typically allied with "name talents." At the same time, the record industry began to seriously ponder the benefits of pooling data that would track "factors influencing sales, determining the relation of turntable sales to record sales and estimating business for the succeeding years" ("Suggest Pooling of Disk Sales Data" 1948). Even in the midst of a recording ban, the recording industry that had once believed that the wartime sales boom had finished in spring of 1947 was delightfully surprised to report that overall business was up 20 percent from prewar numbers ("Disk Biz 20% Over Prewar" 1948). To paraphrase Sanjek, there was no way for the business to go but up, it reasoned, once the major impediment of Petrillo had been beaten (1988, 229).

Upon the announcement of the AFM ban, recording and broadcasting industries responded with a number of strategies to solidify the status of recorded music as a dominant component of mass media production.[3] Among these strategies, one of the first was stockpiling not only popular recordings but classics as well. It is generally accepted and understood that this strategy was one of the more influential in bringing the ban to an end. According to Seltzer, numerous record companies were able to take advantage of their back catalogues through reissues and the willingness of artists to record popular songs before the ban took effect (1989, 52). Although Seltzer is, for the most part, correct, the manner in which the stockpiling took place and the success of this strategy were not nearly as simple or uniform as one might expect. For example, many companies procured compliance from AFM artists to gain an edge and make recordings between the time of the announcement in October 1947 until the beginning of the new year ("Disk Firms Steam" 1947). Other record companies, typically independents, attempted to sign non-unionized talents such as "hillbilly bands" to sidestep the control of the union ("[Chicago] Indie Diskers Scurry" 1947).

Recording companies were not the only ones who rushed the production of their product. Taking advantage of the almost three-month warning, several publishing firms also found a way to capitalize on the recording industry's bid to build a large stockpile of master recordings. According to the November 12 issue of *Variety*, some major publishing firms were listening to "more new songs demonstrated by writers in one week than they did in months before the ban announcement" in order to piggyback on the overtime production schedules of major and minor studios ("1,700 Songs Submitted" 1947). And while a number of publishers entertained thousands of fresh melodies, others reviewed their catalogues for popular songs old enough to have been forgotten by the general public, so they could be revived ("Radio's Petrillo-less Format" 1947). One of the most clear-cut examples of this phenomenon was the rise in popularity of "I'm Looking over a Four Leaf Clover" as a reemergent hit in early 1948. Attributing the success of oldies such as "Four Leaf Clover" to a number of factors, including the AFM's ban, *Variety* reported that the momentum of the trend would persist as record companies continued to release portions of their stockpile ("Public Continues Old-Song Happy" 1948). Still, the fleeting vogue that is pop culture ensured that the practice of stockpiling would result in a number of flops and unusable catalogue, thus leaving a number of companies singing "The Wrong Recording Blues" (see "Pre-Disk Ban Hustle" 1948; "Pubs Sing 'Wrong Recording Blues'" 1948). By the fifth month of the ban, major recording companies began to report that in all probability they would incur significant losses simply because popular tastes had outstripped many of the industry's pre-ban masters ("Major Companies Ditching Many Pre-Ban Masters" 1948).

On the other hand, it is unclear how faithful rank-and-file musicians remained to the principles and practices of the ban. *Variety* claimed that a couple of major diskers had received mail indicating that there were a number of musicians who "violently disagreed" with the ban and would make "their services available for recording services after January 1," thereby relinquishing their union membership ("Many Musicians Offer Bootleg Aid" 1947). Other musicians made more conservative gambles. By making legitimate pre-ban recordings, these players decided that losing significant royalties on records that became hits in 1948 was worth the risk if the song would help ensure future box-office fortunes ("Diskers' Petrillo 'Insurance'" 1947). For example, Nick Tosches points out in his biography of Dean Martin that Apollo, Martin's record company at the time, "optimistically feared" that one of the two records he was contracted to record would become a hit during the ban "and that there would be nothing to follow it up." As a result, Apollo exercised the option in Martin's contract to record more sides as a precaution. Apollo brought Martin back into the studio in November and waxed four more songs including the "*napulitane* classic, Teodoro Cattau's 1849, 'Santa Lucia,'" all at a substantially increased rate that acted as a premium to ensure for themselves the possibility of success (Tosches 1992, 154).

While many musicians refused to cross the picket line into the studio to record the hit songs of the day, there was still a solution of sorts for those record companies daring enough to engage in the popular but illegal practice of bootlegging already-hit records.[4] Given that illicit duplication of one's labors by small-venture capitalists such as independent pressers posed a considerable problem for musicians, we can imagine the threat that the legitimate duplication and production of music without instrumentalists posed. To be sure, bootlegging quite simply indicated the need to continue production, a need that was not limited to upstart labels.

Although stockpiling could temporarily sate the needs of the market, the desire to continue production demanded means by which musicians could be replaced. As in the first ban, recording firms searched for ways of synthesizing instrumental sounds. As mentioned earlier, the most legendary form of synthesizing instrumental sounds occurred in the first ban when a-capella vocal beds were used to simulate string sections. Of course, record companies did not refrain from repeating some of these practices in order to maintain production. For example, *Variety* noted in 1948 that Columbia released an arrangement of "Now Is the Hour" that used the same vocal simulation technique in the second ban as did Victor with the release of "Deck of Cards." At least one other company, Capitol, exhibited an active interest in finding a means of recreating specific instrumental sounds, but it would not disclose the means through which they intended to do this ("Disk Biz 20% Over Prewar" 1948).

While record companies sought a variety of strategies to counter the strike, radio and Hollywood also reacted to the possibility of losing new musical recordings for their repertoire. For example, while NBC and CBS directed their recording and transcription divisions to rush forward and log a significant amount of musical cues, beds, and bridges, the marketing and programming portions of these networks were busy preparing for the worst. Not certain whether Petrillo would even allow live musicians to perform on radio, the networks were forced to establish ersatz programming formulas, as well as lay the groundwork for possible sponsor cooperation ("Radio's Petrillo-less Format" 1947). As networks lobbied sponsors, *Variety* reported that the nets also joined a larger "all-industry" group organized to curry public opinion against the AFM by hiring Verne Burnett Associates of New York, a professional public relations counsel ("All-Industry Group Set for Publicity Tilt" 1947). Regarding itself as a "united" front, the "all-industry" focus was, in the eyes of one *Variety* reporter, no surprise since the biggest questions for the entertainment industry in 1948 would involve the recording industry:

> So much revolves around the spinning turntable today that the second ban against recording will have an even deeper effect that the first. Today, even more so than during the initial ban against the disk industry, it is a monumental, almost impossible, task to build a b.o. name without the impetus and continued support of recordings. And the new ban will exert a strangulation hold on new talent that will have far-reaching effects on all other phases of exhibition—covered by bands and singers—vaude, one-nighters, locations. (Woods 1948)

Even film studios would not remain unaffected by the strike. Some studios such as Metro-Goldwyn-Mayer, which had invested three million dollars into its record label, MGM Records, would most certainly suffer. Without the talent rosters and back catalogue of most major labels, the outlook for upstart investments such as MGM Records was grim, given the ban (Woods 1948).

Another concern for film studios was the AFM's desire to limit the televised broadcasting of film soundtracks that were produced, in the minds of many musicians, solely for theatrical purposes. In a compromise with film producers, the AFM signed a contract declaring that all films produced after February 1948 would be prohibited from being broadcast.[5] This did not mean that the pact would eliminate the musical soundtracks from these films. On the contrary, in an attempt to tally as many jobs as possible, the pact permitted musicians to perform and record scores for new films created solely for television. But by limiting the use of the soundtracks for post-1948 films, the cost of production for those studios interested in both theatrical and televisual markets was significantly elevated. As *Variety* reported, "[for] Those Hollywood studios investigating the possibility of doubling into tele-film production" the main problem was simply that the costs did not add up ("Studios' Music Soundtrack Pix Still Nixed" 1948).

However, the industry that had become most dependent on recorded music since the beginning of the 1940s was radio. As one *Variety* article pointed out, "[radio] more often culls its musical performers from recording rosters rather than spawning its own" (Woods 1948). Assuredly, the foremost manifestation of this dependency was the emergence of the disc jockey during the late 1940s as one of the more popular and cost-efficient techniques of programming stations. While the numbers of radio stations in the United States had begun a rapid postwar expansion in 1946, the demands for cheap programming increased as broadcast networks began to turn their attention to television.[6] As a unit, disc jockeys offered a means through which affiliates and independents alike could produce quality programming during a time when a good portion of previously daytime radio talent was moving on to television.

While local independent stations had relied heavily on transcriptions and "in-home" records, affiliates began to air recorded music as daytime network programming (Sterling and Kittross 1990, 275). The profession enjoyed such a significant rise in 1947 that *Variety* would claim, "James C. Petrillo notwithstanding, the disc jockey is due for a sustained run as an article of commerce in local radio." For example, the DJ had become so popular that a number of major record companies had decided to "pour their advertising largesse on hundreds of disc jockeys." Adhering to a "two-step theory" of mass communication, these record companies believed that "the best way to sell records is through the fellow whom the community accepts as an authority on records" (Bodec 1948). Evidently, the dominant belief among many labels held that neither the local record-store owner nor musicians were viewed as the local authority on records, but rather the DJ. In May 1948, while an informal poll sponsored by record retailers indicated that disc jockeys had claimed first position as an influence on disc sales, other sources speculated that DJs had become important enough "to be cut in on record royalties" ("Jockeys Ride Herd on Disk-Buyers" 1948). As Columbia Records placed 175 disc jockeys on their roster and RCA Victor began to do the same, the ranks of DJs swelled (Bodec 1948), and by July Mercury Records had rescheduled its releases so that disc jockeys could receive new recordings three weeks before the public could purchase them in order to better stimulate prerelease interest ("Mercury to Put Accent On Disk Jockey Platters" 1948).

The AFM had always understood that the disc jockey posed a threat to their job opportunities on radio. As mentioned earlier, in 1944 Petrillo led the union in a campaign to employ musicians as platter turners, technicians who would specialize in operating record players at union wages (Sterling and Kittross 1990, 235). But after the passage of the Lea Act, law prohibited the possibility of forcing this type of arrangement on a radio station. As more and more radio stations began to opt for disc jockeys, the AFM became more and more vocal about their loss of job opportunities. In a cartoon titled "Why the Record Ban" from the January 1948 edition of *The International Musician*, the disc jockey is compared to and equated with other forms of technological displacement such as the jukebox, wired music, records, and electrical transcriptions. In one of the panels a musician's daughter is depicted asking her father, who is visibly disgruntled, "Gee, daddy, why don't you play on the radio any more?" Positioned between a blaring radio set, an even-more irritated mother, and a saxophone conspicuously resting on a coffee table, the father replies, "Well, dear, because disc jockeys are cheaper than live music" (Teaford 1948). With the exception of the recording ban or the occasional affiliate choosing to ban visiting musicians from appearing with a local disc jockey, there was little hope for the AFM in restricting the growth of the disc jockey profession ("Jockeys Ride Herd on Disk-Buyers" 1948; "Omaha AFM Bans Guest Maestros" 1948).

And while the disc jockey flourished on many independent stations, networks were planning and developing television and FM radio as opportunities to duplicate much of their programming and musical entertainment. In a front-page *Variety* article from February 1948 titled "Radio-Television in 'Sister Act'," George Rosen noted that program duplication was already on the NBC agenda, "with simultaneous sight-and-sound broadcasting paving the way." But standing in the way of this was, once again, the AFM. While the AFM agreed to the concept of this particular "system of interchangeability" (Rosen 1948), not every plan of duplication was as warmly accepted. One of the more vocally contested plans to duplicate programming was that of AM-FM simulcasting. In October 1945 the AFM ordered all networks that duplicated AM-FM programming and utilized live orchestras to hire a duplicate "FM orchestra" or abandon studio musicians. The plan backfired, with most stations eliminating their orchestras altogether and opting for recorded music. Despite this drastic move by the radio industry, it was Petrillo's draconian decree that the 1946 Congress regarded as one of the many reasons for the necessity of the Lea Act. Although weakened, the AFM could still remove musicians from the networks at any time. Many network executives must have understood that, as a threat, this was an unlikely prospect. Nevertheless, networks respected the AFM enough that a "gentleman's agreement" *not* to duplicate AM programming was maintained until a written contract could be established ("Not Much Chance of Petrillo Pulling Musicians" 1948).[7]

It became clearer that as a media economy based on the duplication, networking, recording, and stockpiling of programming proliferated in this period, the AFM was losing ground. It is also clear that this new media economy needed to weaken the union in order to make room for this reorganization of mass entertainments. While the ruling body of the AFM resisted these developments by attempting to hinder job losses and placing limits on the use of recorded music, questions about the effectiveness of the union and its strength began to come from its own members. As independent record companies began to sign and record masters using amateur/folk musicians with payments as low as $100 for twenty to forty-five musicians making a recording ("$100 Guarantee for Disking" 1948),[8] reports of AFM musicians willing to cross the line were beginning to be highlighted in the front pages of *Variety* ("Musicians Say They're Willing" 1948, 1).[9] Worse yet, the union continued to lose ground in the public arena. With Petrillo continually singled out and vilified as a greedy despot by much of the press, the AFM began to focus on public relations by promoting the benefits of the Recording Fund ("Suggest Pooling of Disk Sales Data" 1948; "Slice of 802's Record Fund" 1948).[10] Despite the promotions, rumors of an imminent end-of-the-summer settlement of the ban abounded at the AFM's annual summer convention. According to Petrillo, it became evident from the failed preconvention attempts to gain additional employment opportunities for musicians that the counterattack was more than the union could handle and the broadcasters clearly held the upper hand in the negotiating process:

> The cards were stacked against us. We had $26,000,000 in wages tied-up in radio and we were afraid that if we held out too long we might lose that. We realized that it would be wrong to try to recoup the $541,000 we had lost from local stations, and so after holding out as long as we could we made a deal with radio and television.

But Petrillo's closing remarks to the conventioneers were even more troubling, with not one "ray of sunshine to offer": "Industry is now running the show and the Republican candidates I see look like one brother to the other. I know you wanted the truth and I've given it to you" ("Petrillo Opens AFM Convention" 1948).

The industry's legitimacy in calling the shots was not simply the result of a Republican Congress that ensured these conditions. For example, the legitimate recording industry may have suffered from an illegitimate economy of jukebox mobs, bootleggers, scab and foreign recordings during the strike ("End-of-Summer Disk Truce" 1948), but the AFM was by no means a winner as these decentralized means of producing recordings multiplied. The latter issue concerning international solidarity and competition was always a concern for the AFM. The union always hoped to limit the importation of labors and typically attempted to restrict the use of foreign broadcasts by networks.[11] But the second recording ban encountered needy foreign markets that no longer found the basic materials of production inaccessible. By the end of July, MGM invested itself in making new sides by resorting to some old tricks, this time hiring Art Lund and using nonunionized harmonica players to provide instrumental backgrounds for versions of "You Call Everybody Darling" and "Hair of Gold" ("M-G-M Makes 1st Disk since AFM Ban" 1948). And while the ban may have restricted unionized American musicians, it could not restrict imports, and Mexico, for example, expected to increase its number of "south of the border" discs exported to the United States to take advantage of the ban and gain strong American dollars ("Mex Diskers Eye Hop in U.S. Exports" 1948). Other nations' musicians eyed the American dollar and the ban as an opportunity, the most prominent example involving British players. At the 1948 AFM convention at least one resolution to *not* popularize any numbers introduced by imported discs was presented ("AFM in Burn at British Musicians" 1948). For example, Decca planned to cash in on its status as a British label with a significant share of the American market by waxing every American artist on its roster who went "overseas for a theatre, nitery or concert date" using British musicians for musical backing ("Decca Plans Flock of British Discs" 1948). Although it is unknown exactly how many performers recorded with British players, in a number of cases AFM musicians were able to convince marquee names such as Peggy Lee, Frankie Laine, and Bing Crosby to abstain from this practice ("Peggy Lee Nixes British Backings" 1948).

But with the summer polls predicting a Republican sweep of the

House of Representatives, the Senate, and the White House (in the form of Thomas E. Dewey), and uneasiness with British musicians unions' reluctance to cooperate with the ban, the fate of the AFM appeared dark. Even when the British Musicians Union barred its members from recording for U.S. recording companies, many felt that this spelled the end of the ban simply because it would goad many companies into an open rebellion against the AFM, which would then move a number of operations either to Mexico or the Continent ("Crackdown on British Recording May Veer Yanks More to Mexico" 1948).[12] With legislation effectively tying the hands of the union, the AFM began meeting with recording companies in July, and general confidence throughout the industry that the ban could be lifted after Labor Day increased. With sudden drop-offs in the employment of musicians in all musical fields and recording companies appearing open to a compromise by organizing a new form of the Recording Fund that fell within the limits of the Taft-Hartley Act,[13] negotiations between the AFM and the industry opened in October 1948. Agreeing on a newly modified trust fund plan, the Music Performance Trust Fund (MPTF) would be administered by an independent trustee named by the Secretary of Labor. This position would be given the responsibility of acquiring moneys from record companies based on price and volume of sales and would distribute them on a *pro rata* basis in geographic areas coinciding with AFM locals. Intended to be spent one year following their receipt, the funds were designated for live musical performances free of charge to the public. Another condition of the agreement held that musicians both in and outside the AFM could be employed with these moneys. With the desires of industry and the AFM, as well as the requirements of the law, satisfied, the new agreement became effective on December 14, 1948, thus ending eleven months of the second recording ban (Seltzer 1989, 52–53).

As a compromise, the fund, for the most part, fulfilled its purpose. By 1952 the fund was receiving moneys from four sources: "record and transcription companies, producers of theatrical motion pictures (for release of film to television), producers of films for television, and producers of television jingles and spot announcements." Though the fund had spent some $2,350,000 for 16,997 performances that included nearly 189,000 musicians by 1954 (Seltzer 1989, 53), the MPTF was later redefined as an endowment devoted to educating the public through live performances rather than as a means of alleviating unemployment (56). Still, according to Seltzer, the MPTF also created something of an injurious legacy for the AFM as it became the central inspiration for the creation of the Musicians Guild of America (MGA), a competing union composed mainly of film-studio musicians from the Los Angeles area. Beginning as early as 1952, AFM Local 47 issued complaints that one of the prices of the MPTF was the importation of foreign soundtracks for telefilms, or simply their elimination in order to avoid the high price of a union product. By late 1956 and early 1957 members of the local had filed four lawsuits on behalf of film and recording musicians. The suits named the AFM, the trustees of the MPTF, and producers as defendants, and each suit questioned the legality of the fund, claimed past damages against the AFM, and sought to stop payments. Taking seven years to reach a settlement, the plaintiffs emerged as the winners (63). With a dueling union and the attack on the MPTF, Petrillo declined a nomination to return as president of the union, thus bringing to an end his eighteen-year term. Still, Petrillo retained leadership of Chicago Federation of Musicians Local 10 until 1962 and continued on as the director of the federation's civil rights program throughout the 1960s and 1970s.

In 1984, James Caesar Petrillo's heritage and achievements were briefly revisited when he died following a stroke at the age of ninety-two. In its obituary, *Time* noted the war against "canned music," the strikes, and his power as the AFM's "autocratic overlord" as his most significant achievements ("Obituary" 1984). But if history is shaped by less-than-flattering descriptions, it can also be measured by the traces of a legacy. And while this legacy may seem small throughout much of the United States, if you are ever in Chicago you can visit a couple of those sites where Petrillo's presence is still felt. Begin with what remains of the northern portion of Grant Park, Chicago's Millennium Park, the city's "front yard" and its most prized location for gatherings and recreation. On the lakefront in a clearing outside the Loop, in the shadow of the original Chicago skyline that ushered in the modern era of skyscraper architecture, is one of America's great spaces for public performance, what was once the James C. Petrillo Bandshell. Transformed into the Jay Pritzker Pavilion, the bandshell was redesigned by Frank Gehry and is now a venue without comparison. In the past the Petrillo bandshell hosted numerous music festivals, symphonies, popular performers, orators, and celebrations with tens of thousands in attendance, each event free to the general public. Despite the name change to honor the founder of the Hyatt Hotel chain, the tradition of quality free performances has continued, a tradition that has been in place since Petrillo sat as a commissioner on the Parks and Recreation Committee in the 1930s.

If you have a Walkman, turn it on and listen to what they are broadcasting in America's third-largest Arbitron market. You might get some interference as you enjoy the city, but odds are you will find a number of radio stations specializing in both popular and classical music. Undoubtedly you will hear a mix of unionized and nonunionized players, but it would indeed be a rare day if you hear a live broadcast. Of course the same holds true for the majority of the music one encounters without a Walkman: almost all is electronically mediated whether it transpires in the many bars, hotel lobbies, or cars you might encounter from venue to venue, museum to museum. You probably will not be too shocked by this. After all, even in the most sacred moments of death and marriage, those profound occasions of contact and transformation are necessarily mediated with the help of the music and the musician. But nowadays you may find the musician absent as more and more funeral houses offer the services of canned music to efficiently soften the trauma of a loved one lost. In the case of the wedding reception, all too often celebrants spend equal amounts of time dancing and complaining about the choices made by a local disc jockey.

The question is clear: where are the musicians? Some may be in the streets, in an alcove avoiding a chilly breeze. Others are underground. Buskers, some who play with the good graces of the city and others who refuse to bother with permits and fees, fill the tunnels under State and Dearborn with a variety of sounds. But very rarely do these musicians hope for a career providing music for travelers. Almost all musicians dream of recording contracts and hits, of hearing their voices and songs on the radio or on television. Who can blame them? Even the most popular musicians know that you tour to support the record rather than record to increase your return at the box office. How often do we hear of the musical act that refrains from live performance but continues to release records, one after another? How many stories do we read about the great live act that just could not succeed in the studio, as if this reflected some kind of moral or artistic deficiency? And how often is it that artists who wish to enter the marketplace are forced into a form of indentured servitude to a specific record company? Within an economy based on recordings, musicians have become the model agents of production, with individual success measured by one's position within the production, distribution, and promotion of recorded objects.

Walk a few blocks east on Washington Avenue. Just after you cross Dearborn and are about to move under the elevated tracks, you will see the building that houses the historic Chicago Federation of Musicians Local #10. Built in 1936 on dues money, the once-impressive building is now humbled by other new formations in the Loop. If you enter and stroll upstairs you can greet the staff, find out who is in the local, and even have a nice chat with the president about what scale is for any number of jobs. Head back downstairs, exit, and turn left and you run into a record store located underneath the CFM offices in the ground floor of the same building. For years the local rented out this space to the record store, but in February 1996 the owner of the record store purchased the building and now rents office space to the CFM. Go into the record store, take off your headphones, listen and look. It's not a bad shop. They stock a decent catalogue, have a nice variety of genres, and are almost always busy.

PART II

Production, Reproduction, and the Case of My Fair Lady

3

Which Voice Best Becomes the Property?

Stitching the Intertext of My Fair Lady

Miss Hepburn, looking slightly scrawny but lovely nevertheless,
ranges unexpectedly from the raucous to the delicate. She even
appears to be belting out her songs, although our mind does
inform us that it can't be, that it is Marnie Nixon, Hollywood's
most unsung singer, who is being used for what is politely termed
augmentation. This is to say that Miss Hepburn may begin a
song on a note she can handle, but it is Miss Nixon who finishes.
Here there is very little sense of jar, at least for my relatively un-
trained ears, and for this the Warner sound department deserves
much credit. Without being told, we wouldn't have known the
difference.

—Hollis Alpert in *The Saturday Review*

THIS COMMENTARY ON WARNER BROTHERS' 1964 FILM VER-
sion of *My Fair Lady* offers the critical reader any number of analytical options for examination, but nothing is riper for inspection than the
passage's focus on the technology of sound recording. Specifically highlighting technological questions, the reviewer isolates the "trick" of dubbing, noting that the effect is something to be admired when performed
with enough skill to cover its own traces. The seamless seam, if it renders

no audible tear, can both become and strengthen the property of the filmic text as a considerable asset in producing the ideal rendition of any composition. This kind of search for the ideal in the recording was "a quest for perfection," as Glenn Gould would put it two years later in his essay "The Prospects of Recording." Advocating the use of the recording studio and the advantages it offered for the benefit of musical production, Gould was a prominent and vocal proponent of the potential tape offered for musical rendition (Gould 1966, 53). For Gould, it was here, and *hear*, on tape where the scars of performance could be hidden.

Yet the ears of the skilled listener are always problematic; the trick of the dub can never fully eliminate the possibility of its own betrayal. No matter how tightly it is woven, an able listener can detect the splice that grafts the two voices together. Much like the master detective who can pick out significant evidence from the banal residues of an event, the discerning listener can also recast a seemingly competent edit into a serious textual blemish or strength. Though the opening quote slights the application of critical commentaries and applauds the search for pleasure, the critic recognizes that closely listening to a text (or group of texts) can be an act of celebration and of potential censure. This is an important point and one that is easily forgotten by those of us who think of the ear as a particularly passive organ. Indeed, listening exacts a variety of performative potentials, modes, and frameworks that solicit, detect, and judge any number of distinctive acts. For example, according to Alpert, one of the aural delights offered by the film version of *My Fair Lady* is submitted by the fabrication of continuous audio spaces. Achieved despite the possible impediments such as a variety of recording techniques, limits, and circumstances, the sound track's elaborate continuity invites listeners to relish in that which is presumably obscured and no longer beneficial to the narrative itself. The sound track presents itself as a *special* effect, an expenditure whose generosity and grace provide reasons sufficient enough to commit one's ear to the film's audible terrains. Thus operational information such as the fact that Rex Harrison recorded "live" with a lavalier microphone or that moments exist where Hepburn's voice audibly becomes Marni Nixon's are presented as temptations and curiosities that are measured by their artful execution.

But how could a method of audio recording and composition offer pleasures or disappointments that were distinct from the film's story? After all, most of the claims about the fundamental pleasures of classical

Hollywood narrative are predicated on *not* promoting (or following) significant diversions from the demands of the master narrative. Grand designs to incorporate this evaluative practice into the criteria and viewing conventions of audiences and critics alike offer what are almost moral obligations to attend to in the onscreen narrative. Theaters are equipped with management and ushers who provide polite suggestions, and, in extreme scenarios, use their authority to remove unruly spectators from the premises. Our eyes are focused on the screen and our ears, supposedly in subordination, are directed to follow.

But any sensual construct this grand is fated to occasionally break down and fragment. Now and then viewers and critics deviate from the basic blueprints of cinema, tear up the social contracts regulating spectatorship, and pay too much attention to the details offered by cinematic objects. This may include any number of peculiarities including an interest in an actor's style, special effects, the site of exhibition, or any other trivia. For example, Hollis Alpert notes Stanley Holloway's and Rex Harrison's confident and precise singing (Alpert 1964). Though a variety of interpretations could be assigned to these performances, let us try to forge a somewhat historical context, through which we can resuscitate this forgotten memory of the distractions, notorieties, and controversies surrounding the property's multiple forms and configurations.

In 1964 the audience for the film version of *My Fair Lady* was, we can safely assume, at least somewhat knowledgeable about the musical's history. Its then-record Broadway run of six years, its international accomplishments, and, of course, the success of the original cast album were all but legendary by the time of the film's release. Thus many audience members accepted the appearance of both Holloway and Harrison in the film as a repetition involving a major portion of the original Broadway cast. Furthermore, repeating these roles was nothing new to either the actors or their audiences. Both Holloway and Harrison had participated in the play's pre-Broadway tour, its stand in New York and opening run in London, and they had duplicated their performances for at least two popular recordings of the musical. Such a prominent history of repetition invites audiences to relish in their own well-informed opinions and make elaborate comparisons between performances. In fact, this sort of public comparison did take place. In one example, a *Newsweek* critic expended considerable type to assert that Harrison had never sounded better as Higgins than he did in the film. Drawing on a detailed knowledge of

Harrison's past performances, the critic recognized that small but meaningful differences between the film and stage versions could be rendered through the leniency of better recording technologies. "With the security of dubbing and retakes," the critic noted, "[Harrison] does a verse of 'You Did It' that he flubbed in the New Haven tryouts and was too terrified to ever try again onstage" ("Movies" 1964).

Harrison's marked vocal confidence was not the film's only discernible diversion in the soundtrack. According to another critic, the film version offered a significant "blight": the "dubbing over" of Hepburn's singing voice. In fact, for the same critic it was the only flaw that "marred her performance." True, Hepburn had exhibited a charming singing voice in *Funny Face* (Donen 1957) and *Breakfast at Tiffany's* (Edwards 1961) but, in the opinion of the reviewer, Warner Brothers decision to use Marni Nixon's well-known voice (she had dubbed the singing parts for Deborah Kerr in *The King and I* [Lang 1956] and Natalie Wood in *West Side Story* [Wise and Robbins 1961]) offered little dramatic content given the possibility of hearing either another well-known voice such as that of Julie Andrews or hearing Hepburn herself. Whereas Andrews represented the exciting promise of reuniting the three principal leads from the original Broadway and London runs of the stage musical and two cast albums for the film version, the latter possibility would have offered an opportunity for Hepburn to literally *actualize* her role as Eliza by bringing about a similar guttersnipe-to-beauty transformation of her singing voice (Archer 1964).

In fact, Hepburn did spend a significant amount of time taking singing lessons and practicing for the role. As impressive and well publicized as her efforts were, Hepburn could not prevent her voice being edited out of the 1964 release. Nevertheless, Hepburn's performance was received well enough: the film garnered significant box office and critical successes, including the Academy Award for best picture and seven other categories. *Variety's* review claimed that, despite the dubbing, "[Hepburn] is thoroughly beguiling as Eliza," while Bosley Crowther of the *New York Times* stated that Hepburn provided a performance of "profound human feeling and soul" ("Film Reviews" 1964; Crowther 1964). Still, it was hard for many audience members to pardon the fact that her singing voice was not entirely her own. In perhaps the most strident invocation of "voice" summoned by any commentator, *Life's* review of the film was written *as if* the reviewer, Richard Oulahan, had simply transcribed an oral testimony from Eliza Doolittle herself. From the head-line's pronunciation, "It wasn't only 'Iggins, what done me wrong," the review offered a "spoken" account of Eliza's various incarnations from the opening of Shaw's *Pygmalion,* complete with Eliza's cockney adorn-ment. Regarding her voice, Oulahan's Eliza remarked, "I understand it's not all her own voice that puts her low notes on another girl's high Cs. Well, it sounds it. I'll take Julie Andrews any old time. Because Audrey is indeed a lady—I've been one for years and I think I can spot one—she does just fine after Professor Higgins has put polish on her. But down in the gutter she was over her head" (Oulahan 1964). That a critic from one of the most prominent magazines in the United States could so candidly refer to the dubbing process most certainly eliminates any doubt that the general public overlooked the fact that post-production techniques strengthened Hepburn's singing voice. Much like Eliza herself, whose voice and character are simultaneously uplifted through Higgins's regi-mented application of phonetic expertise, Hepburn, much to her cha-grin, was left technologically affected by engineering processes beyond her control.

Observing that "everyone knows that movies are dependent on me-chanics and technique," Phillip T. Hartung of the *Commonweal* posed the question, "What difference does it make who hits the high notes?" Con-tinuing his exposition, Hartung declared that the skill of the filmmakers produced an improvement, a "picture better than the original" for the film exhibited the "great advantage" of making lyrics that were well worth hearing clearly audible (1964, 239). Ever the lady, Hepburn did not complain about the loss of her voice and the resultant controversy over being dubbed, an issue that *Time* magazine labeled as "the burning ques-tion mark of this sumptuous adaptation" ("Cinema" 1964). "I took sing-ing lessons from a New York vocal coach and pre-recorded all of Eliza's songs," she explained almost nine months before the film's release, "but the final result will be a blend [of voices]. It's wonderful what sound men can do with dials" ("'My Fair Lady's' Dream Comes True" 1964).

That so many reviews demonstrate such great concern over the issue of familiar voices may strike modern audiences as peculiar. One could frame this anxiety as a comparative interest in the authenticity of specific substances, namely, bodies. Christian Metz explains that, because sound is basically perceived in an adjectival manner throughout Western cul-ture, we conceive of aural objects as ephemeral, secondary properties that originate through the activities of the primary substances of bodies. For Metz, since "culture depends on the permanence of the object," the aural object exists as a severely misunderstood, almost bad object choice in which one may look for or find "culture" (1985, 157). In Metz's words, our culture has cultivated "the conception of sound as an attribute, as a nonobject, and therefore the tendency to neglect its own characteristics in favor of its corresponding 'substance,' which in this case is the visible [primary] object, which has emitted the sound" (158). Although the practice of dubbing upsets this order, the controversy is typically resolved by recognizing which voices "belong" to whom, whether they be Hepburn's, Andrews's, Nixon's, or even a fictional character's, Eliza's. As such, each individual body is presumably the author of a correspondingly distinct voice to which it *belongs* as a distinct property.

Whatever the case may be, the fact that these voices could be recognized, desired, compared, and contrasted with such ease and adoration indicates that the film's soundtrack exists as a location for the organization of considerable audience pleasures and anxieties. Certainly such affective investments suggest a concern for the soundtrack that seemingly outstrips the restraints of any narrative force that a film could place on it. In fact, the attentive search for voices and their corporeal affiliations demonstrates a specific mode of listening, wherein the listener compares a variety of differing renditions in order to find an "appropriate" voice/body match. This mode may take into account musical styles, the demands placed on the performance by previous performances and recordings, or any other significant fact so long as a rendition's difference can be adequately justified.

This section of *Making Easy Listening* illustrates and argues how and why this comparative mode is continually encouraged and valued by an enterprising recorded music industry. I locate the film version of *My Fair Lady* as one among a constellation of other versions, each of which folds onto the other to form a web of potential intertextual references and comparisons. Through this process of intertextual versioning, a specific media property accrues significant values in both the cultural and economic sense. This, I argue, owes partially to a particular industrial logic in which the music industry both fosters the swift production of numerous versions and actively solicits the repetitive listening of these variants. In this manner the logic unfolds each version with a promise that the listener will recognize significant, audible differences among

This 1964 advertisement for Roulette records is indicative of the many musical tweaks, even by minor labels, that My Fair Lady received.

these products and, through the comparative process, may savor or deride them.

By detailing how and why the *My Fair Lady* property was exploited, promoted, and versioned, I make the case that the recorded music industry forges intertextual logics as one strategy among many to maintain the profitability of its properties. As such, rather than providing a detailed rendering of those actors involved in a property's production and success, I illustrate an *industrial practice* that is committed to exploiting entertainment properties. Thus this section can be viewed as either a detailed, but not complete, elaboration of *My Fair Lady*'s proprietary genealogy from 1956 to 1964, an account of industrial fragmentation and exploitation, or, preferably, both. Finally, the section details how and why the music industry fashioned a *My Fair Lady* intertext ripe with numerous possibilities for depositing the musical or portions of its property into a variety of texts to maximize the property's potential for exploitation. As a result, the following analysis is alternately complex but never complex enough, for tracing intertextual connections consists of portrayals so knotted and intermeshed that a truly "stable" object can never be discovered. As the property is processed it is contorted, spread, affiliated, and advanced to fulfill specific cultural and economic desires. To clarify this point a good portion of the chapter will not only highlight the industry's generation, promotion, and organization of *My Fair Lady* recordings but also offer a number of theoretical frames in order to bring these practices into an adequate focus.

I want to make it clear that one of my purposes in this section is to suggest that the direction of popular music studies needs a different course. It needs to engage deeply intellectual strategies and tactics through which we can better understand particular industrial activities. We need a far more robust and tested understanding of not only present-day industrial practices but past ones as well. So, for a moment, let's take one of the more tossed-about clichés of the industry seriously: the popular music industry cares more about sales than it does artists. If this is true, and indeed it is, then we are obliged to ask ourselves if this is all there is to understand. Is there an art to commodification, and if so, what are the critical consequences that it has on production? And instead of asking whether these consequences are helpful or anathema to self-expression, perhaps we need to nuance our understanding so as to avoid either/or. To illustrate this point I have decided to detail a portion of a property's history. Rather than closely analyzing an artist and his or her work, an audience, or even a specific text, I have chosen a well-known property. Of course, each of these sites—the artist, the audience, and the text—offers rich and satisfying opportunities for intellectual discussion and investigation. But to limit our discussion to these three analytical options ignores the fact that a good portion of the music industry's efforts is firmly rooted in the acquisition, development, and control of properties. To be sure, this involves acquiring the rights to a property's production, reproduction, and distribution. The consequences of these concerns are not simply legal or economic but aesthetic and social as well. In other words, they become the topics for laywers, CEOs, neighbors, and siblings.

Like other mass media industries, the music industry has always understood the need to widely distribute and deliver its properties in various forms. Whether they produce a variety of books, toys, or fashion accessories, modern mass entertainment industries pass their properties into intertextual openings and folds that allow almost anyone, at any given point in time, to enter, open, and engage these investments. Historically the music industry has used multiple musical genres, the production of radio formats, promotional videos, dance mixes, film sound tracks, and so on to develop and process its properties into the large number of versions that result in an ever-expanding intertextual constellation of products and performances. For example, recordings once enjoyed on a long-play record or compact disc may now reappear in a number formats and places in order to increase a property's exposure and subsequent profitability.

For some readers this scenario may simply be indicative of a larger postmodern condition where cultural products are embroiled in a logic of "versioning and reference," as opposed to an earlier era that generated distinct, singular narratives. I do not wish either to counter or to promote such a point. Rather, I would like to revisit the way we look on issues of intertext and versioning in order to imbue them with an industrial and historical specificity that embellishes our perception beyond those debates that would enthusiastically reduce and/or dismiss such concepts as simply part of a postmodern cultural paradigm. As important as the debates surrounding postmodern culture are, and no matter what the appearances may be, the intention of this chapter is to detail an intertextual process rather than hash out the validity of either side of the controversy.

Of the two issues, the notion of intertextuality has received the greatest amount of attention. As a concept, intertextuality has its lengthiest tradition in literature studies beginning with Julia Kristeva's translation of Bakhtin's notion of dialogism. For Bakhtin, dialogism is "the necessary relation of any utterance to other utterances" (Stam et al. 1992, 203). Bakhtin proposes an understanding of dialogism that "suggests that every text forms an intersection of textual surfaces. All texts are tissues of anonymous formulae embedded in the language, variations on those formulae, conscious and unconscious quotations, conflations and inversions of other texts" (204). Kristeva's use of intertext positions texts within a larger dialogical system, wherein texts exist as a "'mosaic of citations', a palimpsest of traces, where other texts may be read" (204). Within media studies, those involved in television studies have most prominently adapted the notion of the intertext. This is particularly true of those theorists interested in the reception of television such as John Fiske (1987) and Henry Jenkins (1992). Both scholars profit handsomely from using the concept to forward an awareness of how audiences actively read, understand, and pursue pleasure from popular culture in general and televisual texts in specific. In short, the consumer of popular culture becomes an active participant rather than a passive vessel. Despite the gains from mobilizing intertextuality as a concept, critics such as Andrew Goodwin (1992), David Morely (1992), and Eileen Meehan (1991) have vocalized a clear-cut resistance to embracing the concept without properly scrutinizing the details involved in intertextual production and distribution. Morely notes that intertextuality all too often exists as a form of theoretical shorthand whereby scholars position readers outside a "simple minded effects model," thus steering media audiences into an equally implausible form of "cultural relativism" and a neoliberal rhetoric of reader's rights (1992, 26).

Both Goodwin and Meehan raise similar concerns. Goodwin contends that the use of intertextuality as a theoretical tool to explain the textual workings of music videos all too often ignores political economic critiques by conflating "political economy with cultural pessimism" (1992). Meehan is much more pointed about the cultural insights gained when we generate a better understanding of the political economic processes that go into producing intertextual connections. Examining the intertextual nexus of Warner Brothers' 1989 film *Batman* and all of its accompanying commodities, Meehan notes that

> this web of cross-references creates an intertext into which we fit ourselves, positioning ourselves to construct readings of the film and position the film and its intertext to suit our own particular purposes. [But] when a text like *Batman* generates such a rich and complex intertext [of references and products]—in short, when Batmania takes the nation by storm—cultural critics are naturally drawn to analyze the text and intertext in order to discover why that text resonates with so many people, why it activates such widespread participation in the intertext. . . . Economics must be considered if we are fully to understand the texts and intertexts of American mass culture. (1991, 47–48)

Meehan's appeal for an economic analysis of media texts may not offer us all the missing pieces to complete a fuller cultural understanding at which she hints, but it does advance a clearer understanding of the formation of intertexts as an economic aspiration.

Given that the creation of intertextual webs such as *Batman* is by now a regular if not seasonal occurrence in the widespread exploitation of media properties through "blockbuster" adventures, it has become easier for media scholars to point out and identify the standard set of textual forms that go into producing such a constellation. Books, comics, television shows, toys, games, park rides, records, fast-food meals, and more combine their distinct and differing forms to simultaneously envelop and promote a specific property. The formal variety of such products is not so much an epiphenomenon resulting from an intertextual logic as it is a necessary element in the formation of that logic. Without the dissimilar, differentiated products there would be no *inter*, that is no space through which subjects could travel from text to text.[1]

Not surprisingly, the intertextual need for formal variety makes the concept a prominent one for theorists interested in the film musical, though this concern is typically expressed through the more literary terms of genre. For example, Rick Altman notes that the assembly of intertextual elements is absolutely paramount for the musical's "generic" construction. As a genre the musical activates a specific set of well-understood intertextual rules, whereby "text after text is generated from the same mold, thus highlighting certain textual relationships, repressing others, and eventually limiting the field of play of the [genre's] interpretive community," a community that consists of both audience and producers (1987, 4). Echoing Altman's observation, Jane Feuer argues throughout her book on the Hollywood film musical that the genre employs intertextuality as a generic convention. For Feuer, intertextual filmic references are actively invoked in a form of reflexivity that she views as a basic building block for musicals in the 1950s (1993, 102). Feuer argues that this referential process continued well into the 1980s.[2] In each case the writer views the musical as a genre that utilizes a dynamic industrial space for the intertextual referencing of styles, forms, performers, and its own generic conventions.

Let us follow Altman's and Feuer's thoughts in order to highlight a feature particular to *My Fair Lady* as a text: the musical is a version, a variation on the well-known myth of Pygmalion. This may strike some readers as elementary, banal in fact. Yet this banality is involved with an interesting if overlooked logic of interpretation and re-interpretation, whereby each version of the story is judged by the skill involved in its alterations and the delivery of these significant differences. In short, throughout its continual re-articulation, the myth is continually involved in the production and exhibition of difference. This may run contrary to what many consider to be the way in which myths operate. To state that Pygmalion enjoys a mythic status is, in the minds of many, to say that it is kept in circulation because of its ability to express unchanging, timeless, "fundamental" truths.

The claim that these or any "truths" are fundamental is often assailed as an ideological formation by critiques adapted from Roland Barthes's work on mythical speech. Barthes claims that myth is a type of speech that "has *already* been worked on so as to make it suitable for communication: it is because all the materials of myth presuppose a signifying consciousness, that one can reason about them while discounting their substance" (1972, 110). Barthes suggests that massive social efforts are incurred in establishing the signifying consciousness that accepts mythic speech as natural, organic explanations for social desires, occurrences, or hierarchies. Typically Barthes's point is taken as the first step in understanding the creation of mythic speech as a form of depoliticized speech, that is, speech that does not investigate the materials that form the myth's ostensive "naturalness." Within the Barthesian model, the popularity of mythical thought is predicated on developing and maintaining the appropriate socio-ideological framework to ensure the narrative's unnoticed employment.

The importance of this is the temptation one has to draw from Barthes's analysis that a myth's long-term popularity is indicative of a sort of socio-ideological stasis. But we should never assume that stasis does not necessitate constant change. Indeed, stasis is often an illusion that is fabricated through the ongoing processes of social maintenance. Even so-called canonical narratives, to sustain their status, need a number of continual institutional supports that range from their subsidization by the state to their discussion in university classrooms. Such processes have their effects on the canon, as alterations often come in the form of so-called classic fare. But these alterations are often forgotten if not hidden. Indeed, as the alterations are made, we are still given the impression that myths and legends are somehow cast in stone. Yet, like most forms of popular and classical literature, myth often claims no specific author or definitive version through which its existence is maintained. The lack of an authoritative version derives from the fact that myth is often generated in the world of oral rather than written, literary tradition. As such, a myth's vitality resides historically *not* in continually retelling the same version but through effectively restaging of the myth as a current, relevant narrative. This *is* the power of the storyteller: his or her ability to recite, reframe, and reestablish the story for his or her contemporary audiences in order to ensure its continued success. In each case the basic story is flexed and altered enough to allow for one specific articulation after another. In each articulation, each restaging individuates itself through the exposition of significant differences in elements such as timing, the intensity of expression, locale, use of effects, music, and so forth. This proposal that re-articulation and repetition convey the expression of differences rather than similarities is Deleuzian in its basis. To paraphrase Ronald Bogue, Deleuze views repetition as a process of individuation whereby difference, a metastable substance of potential energies (for example, clay that can become a pot or a sculpture, or sulfur that, under proper circumstances, can become crystalline or powdered), articulates itself through the processes of its own becoming (1989, 62–63).[3] It is within this Deleuzian paradigm that I situate the process of versioning musical properties.

For example, to convey the basic elements of the Pygmalion myth one needs only the briefest amount of time. A sculptor and king of Cyprus, Pygmalion, carves an ivory statue of a young woman. The statue is so beautiful that the Cypriot king prays to Aphrodite to bring it to life, after which Aphrodite grants Pygmalion his wish and the statue is given life. Pygmalion marries the woman, Galatea, and the two beget a child, Cinyras. There is nothing outstanding let alone pleasurable about this variation, yet it exists as the most basic framework of the story. It is through the actualization of this virtual (ideal) story of Pygmalion that a skilled narrator may plait her particular rendering. To be sure, a number of writers have used the myth for a variety of purposes. For example, Villiers d'Isle-Adam summons the myth in his book *Tomorrow's Eve*. Using Thomas Alva Edison as his central character in place of the Cypriot king, Villiers d'Isle-Adam builds a commentary on a variety of late nineteenth-century European issues concerning modernity and technology (Villiers de L'Isle-Adam 1982). Perhaps the most famous version of the myth exists in the form of Bernard Shaw's 1916 play simply titled *Pygmalion*. Replacing Pygmalion with the Higgins character and Galatea with Eliza Doolittle, Shaw uses the myth, as Lynda Mugglestone has pointed out, to express an admiration for phonetics as a powerful modern science that wields an egalitarian potential for society: "The *Pygmalion* myth in Shaw's hands, predictably endowed with social meaning, becomes therefore not only a paradigm of social mobility, but also a paean to inherent equality, with its thesis, as Nicholas Greene has pointed out, that 'a lady is only a flower-girl plus six months of phonetic training, a gentleman only a dustman with money'" (1993, 373). The play's immense popularity resulted in a number of extended runs throughout many of the world's major cities. Its success continued in the form of a 1938 film adaptation featuring Leslie Howard as Henry Higgins; the film gained two Academy Awards (Best Adaptation: Screenplay and Best Adaptation: Writing) and two nominations (Best Actor: Leslie Howard and Best Actress: Wendy Miller as Eliza Doolittle) (Asquith and Howard 1938).

One distinctive mark of Lerner and Loewe's version of the myth from Shaw's is the articulate circumvention of Shaw's concern and rhetoric for social justice. In lieu of this theme, Lerner and Loewe substitute a more prominent theme of romance. According to Lerner, the reason for this specific rewrite is that Shaw's *Pygmalion* is a play where, "unlike the original legend of Pygmalion and Galatea in which Pygmalion brought his statue to life because of his love for her, in Shaw's play Pygmalion brings Galatea to life by *not* loving her" (Lerner 1994, 36). Lerner and Loewe marry the musical to the romantic potential of the myth, a fact that Lerner was proud enough to note in discussing a number of the details that distinguish *My Fair Lady* from Shaw's *Pygmalion.* For example, Lerner points out that

> for the published version of *Pygmalion,* Shaw wrote a preface and an epilogue which he called a sequel. I have omitted the preface because the information contained therein is less pertinent to *My Fair Lady* than it is to *Pygmalion.* I have omitted the sequel because in it Shaw explains how Eliza ends not with Higgins but with Freddy and—Shaw and Heaven forgive me!—I am not certain he is right. (Lerner 1956, 7)

As a romantic enunciation, *My Fair Lady*'s elimination of the preface and realignment of who is coupled with whom may seem trivial at best. But as a specific version, *My Fair Lady* fashions the Pygmalion myth into a particularly new form through the process of translating the ideal text into a new genre complete with new formal languages and requirements. In this case the genre is the stage musical and the language is music, thus subjecting the mythic text to the influence of this unique form.

Indeed, the fact that *My Fair Lady* is a specific version among other versions of the Pygmalion myth was well understood by many of its audiences. Take, for example, a 1964 review of the Warner Brothers' film version, which appeared in *Seventeen,* at that time the most popular magazine for young women in the United States. Titled "Love Letter to Eliza," it details the basic evolution of the narrative that informs the musical:

> Fifty-one years ago, Bernard Shaw wrote a witty comedy he called *Pygmalion* after the name of the Cypriot king who carved an ivory statue so fetching that he prayed the goddess of love to grant it life. The Irish playwright, a man who delighted in having a joke at his audience's expense, amused his status-conscious British viewers by suggesting that the only difference between the upper class and the poor was the way each spoke the King's English. . . . Shaw had a hit then, and it became even more popular nearly a decade ago when songwriters Alan Jay Lerner and

Friederich Loewe transformed it into a marvelous musical opening in 1956. *My Fair Lady* first captivated Broadway, then went
on to charm the world: as a movie it now promises even greater
pleasures. (Miller 1964, 194)

Although a few of these greater pleasures may have been the expected
spectacularization that Hollywood lends its adaptations, certainly some
of the anticipated delights must have come from the prospect of viewing
an updated, well-known myth in yet another media form.

The transformation of the Pygmalion myth may know no limits
and we most likely have not seen its final articulation. Certainly one
could envision a detailed study and analysis of these textual alterations
through an interesting if ambitious project. As indicated earlier, this is
not the goal of this section. Rather, I am interested in the *My Fair Lady*
property inasmuch as this musical version of Pygmalion directly participates in the process of generating numerous recorded musical versions.
Whereas literary analysts may make structural comparisons in search of
substantial variations, I am more interested in those specific industrial
processes of intertextualization that encourage the production and promotion of textual versions that flaunt their significant differences among
a palette of similar texts. Thus the specific *rendition* of each text, rather
than the composed text, becomes the basis for each text's promotion. It
is in this manner that the music industry develops, through a seemingly
indiscriminate industrial logic of production, an intertext within which
it can position its properties.

Before we enter an investigation of versions we should examine the production of at least one original, Columbia Records' "original" Broadway
cast record of *My Fair Lady*, to gain a foothold with which to begin our
understanding of this particular intertextual investment. As an important dimension of William Paley's CBS media empire, Columbia Records
was one of the most important record companies of the late forties and
fifties. In conjunction with RCA Victor, Capitol, and American Decca
(MCA), CBS was part of a formidable quartet of major labels. Each of
these four companies boasted well-organized systems of distribution,
significant rosters of stars, and contacts with radio, film, and Broadway
that assisted each in controlling which songs made it to the public's
ears. As a result, these labels were able to concentrate the majority of the

United States' record industry throughout the postwar period in a fashion that has not been equaled since (Peterson and Berger 1990, 104).

In addition to these factors, RCA-Victor and Columbia wielded a technological leadership within the record industry through coordinated efforts with their parent companies' research divisions. The most infamous case of this dominance resulted in a competition between the two companies' desire to establish their basic playback equipment as the industrial standard. The struggle between the two different forms of electronic equipment initiated a series of events in the late 1940s and early 1950s commonly known as the "speed wars." Out of this contest RCA-Victor's 45 rpm 7-inch record and CBS's 33⅓ rpm 12-inch long-play record became the two dominant playback standards for almost the next forty years (Sterling and Kittross 1990, 250–51).

As the two companies developed throughout the postwar boom, so did the industry in general. After two years of consecutive declines in 1948 and 1949 following its all-time high in 1947, the industry saw steady growth from 1950 to 1954. "Then," as Richard Peterson points out, "every year for the rest of the decade sales grew rapidly so that the total records sold in 1959 was well over double what it had been in 1954" (Peterson and Berger 1990, 105). Given the enormity and speed of the growth in the fifties, this boom must have felt limitless. And by 1956 the U.S. recorded music industry was sufficiently confident, as one *Billboard* article recognized, to flaunt a newfound optimism envisioning a "new global record market," complete with new vistas for both the publication and pressing of U.S. popular music ("Pop Music's Global Vistas" 1956).

While such sweeping enthusiasm may have been a prevailing industrial sentiment, the recorded music industry considered a number of more pragmatic interests, such as methods for marketing its wares. Some of these included the promotion of many of the new "hi-fi" technologies, such as stereo systems and their accompanying softwares (reel-to-reel tape, long-play, and 45 rpm records). Other cases simply involved the elaboration of old-fashioned, tried-and-true methods of music industry exploitation. Among these methods, *Billboard* reported, was continuing the practice of "tying up" music with other media adventures, particularly major film releases. According to a 1956 article, "the promotion of films via records and vice versa is better than ever this summer, with a flock of film themes—vocals, instrumentals, revivals and new tunes—

dominating the current singles release schedules of the major labels" ("Disk-Film Tie-Ups" 1956).

Earlier in the same year this form of mutual promotion was highlighted when RCA Victor released a song from *The Eddie Duchin Story* before Columbia Pictures and music publishers Shapiro-Bernstein could release their products on the market. Vigorous protests from Columbia and Shapiro-Bernstein that RCA Victor had broken an agreement to respect a common release date only emphasized that, as *Billboard* noted, "the degree of interdependence between films and records at the economic and promotional levels has been markedly increasing," and that it "is expected that this is only the beginning" ("Release Protest Highlights Growth" 1956). As record companies continued to provide disc jockeys at independent radio stations with more and more records for airplay, this new practice, in addition to earlier forms of coordinated ballyhoo, became a new means of programming promotional efforts. Of course, as the freelance army of DJs grew and became ever more extensive, it also grew exponentially more difficult to control.

With these factors in mind it becomes clearer why the investment in Broadway musicals was regarded as a prime arena for major label exploitation. As a popular form of entertainment, a successful stage musical could bear an abundant harvest replete with a variety of fruits. A fortunate musical property could realize profits from hit songs, a Broadway show, a touring company version, a film version, and, of course, records that could be produced ad infinitum for a steady stream of revenues. It is within this framework that we need to view Columbia's decision to finance the initial production of *My Fair Lady*. Accounts of the amount invested vary. In his memoirs William Paley purports that CBS's initial investment was around $360,000 (1979, 335), while other estimates put Columbia Records' budget anywhere from $500,000 (Dannen 1991, 61) to $400,000 ("'Fair Lady' a Palpable Hit," 1956; Lerner 1994, 71) to $340,000 ("Inside Stuff-Legit" 1956). But throughout each account one item remains constant: CBS's venture purchased a 40 percent ownership of the *My Fair Lady* property. Along with this percentage, CBS procured the mechanical rights to produce a number of *My Fair Lady* products, including the "Original Broadway Cast" record (Lerner 1994, 71) as well as "the priority on at least one telecasting of the musical ("Inside Stuff-Legit" 1956).[4] Certainly, Columbia Records expected nothing less than outstanding returns on the investment. A May 23 edition of *Variety*, drawing on an estimate from Hal Cook, Columbia's then-director of national sales, asserted that "the recorded music from *MFL* on the Columbia label alone [would] net $5,000,000 at the retail level" ("See $5,000,000 As Jackpot" 1956).

These expectations were swiftly fulfilled. Shortly after the show's opening, while rumors abounded that the three major shareholders had already begun to consider the value of *My Fair Lady*'s film rights ("No Pic Deal in Sight" 1956), CBS's original cast record almost immediately blossomed into a substantial prize. Riding a wealth of positive press regarding both the pre-Broadway performances and the musical's Manhattan premier, *Variety* reported that Columbia's cast record was "off to the biggest advance in the label's history" with a national order of 100,000 long-play records ("Col's 'Fair Lady'" 1956). Although a number of critics and reporters hailed both the record and the play with extensive praise, at least one journalist was puzzled by the size of the advance, asserting that the large amount of LP sales was "particularly interesting, in that unlike most of the past original-cast best sellers (e.g., "South Pacific", etc.) 'MFL' would ordinarily appeal to a more specialized market." The journalist maintained that although the musical's lead actors—Rex Harrison, Stanley Holloway, and Julie Andrews—were excellent actors "and strong in showmanship," with the exception of Andrews' particularly strong voice, singing was a sideline for these actors ("'Fair Lady' Album" 1956). Just whom this "specialized market" consisted of was never adequately defined. But one thing was certain: the large advance sales of the LP were followed by seemingly endless popularity.

By May, Bennet Cerf would write in *The Saturday Review* that "the big sensation in recording circles today is the new 'MFL' album" for it offered a score of "the greatest musical show to come to New York in many a moon" (Cerf 1956). Offering a less aesthetically oriented accolade in its tribute to the "bottom line," *Billboard* described the original cast record's sales of 250,000 units as "astronomical" ("'Lady' Disk $$ Astronomical" 1956). With no slowdown in sight, a late-July issue of *Variety* proclaiming that the record had exceeded the 300,000 mark confirmed that the "original cast version of *MFL* [was] bidding to become one of the top best-sellers of all-time" ("'Fair Lady' Tops 300,000" 1956). By 1962, *Variety* noted that along with *South Pacific*'s 393- and *The Music Man*'s 198-week tenures, *My Fair Lady*'s 298 weeks on *Variety*'s best-selling LP charts indicated that original cast records were nothing short of a mass cultural phenomenon ("Disk Business in 3 Words" 1962), a fact that remained true almost two years later as *Billboard* reported a 416-week-long chart streak and over 5 million units of *My Fair Lady*'s original caster that had been moved (Gross 1964).

The phenomenal success of *My Fair Lady*'s original-cast long-play record is well known to those with an interest in the history of recorded music. In the pre-Beatles history of recorded music, only Vaughn Meader's comedy record *The First Family,* a spoof of the Kennedy administration and relatives in the form of musical theater, equaled the extraordinary sales success of the *My Fair Lady* original-cast album in terms of LP sales in the United States. Yet, despite the continued popularity of long-play recordings of popular music, little scholarship is devoted to understanding how they operate textually, let alone industrially. No doubt every genre and group of listeners may utilize the form to create substantially different texts for different pleasures. Thus the analytic task takes on an appreciative form that is concerned with how the formation of the original-cast record of *My Fair Lady* operated to intersect and promote the stage version of the show.

First, the use of the adjective "original" for this or any other original-cast recording is one that invokes the term's representative, rather than source-oriented connotations. As a result, original-cast recordings are almost always positioned as adequate approximations rather than accurate reproductions. Alan Lerner makes this point in his autobiography. Regarding the original-cast album, Lerner acknowledges, "A cast album is *not* merely a matter of recording what is heard in the theatre" (1994, 118; my emphasis). While referring to Goddard Lieberson, the producer of two different *My Fair Lady* cast recordings, Lerner recalls,

> He was a firm believer in never, nay never, including any dialogue from the play [in original-cast records]. His reason was that a recording is for *music* and *lyrics,* and that although a few lines of dialogue may fertilize the memory of those who have seen the play, for the rest it will mean nothing and in time it will become a bore to everyone. (119; emphasis added)

Although Lerner's words may be less than shocking to today's reader, the stridency of this extraction and isolation of the songs from their diegetic context is interesting when one considers Lieberson's reputation as a man obsessed with precision and authority in musical style and aesthetics.[5] In the words of Fredric Dannen, "Lieberson was perfectly tailored for a corporation like CBS, the 'Tiffany' network" (1991, 59).

Assuredly, CBS did not engage in vulgarities like the decidedly low-brow genres of rock and roll or rhythm and blues. Instead, the record division under the direction of Lieberson signed artists like Vladimir Horowitz and Leonard Bernstein and plowed back moneys into "'important' music that sold poorly, such as the jazz of Duke Ellington." Without this direction it is unclear whether Columbia could have afforded to print and distribute catalogues of "the complete works of Arnold Schoenberg and Anton von Webern." Lieberson and Paley's CBS satisfied popular appetites for recordings throughout the fifties and early sixties with tasteful acts like Tony Bennett, Andy Williams, Barbra Streisand, and family entertainments were honored with acts such as Mitch Miller's renowned sing-along records. The prestige acts for CBS included artists like Mahalia Jackson, Johnny Cash, Pete Seeger, Dave Brubeck, and Miles Davis, who, though their records enjoyed the occasional moderate success on the market, all too often produced properties and recordings that many other companies would consider failures. But in most cases, despite their inconsistency as financial frontrunners, these artists were held in high regard by Columbia. Indeed, one could argue that the company's bankroll was invested not only in a market position but in maintaining a cultural reputation as well (Dannen 1991, 58–61).

Given CBS's and Lieberson's reputations, both their concern for not boring their audiences and their decision *not* to release a full-fledged presentation of *My Fair Lady* on record are of significant interest. One could easily dismiss the decision to eliminate large amounts of the musical's text in order to fit it onto one (or two) long-play records as a standard industrial practice, one involving both technological and promotional considerations. But if this is a standard practice, then it might be profitable to quickly analyze why these decisions are made time and time again by the record industry. This is especially the case today when compact disc and MP3 formats eliminate the storage concerns. To this day, most original-cast records exist as reduced, almost concentrated forms of the musical. As a type of reduction, *My Fair Lady*'s original-cast album highlights those textual elements that significantly distinguish Lerner and Loewe's rendition of the myth from Shaw's popular predecessor: the songs. This is no trivial difference, for it is not so much the addition of music to a theatrical version of a play that turns a play into a "musical." Unlike the use of music on the dramatic stage and cinema, the musical's use of the popular song is fashioned primarily to entertain rather than abet narrative progress. This is not to say that the genre's musical moments have little or nothing to do in forwarding narrative objectives. But, unlike most forms of narrative drama and cinema, the primary objective of the musical is to champion spaces of immediate delights and amusement. Music can support or serve as climactic portions for the aims of the narrative, but only as much as that is coincidental with its ability to entertain. Most often these musical spaces are developed through the very items that have been integral to the success of the recorded music industry: popular songs.

The emphasis that both industries have placed on popular songs for both recorded objects and the film musical is not simply coincidental. The popular song is not only the dominant aesthetic unit of personal audio recordings,[6] but also *the* most distinctive and important site of aesthetic expression for the classical Hollywood film musical. In the words of Jane Feuer, one of the primary goals of the Hollywood film musical is to "celebrate the popular song." Feuer finds this particularly evident in the genre's use of "the reflexive song lyric," which is pronounced in popular song performances. For example, Feuer cites Gene Kelly's character from *Summer Stock* (Walters 1950), a film musical about the production of a stage musical. Kelly's character claims, "We're trying to tell a story with music and song and dance and not just with words. For instance, if the boy tells a girl that he loves her, he doesn't just say it, he sings it" (Feuer 1993, 49). Reflecting an intense belief in the powers of lyricism,[7] Feuer claims that the reflexive song lyric often "redefines music as singing." Therefore, "in order to sing the praises of music, the general term 'music' must be particularized as 'song'" (51). Within this context the popular song can simultaneously "proclaim" and "expose" emotions through privileging the musical elements of the lyric. As Feuer notes,

> In the very act of privileging the non-representational language of music over the representational language of words, a switch is made so that what at first seems to be a contrast between modes of representation actually becomes a contrast between modes of *presentation.*

> What the musical can do that "third-person" forms (such as narrative films and classical music) can't do, according to this line of reasoning, is to show the process of transformation from one mode of presentation to another. In becoming song, language is in a sense transfigured, lifted up into a higher, more expressive realm. (52)

In short, the popular song operates as a conventional means for showing rather than explaining emotional states.

But showing is not simply an act whereby emotional desires, meanings, and intents are revealed or expressed. As Dennis Giles argues, the "show" not only exposes psychic states through mediums other than language but it aspires to

> arrest the flow of time. Temporality was previously to be desired, since only in time could the show be developed. But the purpose of the show is to be shown. Any further passage of time is regarded as an evil, since it can only disrupt the harmonies of this moment, only degrade the beauty so previously achieved. In sum, by virtue of showing the show, the performers pass to a transcendent realm of being. (1981, 87)

While the musical attempts to temporarily halt the linear logic of narrative time, this is different from ridding itself of temporal linearity. The narrative time of the drama is arrested by "the show" so that spectators may fully caress the intensities of a particular narrative moment in much the same manner that an epicurean exhibits her appetites as she slowly relishes the introductory sensations of a treasured entrée or wine. These moments of show may involve a romantic coupling, or a character's wish or desire, for example, but each presentation necessitates the sensual inflection of the textual event in order that the full impact of the sensational can be embraced.

In the most extreme applications of the form, the demand for the "show" leads the narrative into what Thomas Elsaesser regards as a "psychic law and not an intellectual one, and thus achieves a measure of coherence which is very difficult to analyse" (1981, 15). For Elsaesser, this is best epitomized in the films of Vincente Minnelli, wherein

> the world of the musical becomes a kind of ideal image of the medium itself, the infinitely variable material substance on which

the very structure of desire and the imagination can imprint itself, free from all physical necessity. The quickly changing decor,
the transition in the lighting and the colours of a scene, the freedom of composition, the shift from psychological realism to pure
fantasy, from drama to surreal farce, the culmination of an action
to a song, the change of movement into rhythmic dance—all this
constitutes the very essence of the musical. In other words, it is
the very exaltation of the artifice as the vehicle of an authentic
psychic reality. (1981, 16)

If the musical demands these lyrical and entertaining periods that
show emotional states, then the genre must incorporate formal elements
designed specifically to arrest the linear flow of narrative tempo. This is
one of the reasons why musicals emphasize a constellation of what are
typically regarded as "emotional," primarily nonnarrative forms of expression such as dance, popular song, and visual design. Though these
elements can be "narrativized" or assist in narration, they also include
properties excessive enough to easily supersede the most basic formal
limits of narrative film. This is most evident in the "musical number."
In the words of Alan Williams, "the space of the musical number becomes *larger* than the space of the narrative." Yet this enlargement is
not a radical rupture. Rather, "this sense of expansion only occurs as
the distortion (but not the destruction) of an initially coherent space"
(1981, 149). Williams contends that the popular song effectively distorts
narrative film spaces for a number of reasons, some of which are bound
to issues of recording technology, while others involve compositional
forms that emphasize the piece's autonomy. In either case, it is important
to recognize that the popular song is able to separate and present itself
as a specifically distinct audio and textual space that is distinct from the
classical principles involved in the creation of narrative spaces by musical and audio soundtracks (Williams 1981).

While the distinct spaces of the popular song may be functionally
deposited into a musical's narrative, the relative autonomy of the space
allows for its rather uncomplicated detachment from the master text. For
example, think of the many times you have been pleasantly surprised to
find that a favorite song originated in a musical play or film. Although
the "detachability" of the popular song is not essential to the musical
as a genre, this particular potential allows the textual fragment a dual
existence. This existence is peculiar because it claims an existence with-

in the larger narrative of the musical and an independent position as simply a popular song. This second, more independent existence is of particular importance for understanding popular music. Because of this independence the popular song can be performed in a variety of forums and styles and/or deposited into other textual sites such as recordings and radio playlists. Altman notes that the song's flexible detachability is a long-standing tradition in Hollywood's formation of musical genre. Indeed, one manner in which the popular song's detachability operated to simultaneously "fund" the musical and exist independently of the narrative was through sheet music sales:

> For decades the musical—with its tendency to prefer "hum-mable" tunes—joined hands with the sheet music industry to keep American pianos playing and American voices singing. Or, rather, I should reverse the formula because the musical's music was destined for the sheet music industry and the family piano, it remained hummable, i.e. appropriate for the amateur musician. In short, for over a quarter-century the musical and the sheet music industry together combined to provide the nation's most powerful defense against mass-mediated passivity. (1987, 352)

Altman's assertion that, "the film musical's history takes on a new meaning when placed in this context" is certainly interesting (352). The very suggestion that the American film musical activated an engagement with musical production deserves serious attention if not vigorous research. For example, Altman claims a connection between the beginning of the film musical and the sale of pianos, since the genre "begins at the very high point of piano sales in America." From this coincidental evidence Altman infers that the American "desire to sing was at an all-time high" (356). Following this logic Altman continues,

> the decline of the musical as a whole in the late fifties is closely tied to a generalized change in the consumption/production configuration of the musical's operational role. With the rise of the original-cast recording in the late forties, along with the long-playing record, Hollywood rapidly abandoned the sheet music industry in favor of the disc industry, going so far as to bankroll Broadway shows in order to assure lucrative rights to title, plot, and music alike. (353)

For Altman, the height of the film musical's popularity is indicative of a culture that, in general, actively practices the reproduction of music rather than the consumption of musical recordings.[8]

This may be partially true, but Altman's line of thought does not consider any number of other elements that may have played an integral role in the rise and fall of the film musical genre. In particular, larger social changes such as the rise of live variety productions on television, coupled with suburban growth, may have hindered Hollywood's desire to invest in the genre throughout the 1950s. But more importantly, the rise of the film musical is directly related to the widespread introduction and acceptance of recorded sound to standard studio filmmaking. This historical fact would seem to cast significant doubt on the proposition that recording, whether it involves public or private means of exhibition, necessarily entails the general passivity vis-à-vis music that Altman suggests. Instead, I believe that the rise in the popularity of the record suggests an active interest in the practice of listening. It is an issue with which I will grapple throughout subsequent sections of this book.

First, however, it is important that we begin to scrutinize Altman's observation that Hollywood found itself interested in the production and sales of records, particularly those involving original casts. Jeff Smith's substantial research concerning Hollywood's textual and financial investments in the musical soundtrack as a popular commodity designed for ancillary exploitation throughout the 1960s and early 1970s bears out Altman's claim that Hollywood abandoned the sheet music for the disc industry (Smith 1998). And there is no doubt that this aesthetic and financial transformation had a widespread effect on the products that Hollywood produced and promoted. But it is too simple to focus on Hollywood or even a few record companies as a network of coordinating "prime movers" that independently chose to move into the disc business. Given the form's relative independence, we can begin to better understand how and why the recorded music industry was able to deposit elements of the musical in a variety of spaces. Alongside the popular song's formal independence we can begin to discern another logic particular to the music industry. It is through this logic of the substantial development and exploitation of both the film soundtrack and cast records as continually repeatable forms of the show that the music industry is able to profit. In short, this is another version of My Fair Lady's story.

Listening to My My Fair Lady

Versioning and the Recorded Music Object

4

Because of hindsight it is possible to find in Shaw's *Pygmalion* something humorous. Perhaps it is the mixture of his confident tone with the fact that it was this play that was processed into a romantic musical rather than retaining its instructive airs. Shaw's rendition of the Pygmalion myth would become one of Hollywood's last successful musicals, a genre whose primary aim is entertainment. The musical is so fixated on every aspect of what the term "entertainment" embodies that it is now regarded as the most garish of American film genres and, as its presence has receded, it has come to be considered almost a contemptible one. "Low," for reasons of its blatant disrespect for a realist film aesthetic, the musical revels in its artifice, but it has transformative potential precisely because of its ambitious engagement of the artificial in a modern world in search of novel sensations. Thomas Elsaesser celebrates Vincente Minnelli's musicals because they alter "the movements of what one is tempted to call, for lack of a better word, the 'soul' of the characters into shape, colour, gesture and rhythm" (1981, 16). The characteristic most often ascribed to the musical, by viewers and critics alike, is "excess." As scenery, actions, and words seemingly flow over the limits of realistic conduct, it seems that the musical becomes one of the few arenas where, aside from the "blood, guts, and screams"

77

aesthetic of horror and action films, we expect (and accept) good taste to be cast aside. If horror and action fulfill a desire to change the social order through the poetic force of "unlawful" violence, the musical offers us the fantasy of changing our social position through the violation of social proscriptions and genteel behavior. The drop-of-a-hat appearances of outlandish fashions, choreographed groupings, and public sing-a-longs are, in their own way, social offenses. One need only think of how out-of-control subcultural groups such as punks, hip-hop kids, and metal heads are often disparaged for these same social wrongdoings to understand that there are, indeed, very real penalties involved in defying well-mannered behaviors.

Higgins, of course, hoped to refine poor Eliza, in his eyes a veritable amalgam of poor speech, dress, gesture, and self-image. Under the tutelage of Henry Higgins, "Eliza the guttersnipe" becomes "Eliza the aristocrat." Higgins reforms Eliza through a dazzling combination of technical competence, exercise, and machinery. Most prominent throughout both *Pygmalion* and *My Fair Lady* is the turn-of-the-century miracle of the phonograph. Capturing and returning the voice to oneself, the phonograph repeatedly defines Eliza to herself in order to redefine her. She is forced to listen, pick out her "mistakes," extract the cockney from her English, and render forth a new, uplifted Eliza. With Higgins's methods based in phonetics, Eliza's transformation is dictated by an essential anti-essentialism: the belief that the autopoetic powers of self-becoming can literalize our most ideal fantasy into corporeal reality. Listen to any recommendation for any "phonics" or "word power" educational program and it is clear that Shaw's politicized vision of fashion, a vision wherein class divisions are as artificial as the clothes one wears, remains as charged today as it did at the beginning of the twentieth century. This belief in the flexibility of our selves is open to quite a bit of analysis and debate. But there is little doubt that its pronounced position in popular culture is partially the upshot of our investment in modern technologies of self-transformation. Whether it comes in the form of scientific discourse or over-the-counter cosmetics, there is a very modern appeal to "versioning" ourselves for each and every particular space, club, and occasion. No matter how much we believe in a "fundamental self," there is also a belief that we must present multiple facets of ourselves contingent on the many circumstances of our lives.

The appeal of this fact is aggressively explored throughout modern popular music culture. Spend a couple of nights in club forums of disco, techno, jazz, and reggae and you quickly recognize that versioning is a vigorous and vital process for these spaces and genres. But it is hardly limited to dressing and becoming another facet of oneself. Songs that spend their three-minute lives on radio playlists often morph into ten-minute dance epics in the hands of the club disc jockey. Indeed, it is possible that you might hear the same song in each "genre space" (techno club, reggae club, etc.), and hear how each genre physically alters the sonic design of each rendition. This is nothing new and should come as a shock to no one that the practice of generating multiple recorded music versions of a particular composition is not merely alive but actively encouraged by composers, musicians, fans, and, of course, producers. To offer an explanation of how each genre values this practice would not only be a tall order; it could never account for the sheer variety of distinct aesthetic styles and popular music traditions. But to ignore the fact that each contemporary genre produces a number of recordings that include an "original" and an assembly of "other" versions, whether they be remixes, dubs, or alternate takes, simply denies the vitality of the practice. Take a walk through any record store specializing in any one of these genres and you will discover that the practice is thriving. Nevertheless, with few exceptions, the practice continues to be ignored by mass media and popular music scholars.

Although the exact reason why music scholars do not adequately investigate this practice of "versioning" is not entirely clear, I would like to offer a few historical and present-day influences to contextualize this ignorance. For instance, many modern-day listeners, critics, and scholars still adhere to a particularly "romantic" vision of popular music. This vision of individual, artistic expression continues to be aggressively advanced as a particular ideological support that simultaneously sets the field and campaigns for rock as a dominant popular musical genre. As Simon Frith has pointed out, rock fans and musicians are not blind to many of the limits and contradictions involved in the production of this or any other popular form of expression within capitalist economies (1996, 60).

Nevertheless, both rock fans and musicians continue to champion an ideology based on a "double articulation of originality" that provides a discursive and legal foundation that simultenously asserts that rock is an art and an ownable property (Frith 1996). Therefore, both aesthetic and financial judgments in rock music are made with reference to a specific "originator," whether it be an artist, a composition, or a copyright. As a result, a form of critique, influenced by what Frith identifies as "two familiar positions" that act as "the most common critical arguments about musical production," is developed and maintained in day-to-day pop music discourse.

The first is that music is judged in the context of or in reference to a critique of mass production. Bad music is "standardized" or "formula" music. Good music is implicitly "'original' or 'autonomous,' and the explanation built into the judgment depends on the familiar Marxist/ Romantic distinction between serial production, production for the commercial order, to meet a market, and artistic creativity, production determined only by individual intention, by formal and technical rules and possibilities" (69). Frith supplements this distinction with a second point: When musical formulae are judged *not* to be engaged or developed by capitalist machinations for the purpose of being exploited (for example, a localized "folk" genre such as Appalachian coal miners' songs) these formulae are viewed as *honorable,* even healthy examples of collective activity. But when the genre is actively exploited by artists and industry alike, the genre is perceived to be *unsatisfactory* and vulgar, thereby activating a recognition that the genre lacks the appropriate cultural capital that the Marxist/romantic critic honors (69). Not surprisingly, the same critique all too often is the convenient prejudicial obstruction to the analyses flexible enough to understand or celebrate the pleasurable aspects that the many genres of popular music continually develop and deploy.

For Frith, it is exactly this "sort of criticism, which refers to production but without a Marxist edge, [that] equates bad music with imitative music." The critical contrast is with an "original" composition or an "individual" sound or voice. The result is that records and artists are "dismissed for sounding just like someone else (or, not least, for sounding just like their own earlier records or songs)" (69). One consequence of these standards is a perception that the production of analogous versions is a "cynical or pathetic production decision," wherein authentic expression is cast aside in order to invest in already known aesthetic commodities. Continuing this logic, Frith notes that one variation of this position "is the distinction between 'the cover version' and 'the version':

The cover version is almost always heard as bad—this is now the usual attitude to white pop versions of black songs and records in the 1950s, for example: Pat Boone's "Tutti Frutti" is probably the nearest thing to a consensual bad record in popular music history, a track that is both exploitative and feeble. The fact that Pat Boone's "personal stamp" was put on Little Richard's music is clearly a bad thing.

Frith recognizes the importance that this lesson holds for becoming a rock fan:

One aspect of learning to be a rock fan in the 1960s was, in fact, learning to prefer originals to covers. And this was, as I recall, something that did have to be learned: nearly all records that I had bought in the late 1950s had been cover versions. (69–70)

The key to Frith's testimony is not that he can now distinguish a "good" version from a "bad" one (though this is probably important in his other discursive arenas as a fan), but rather that he was encouraged to learn how to listen to rock music covers and how to distinguish "good" rock music from "bad." This type of everyday aesthetic education is common to all music fans, popular or otherwise. In fact, as Pierre Bourdieu argues, without such a specific degree of education or cultural capital it is questionable whether one could actively, or competently, engage in making aesthetic distinctions (1984). This fact holds true for any mode of listening that bases its judgments on noting which distinctions significantly differentiate one text or performance from another. Since value (that is, significance) is a cultural byproduct that is social and learned, all cultures instruct their members what is aesthetically valuable and how to recognize it.

Put simply, active fans are acute social formations primarily constituted around the process of making (and marking) distinctions within a particular constellation of products. These products can include any number of popular texts and properties, such as film stars, television shows, popular forms of literature, or musical genres. Whatever the case, fans vigorously inspect specific moments and innovative displays to sort the proverbial treasures from the trash. For music fans this mode of attention is typically manifested in active forms of listening. Most often these forms represent a *comparative mode of listening* and are therefore contingent on uncovering distinct differences between generic similarities, performances, and/or versions. Fans in a number of ways can exert this mode at their will and convenience. For example, there are those fans who "hear" the trace of an influence in a player or composer's style, while others may simply be able to recognize a composition or player without the aid of any visual clues. Still other fans may compare versions of a composition to hear what performative possibilities are (or have been) available to the work.[1]

In every case, the comparative mode offers a number of pleasures for the popular music listener. These pleasures are exhibited not only in those game shows and magazine columns that invite listeners to demonstrate their abilities to discriminate one piece of music or artist from another but in the purchase and playback of all recordings. Assuredly, for a listener, every new recording demands the investment of time so that it becomes familiar enough to be positioned in educated and "appreciative" comparison. It would be hard to overstate the pleasures offered through this mode of listening, particularly the critical components of appreciation as activities devoted to the recognition of significant differences and the subsequent assignment of value. Through the repeated practice and engagement of this mode vis-à-vis a system of objects, the music fan accrues worth and authority among other enthusiasts. In this case, a fan's expertise may lie in her ability to detect nuanced differences between recordings that she has repeatedly heard but a novice could never appreciate in his first few listens.

It is tempting to equate the practice of repetitive listening with the practice of rereading. Yet the latter is distinguished from the former in at least one substantial manner. Whereas Roland Barthes notes that the practice of rereading specific pieces of literature is widespread but is only tolerated for those "certain marginal categories of readers" such as children, old people, and professors (1975, 15–16), the practice of repeated listening is, in general, actively encouraged. Not only is this reflected in the fact that listeners of recorded music very rarely purchase recordings with the intent of playing these records once and one time only. Take, for example, the 1946 music-appreciation text titled *Listening to Music Creatively*, written by John Edwin Stringham, a former faculty member of Columbia University and the Julliard School of Music and head of the music department at the U.S. Army University. Stringham asserts in his "postscript to the listener" that there is a both a need and a joy involved in hearing pieces again and again. As he sees it, this repetitive behavior is unlike the accumulation of certain forms of academic knowledge involved in the rote memorization of facts and trivia. Stringham argues that repetitive listening stands out because it imbues the ability to influence the creation and performance of music, and to better people. To achieve these effects on music and society, he writes, "nothing can ever take the place—nothing can approach it in the slightest degree—of listening to great works over and over again until they are really and wholly the 'personal' possession of the listener. Thus music can become a vital force in everyday living, making it the happier and nicer for its benign influences" (1946, 457–58). In the expressed "modern" desire to tame and listen to music at one's everyday convenience lies a comment on the value of repetitive listening. In some facets this sentiment echoes Barthes's argument that rereading *is* a form of play and results in the "playing" of texts. Yet Stringham's interests are in no way playful (let alone poststructural). Whereas Barthes argues that the amusing aspect of rereading lies within one's ability to recall different textual influences and opens these texts to a number of influences, Stringham advocates the practice of repetitive listening for its utopian possibility of enlightening social subjects. And though both authors may appear to offer oppositional ideologies, each valorizes the transformative effects of repetition. In each case, repetition *produces* something: whether its products are new social subjects or texts, the outcome is generative.

In narrative literature the repetitive production of a text may result in accenting or minimizing the specific material attributes and influences on a specific text. But in the case of music, repetitive production is championed because its physical rendering is contingent on a variety of distinctive performative styles and possibilities. These possibilities are manifold and may result from any number of influential parameters such as elements of exhibition, editing, the performers themselves, and so forth. Thus the composition is always in competition with the more ephemeral aspects of performance. No matter how much the composer and librettist may otherwise desire, it is the performer's ability, whatever that may be, that exists as *the* most significant difference for listeners regarding a composition's rendering. In fact, often it is the performer's ability that separates one listener's pleasure from another's boredom while listening to well-known compositions. Certainly the music industry understands this and has embraced the fact that the production of

competing versions is an important means of engaging audience pleasures. Thus the recorded music industry engages in a production logic
designed to service its audience's desires and tastes, no matter how fragmented or unified they may be, as well as satisfy its own appetite for
profits and market shares.

It should be noted that as an industrial and aesthetic practice, versioning should not be confused with the more common practice of copy-
ing. While the basic principle behind the copy is the reproduction of a
specific, already rendered, original work (a distinct painting, a photograph, etc.), the production of music involves a more complex logic
than the simple capture and reproduction of a performance or event.
The Chicago Recorded Music Workgroup has pointed out that because
music has historically been conceived as separable from the recording
medium, a number of unfortunate mistakes are continually made in
understanding how and why recordings are produced and distributed
by the music industry (Chicago Workgroup 1993, 172). To understand the
recorded music process we need to "look *at*, rather than *past*, the material
of music" (Corbett 1994, 37). This material investigation may include a
number of techno-aesthetic components that produce and constitute the
recording (specific materials, recording processes, techniques, etc.) as
well as the industrial logics of production, distribution, and exhibition
that circulate and affect specific receptions of the product. For our purposes we need to treat versioning as an industrial logic that has distinct
material effects on the production process.

As a first principle, we must recognize that multitudinous versioning
is not an anomalous practice for the recorded music industry. In fact, as a
rule, it is the rule. As a specific logic, versioning exists at the very heart of
the music industry—an industry based on the acquisition and development of copyrightable properties. Although the exclusive "right to copy"
is typically understood as a license that deters the illicit proliferation of
versions, "copyright's monopoly grant," as Jane Gaines argues, "whether
we like it or not, *does* work as an incentive to publish and consequently
to disseminate [one's product]. Copyright *protection* is always and at the
same time circulation and restriction" (1991, 122).

Forms of copyright vary, but for our understanding we should realize that the music industry administers and is composed of two basic
sets of rights: "performing rights" and "mechanical rights." Performing
rights are typically assigned to composers and publishers. In the United

States two main organizations license the public performance of songs, American Society of Composers Authors and Performers (ASCAP) and Broadcast Music, Inc. (BMI), both of which are nonprofit organizations funded by publishers themselves. As Frith has pointed out, these organizations license the public use of music and distribute the resulting fees through a variety of formulae. The basic principle that underlies each organization is that music exists as a form of *property*, through which the composer, by controlling its use, can earn a living. As a result, one may purchase sheet music or a recording of a song, but one does not necessarily gain the right to perform the song. In each case, the permission of the composer, although it can be granted through a number of means (for example, through the purchase of the licensed sheet music, legal written permission of an agency or composer, etc.), is necessary to *legally* render the composition (Frith 1981, 132–33). Through this system of policing illicit performances and plagiarism of copyrighted material, the interests of both the composer and the publisher are protected.

Distinct from performance rights is the less-understood mechanical right. Mechanical rights are simply "the royalty rights on the use of a song as a recording, [with] the mechanical rights resulting from record sales [being] the most significant [form of the right]" (Frith 1981, 132). Those invested in mechanical rights encourage the purchase and placement of specific recordings within other possible profit-gaining ventures.[2] These two forms of rights may seem to promote distinctly different ambitions, yet together they work to proliferate the number of legitimate recordings. While holders of performing rights hope to see their compositions rendered in as many styles and by as many artists as available, those vested with mechanical rights aspire to maneuver their recordings into not-yet-saturated niche markets. Since the good majority of these markets are divided by reference to genres and subgeneric distinctions ("Latin" or "jazz" may be viewed as at-large genres, "soca" or "big band" may operate as specific subgeneric divisions therein), a popular, in-demand property may be forged into a wide variety of interpretations in order to explore all possible profit sources. In short, these two copyright logics operate synergetically and result in the industrial logic of what I refer to as "versioning." Through this logic we begin to understand a specific industrial motive to account for why a specific composition may be recorded in a variety of musical arrangements, and popular genres and by any number of performers.

The importance of these rights and the logic of versioning is best expressed in the prominence given to songs and recording catalogues. Indeed, music publishers, artists, and recording companies understand that their most important assets lie in the respective catalogues they develop and maintain. As a bundle of rights, the catalogue exists as a continual source for possible profits. Through rereleasing numerous versions of the properties therein, no matter how antiquated that property may seem, songwriters, publishers, and record companies can collect earnings long after a composition's initial release. Thus there is no such thing as a "dead" catalogue of music. All catalogues are only "dormant" properties that can become repopularized through any number of strategies, among them the occasional commercial tie-in such as a film sound track, commercial and/or proper rerelease, and promotion of the property. For these reasons, musicians from the most elementary pop group to the most sophisticated artist are well advised to obtain competent legal counsel when negotiating any contract where a possible transaction of copyrights is involved. Of course, fair and equitable relationships can and do exist, and when a property is successfully exploited, the benefits for both parties can be immense.

Again, a good portion of this industrial logic predates the rise of the recording industry as the dominant mode of industrial production and distribution. In pre–World War II America the traditional measure of a song's success was the number of sheet music units the property was able to move. These sales could be promoted through a variety of media, including but not limited to Hollywood films (typically musicals), vaudeville productions, the occasional radio broadcast, or simply through salesmanship and off-the-cuff performance from door-to-door marketing. As I argued earlier, by emphasizing the sale and production of recorded music the industry's postwar emphasis on new technologies (particularly recordings) altered the means by which we experienced the performance and reception of musical labors; and as I will argue later, this ultimately had a profound effect on both our general reception of music and our conception of it as well. Of course, throughout this change one thing remained constant: the music industry continued to base its success on the maximum exploitation of its properties. Therefore it should not be a surprise to discover that a record company such as Columbia would carry on the practice of versioning in order to generate an assortment of recorded music versions of *My Fair Lady*, a property in which they held significant vested interests.

In order to capitalize in numerous popular music markets Columbia did not limit itself simply to the production of *My Fair Lady*'s original cast record. At the same time it released the original cast record, the company announced the release of two other long-play versions and a number of single, 45 rpm, 7-inch recordings featuring songs from score performed by popular vocalists. From Columbia's recording artist roster, Percy Faith and Sammy Kaye each released long-play recordings of the score that showcased their own aesthetic specialties. While Sammy Kaye's orchestra arranged the score in Kaye's style (placing a specific emphasis on "dancing with [his] familiar bounce beat and smooth ensemble vocal choruses") ("Album Reviews" 1956), Columbia boasted that Percy Faith's instrumental arrangements brought out "the *singing line* of the melodies" (Faith 1956; my emphasis). Though each version was distinct in its arrangement and rendition, Columbia did not hesitate in openly comparing the Faith and Kaye LPs to the original-cast recording of the musical, the flagship product of the three. For example, the Faith liner notes announce:

> The recording by the original cast is available on Columbia Records, where the bite and the charm of the lyrics can be heard in their proper setting. Here, in Percy Faith's imaginative arrangements, the melodies of Frederick Loewe are the focus, and provide not only a fine complement to the original cast recording, but a bright and tuneful souvenir of one of the theater's most resounding hits. (Faith 1956)

Another variety of *My Fair Lady* versions resulted from Columbia's recruitment of popular vocalists for single recordings. Rosemary Clooney recorded both "I Could Have Danced All Night" and a modified version of "I've Grown Accustomed to Her Face" that replaced the gender-specific pronoun "her" of Lerner and Loewe's composition with "your," while Vic Damone lent his melodramatic talents to a rendition of "On the Street Where You Live." And in case customers or radio stations simply wanted a single, instrumental interpretation of one of the songs, Columbia released "The Rain in Spain" backed with "With a Little Bit of Luck" from Percy Faith's album as a 7-inch record ("See $5,000,000 as Jackpot" 1956). In each case, the artist's fare, no matter how generic, was continually positioned alongside the original-cast record. Take, for example, a Columbia advertisement from a 1956 issue of *Billboard*. Although each artist is highlighted with a headshot and an emphasis on the name, the advertisement promotes "the many sounds of My Fair Lady" and the original Broadway cast album version of the score ("The Smash Hits" 1956).

This promotional strategy of associating the original-cast LP with other versions of *My Fair Lady* is indicative of the substantial stress placed on the strength of the property itself. That is, the *My Fair Lady* property held a substantial promotional cachet, a value that rivaled that of the performing artist. We see this pattern repeated almost eight years later when *My Fair Lady* was released as a feature film. In an attempt to piggyback onto the popularity of the film, several companies released or rereleased a number of *My Fair Lady* albums, of which there was no lack. Opening his article for the *New York Times* on the *My Fair Lady* album phenomenon, Robert Alden noted, "Like the heart of an artichoke, 'My Fair Lady' has a leaf for everyone." Accentuating that the property exuded an "extraordinary versatility" and seemed to take well to various differentiations, Alden continued, "Each musical artist can take his leaf, and, to a remarkable degree, make the score his own." With close to fifty-five long-play recordings of *My Fair Lady* on the market (and several more expected), the reviewer noted that "in the history of the music business, classical or popular, there has been nothing to compare" (1964, 23).

Given the enormity of the catalogue it is hardly surprising that both independent and major labels promoted their roster of *My Fair Lady* variants on the release of the Warner Brothers musical. For example, corresponding closely to the release date of the film, Roulette, an independent record company, placed an ad in *Billboard* promoting Tito Puente's *My Fair Lady Goes Latin* and Johnny Richard's big band jazz version of the score, *My Fair Lady My Way* ("Bet on Roulette's 'Fair Ladies'" 1964). And anticipating the film's success, Columbia put forth no fewer than nine different *My Fair Lady* LP records, including two "original cast record" versions and two recordings featuring Andre Previn (one of his quartet, the other of his film soundtrack arrangements). One Columbia advertisement in *Billboard* promoted the release of the film soundtrack and seven of these other LPs, including the rereleases of Percy Faith's and Sammy Kaye's renditions, a collection of Andy Williams's performances, and

We've Got The "Lady" Covered

CL 2205/CS 9005*

OL 5090/OS 2015*

CL 895/CS 9004*

CL 2195/CS 8995*

HL 7321

Coming Soon!
The Exciting
"My Fair Lady"
Original Sound Track
Album

The Many Sounds of "My Fair Lady" on Columbia Records

Anticipating the release of the film musical, this Columbia Records advertisement promotes the "many sounds of My Fair Lady," including the rerelease of the original cast's 1959 stereo version recorded in London as well as two previous 1955 versions recorded by Sammy Kaye and Percy Faith. The Percy Faith version is depicted here with a new Audrey Hepburn record jacket.

three foreign-language versions in Spanish, Italian, and Hebrew ("The Excitement Is about to Begin" 1964).

Also depicted in the same advertisement is the stereo version of the original-cast record. Perhaps no better example of the practice of versioning involving the *My Fair Lady* property exists than this LP, Columbia's

This Columbia Records advertisement depicts its new release of the film sound track as well as versions in Spanish, Italian, and Hebrew for international markets.

second "original cast record." In an effort to profit from the interest in listening to stereo recordings, Columbia hoped to reassemble the same successful cast from the original-cast record to rerecord the score. This process was by no means sluggish. By December 1957, little over twenty-one months after the release of the first original-cast record, a *Variety* article mentioned that "[My Fair Lady] is due for the stereophonic trimmings" and executives at Columbia were well at work in planning the project. With many labels having adopted the practice of cutting two different audio versions of major releases at the same recording session, one for the regular LP market and the other for stereo enthusiasts for release on both LP and tape, Columbia believed another original-cast version of a record that had already sold 1.3 million copies could actually earn significant returns ("'Fair Lady' in Stereo" 1957).

Produced in London in 1959, the album featured the four principal leads, Rex Harrison, Julie Andrews, Stanley Holloway, and Robert Coote, re-creating their Broadway roles. It was promoted by Lieberson in the gatefold jacket as a sort of "second honeymoon" for those listeners who had already established an intimacy with the score. As the initial conjugations were repeated, Lieberson's notes encourage listeners to notice significant differences in the actors' performances as well as the improvements brought forth by the stereo process. Most conspicuously improved was, according to Lieberson, Rex Harrison. For Lieberson, the stereo record exhibited Harrison "giving what is far and away his best, his most touching, his most sensitive performance of *I've Grown Accustomed to Her Face.*" It is the intimacy that is attained through a particularly repetitive/comparative listening that Lieberson honors and encourages:

> How could all of us who were working on this project, after all of these hearings, be caught up again in the humor pathos of this musical story? Certainly, the answers to these questions are to be found in the professionalism and the consummate artistry of Rex Harrison and his confreres.
>
> But, in addition, we learn something else—something very important about the words and music. We learn that these elements are so genuinely moving, so irresistibly appealing, so in accordance with basic emotional needs, that repeated hearings enhance the love we felt at first hearing, and an authentic romance begins. (Lerner and Loewe 1959)

Given CBS's proliferation of recorded versions of the musical's score, it should not surprise anyone to learn that Chapell Music, the music publishing company responsible for licensing the performance and recording of songs from *My Fair Lady*, would want to profit from the practice of versioning. Along with CBS's roster of artists who released versions of *My Fair Lady* songs in 1956, *Variety* noted that Chappell had set up considerably more artists, including Dinah Shore, Charlie Applewhite, Gordon McCrea, and Frances Wayne, to record versions of the play's "three most commercial tunes—'I Could Have Danced All Night,' 'On the Street Where You Live,' and "I've Grown Accustomed to Her Face" ("'Fair Lady' a Palpable Hit" 1956). But advertisements published in 1956 editions of *Billboard* reveal that many more renditions were produced than the *Variety* article indicated. For example, Lawrence Welk released four songs from the musical on two singles for Coral Records, which eventually became a *My Fair Lady* EP ("America's Hottest Band" 1956). While RCA Victor placed an Eddie Duchin rendition of "On the Street Where You Live" on the backside of his "Sweet Heartaches" single ("Eddie Corners the Hit Market Singing" 1956), they recorded a Julius LaRosa single featuring two selections from the play ("Double Scoop!" 1956), and RCA's budget label, RCA/Camdem, offered a four-song EP from Domenico Savino and His Orchestra ("Profit Pick of the Month!" 1956). Even the jazz genre had its initial participants in the *My Fair Lady* sweepstakes with Decca Records' single release of "I Could Have Danced All Night" by Sylvia Sims ("America's Fastest Selling Records" 1956). Riding the unprecedented success for Broadway original-cast albums, labels produced enough "differing" versions of *My Fair Lady* as well as other musicals that by mid-December 1956 *Variety* recognized that "in addition to original cast set releases, the diskeries are now covering the tuners with instrumental, dance tempo, pop vocal and even jazz packages" on a more regular basis. Among these included another Columbia *My Fair Lady* album of pop vocalists collected from the already released singles plus new renditions, as well as a jazz label, Contemporary, production of a Shelly Manne long-play version of the score ("Diskeries Putting Showtime Albums" 1956).

As both Broadway and road shows continued to prosper well after the show's 1956 opening, recording companies exhibited a seemingly endless appetite for *My Fair Lady*–related productions. Almost two years after the musical's opening and the release of the original-cast record, a 1958 *Variety* article noted that more than twenty *My Fair Lady* albums from "instrumental, jazz and vocal veins" had been issued. According to the same article, the massive success of the original-cast album, combined with Columbia's other *Fair Lady* projects, made it clear to record companies that the value of an album tie-up with a successful Broadway show could certainly be immense and that *My Fair Lady* was only the beginning of this "tie-up" trend. *The Music Man* provided another example of this phenomenon. Although Capitol purchased the rights to the original-cast version, a dozen other albums of the score were scheduled for release well before the show's opening in order to capitalize on the musical's much-anticipated popularity ("Disk Yen for Legit Scores" 1958). That record companies had lined up album versions of a musical well before the premier of the show reflects a tough financial lesson that many had learned from the massive success of *My Fair Lady*: because so many labels had waited for the musical to shape up as a hit, when distributors of companies other than Columbia began "putting in p.d.q. calls for numbers from the show," these labels were forced to cover these songs and, for the most part, "take second money" on recordings they tried to push into specific yet profitable niche markets ("'Singling Out' the Showtunes" 1956).

The benefits of the "tie-up" are best reflected through its ability to develop and engage a system of ever-constant promotion. A nationwide event, the success of *My Fair Lady* as a show and recording was possible not only through the extensive magazine and newspaper coverage of Broadway but through the recent cross-country phenomenon of the disc jockey. Major labels had learned to skillfully access, corral, and supply these independent publicists with a variety of products. The multiple versions of *My Fair Lady* were no exception ("Disk Yen for Legit Scores" 1958). The network that connected disc jockeys with major labels was firmly established by the mid-1950s, a fact that Hollywood, Broadway, and the general music industry had certainly grasped (Grevatt 1956; Zhito 1956). As a result of this nationwide network the demand for original-cast records could be expanded far beyond the New York area. In a *Variety* article from February 1957, the reporter noted that records would be the "key media" in exploiting the road-company version:

> The groundwork for the disk-tuner tie in already has been laid
> with such labels as Columbia, RCA-Victor, ABC-Paramount and

Contemporary pitching in on the promotion. The record distributors in cities where the musical is scheduled to play already
have been alerted to special deejay promotion campaigns on the
show's waxings. Columbia, of course, is most active, because of
its original cast albums as well as [others]. The Victor distribs are
pitching the diskerie's album by Melachrino, while Contemporary and ABC-Paramount promote their jazz albums of the Lerner
and Loewe music. ("No Disk Jockey Left Unturned" 1957)

Of course one could presume that both Broadway and touring productions
of the show saw the use of disc jockeys as a source of cross-promotion
from which they also benefited. In other words, as the tour promoted the
record, the record promoted the tour, and so forth. This coordination of
disc jockeys with distributors and "the tour" would become a standard
"rock practice" by the end of the 1960s.

Unsurprisingly, the proliferation of textual versions also creates numerous opportunities for considerable problems to arise. As the constellation of any copyrighted text reproduces and exerts its influence,
the limitation of unauthorized renditions, variations, and sales of these
properties opens numerous doors through which various conflicts and
debates can enter into the intertextual process. Because the music industry is firmly grounded on the principle of exploiting specific properties
through as many venues as possible, the most popular investments engender their own policing difficulties. This, coupled with the fact that
audiences and authorities alike seemingly care more for the performer
and her performances than the law, makes the task of controlling the
manner in which these properties are exploited even more complex.

Because the musical requires such a substantial investment, the proliferation of nonsanctioned versions can pose a sizable threat to satiate
or capitalize on markets that have not yet been fully mined by the legitimate bodies of production and investment. Whereas someone may
easily purchase the right to play or perform a song, purchasing a right
to perform a musical involves a substantially riskier investment in terms
of both initial capital and the possibility of returns. Thus, in order to
develop and foster large-scale cultural investments such as a musical, its
cast recording, and so on, the same industry must incorporate, restrict,
and legitimate its properties where potentially significant markets are at
stake. This point cannot be stressed enough. The legitimation process is
continual and ongoing for the music industry. Unlike radio, television,

or film, the modern music industry of recordings, copyrights, and modern modes of distribution must deal with a substantial history of musical production, a history that predates both capitalist economic formations and modern technologies. As a result, the industry is involved in a continual negotiation between musicians, composers, and audiences who often hold many of the earlier, premodern attitudes that position music as something belonging to a collective culture rather than private entities. Sometimes this concern embarrasses the industry because it betrays an unseemly, almost crass desire for profits in an artistic arena. In other cases the legitimation process tills unharvested markets for brazen speculative purposes. By acquainting a new market with "proper methods" of receiving and using its wares, the music industry does what it can to control growth on its own terms. In the case of *My Fair Lady*, three "legitimate" interests—the music publishers, the show's producers, and recording companies—worked, sometimes together, in order to dominate the processes of the property's simultaneous growth and containment.

As one might guess, not every version of *My Fair Lady* was welcomed. For example, those record companies that produced legitimate recordings viewed bootleggers as a threat. As mentioned earlier, bootlegging has always been and continues to be something of a nuisance and the site of much debate for the official record industry. But for the producers of *My Fair Lady* a much more urgent concern was what they felt were a variety of inappropriate and unauthorized performances of the show's material. In one case, Lerner and Loewe vocally objected to the J. Walter Thompson advertising agency's use of "On the Street Where You Live" as the basis for a radio commercial promoting Ford automobiles. According to one Thompson vice president, the protest was simply hypocritical considering that the songwriters' publishers reportedly received close to $3,000 and that "a play like 'Fair Lady' was created not to improve the breed of theatrical horse flesh. It was for cash gain. It's a commercial product. Its songs are commercial products . . . sold to record companies for cash gain." And, of course, the same songs were "okayed" to help the sale of products as well ("'My Fair Lady' Authors' Blast Unfair" 1956). In another case, *My Fair Lady*'s producers were able to delete portion of a Nevada nightclub act's show that included a twenty-two-minute "capsuled version" of the musical, complete with shortened songs and bits of dialogue ("Gordon MacRae's 'Fair Lady' Medley Unfair" 1956; "Threatened with Suit, MacRae Drops" 1956). One could presume that the incentive behind this type of litigation was to preserve the novelty of the play and spur demand for other "official" versions. Although there is no evidence that this was the impetus behind this specific act, it certainly was the case in restricting other "unofficial" performances.

This desire to restrict the appearance of unlicensed versions is best displayed in the policing of two cases involving live performers' use of the score in the South Pacific before the specific, sanctioned tour and recording of *My Fair Lady* could appear. In March 1958, during an Australian tour, Liberace reportedly received an injunction from Chappell Music to cease and desist from featuring numbers from *My Fair Lady* because it breached a local copyright setup that was geared toward having an Australian company perform the play. Incensed that he had been forced to eliminate these songs from his act, on March 5 Liberace shortened the duration of his tour, apologized to his audience for not being able to "perform the music of [my] country, for which I am noted," and claimed that this restriction violated the laws of the United States, muddied a democratic vision, and must be communist ("Liberace, 'Lady' and Truncated Trot" 1958). One month later, *Variety* related a similar story involving New Zealand musicians who had been performing songs from the musical for over a year. A warning issued from Chappell informed New Zealanders that none of the music from *My Fair Lady* could be played in public. The ban applied to the musicians who performed in local pubs and other gatherings and also to any public playing of the Columbia original-cast album. According to the article, although the record was not for sale in New Zealand record shops and would not be released until the Autralasian company of the play arrived, some eighteen months later, "most [New Zealand] travelers to the U.S. and other dollar countries return with at least one copy" of the much-in-demand record. And if they had no intention of keeping the record, their copy could easily gain a significant profit ("'Fair Lady' Score Nixed in N.Z." 1958). Two years earlier the same restriction on the public exhibition of *My Fair Lady* records was enacted overseas as publishers moved to eliminate the score from the Armed Forces Network. While this case involved British publishers who had bought an option on the American musical, the act exacerbated a sore spot for American servicemen stationed in Europe, who would repeatedly find Armed Forces radio broadcasts sans the biggest musical hits because of restrictions like these. Despite the loss of radio airplay, the original-cast record remained a popular seller for American troops ("O'Seas Pubs Nix Airing" 1956).

While playing sanctioned versions of the *My Fair Lady* score in "unsanctioned" markets posed a number of difficulties, the creation of parody scores and records existed as another problematic practice. In the words of a 1957 *Variety* article concerning Foremost Records' parody of *My Fair Lady, My Square Laddie*, "the issue of 'justifiable satire' has been brought into focus." Although the independent label transformed such hits as "I Could Have Danced All Night" and "I've Grown Accustomed to Her Face" into "I Could Have Boozed All Night" and "I'm Kinda Partial to Her Puss," questions of taste were kept subordinate to the legal principles of music publishing. Through their attorneys, Lerner and Loewe informed *Variety* that actions taken would be similar to those made against the Ziegfeld Follies: first, a formal protest in the form of a letter and then, if necessary, litigation. According to *Variety,* the major complaint of the writing team as voiced by Lerner was that these parodies were simply made "without authorization." Articulating the sentiments of the publishing industry, Lerner noted that without creating a record of objections, their silence might "constitute blanket licence to parody," whether it be *My Fair Lady* or other popular musicals and songs on Broadway, television, and film ("Is 'My Fair Lady' a Fair or Unfair Game for Parody" 1957). Later that same year Lerner and Loewe continued to register their disapproval of these parodies by issuing a similar complaint to Jay-Gee Record Company, whose label, Jubilee Records, released another *My Fair Lady* parody titled *My Fairfax Lady* ("'My Fair Lady' Has No Sense of Disk Humor" 1957). And almost two months later the duo filed suit in a New York federal court to stop the label from continued production of the record ("Lerner-Loewe vs. Jubilee Label" 1957).

In other cases mild controversies were generated when international recording companies began to exploit nationalist sentiments in order to ride the property's remarkable potential for flexible marketability. As mentioned earlier, Columbia released three foreign-language versions and expected its English-language versions to succeed in all Anglophone countries. Yet, as one *Variety* article claimed, if an enterprising recording company would have distributed the original Australian version of *My Fair Lady* starring Robin Bailey and Bunty Turner, there would have been little doubt of its down-under success (Stanley 1961). This form of differentiation through the invocation of specific national properties was perhaps best exemplified in the dispute between Philips and Polydor record companies, each of which produced a German-language version of the play. The dispute focused not so much on whether the two could compete with different versions as on Philips's opinion that the two LPs were not distinct enough. With the rights to the original-cast recording of the highly successful Berlin staging of the show, Philips's main objection was to Polydor's claim that it had produced "the German Ideal Cast" version of the LP, an assertion inscribed on the record sleeve. Oddly enough, as *Variety* pointed out, Polydor's LP spotlighted two Hungarians, two Austrians, a Swiss orchestra, and only two Germans ("Polydor 'Ideal Cast' Tag" 1962).

As varied and distinct as each controversy may be, a common thread of legitimation and containment runs throughout and tethers the concerns of copyright from medium to medium and nation to nation. With each market involving its own set of contingencies, it is unthinkable to propose that they adopt a large set of uniform concerns. However, the "right" to exploit a property remains constant. Among a sea of versions, each containing a seed of industrial hope that it, too, will germinate into a sizable hit, and with liberties taken at the production level wide and varied, the individual version is to be created with deference to a granted privilege. Without this license the version must be challenged if the license is to remain sheltered. Although one can create a copy of "Show Me" after listening to the Oscar Peterson, Shelly Manne, or Julie Andrews version (or all of them), to enter this rendition into the marketplace, a right of origination rather than any "original" needs to be continually acknowledged. Without such a recognition the license is defrauded, the property is redistributed, the author is forgotten, and the mechanism—through which the industrial process of versioning is managed—is jammed.

Which brings us back to the controversial question echoed in the title of chapter 3: which voice best becomes Eliza after all? Answers are multiformed, from stock approvals to protests, but only one conveniently flees the seduction of continual dispute: indifference. To compare and argue over the versions is not so much to debate a red herring as it is to embrace it. As audience to all of these forms, we are not critically distant. Rather we are enfolded within a comparative practice of listening. It is not the discovery and validation of evidence that is ultimately deter-

minant but a comparative practice that invokes a specific field of differentiated recordings. In this case the field is conveniently limited to
the voices of Andrews and Hepburn/Nixon, each of which continues to
reside within Columbia/Sony products. We may argue and reason with
enough evidence in hand to decide that yes, X is better than Y, and so
on. But it is our investment in acquiring the evidence that betrays our
industrial capacities.

If there is one axiom of the recorded music industry, it is that there is
no such thing as a definitive version, no matter how much ballyhoo and
publicity to the contrary. One need only think about a favorite recording
artist and her catalogue. All too often we witness how so-called comprehensive anthologies can always add material originally suppressed by
an artist's or producer's decision. Our favorite albums and compact discs
can always be appended through the attachment of a couple of "previously unreleased" tracks, thereby making them valued once again. Even
that definitive box set can be updated with a few "lost recordings." And
when every option seems exploited, a property can be rereleased in a
new recording medium or remastered with the latest audio technologies. Perhaps a slogan from Arista puts it best. Promoting their own
Arista Masters line, the label promises "More than just re-issues" in an
extensive search through their archive of artists in search of the "never-
before-seen": the rare photo, liner notes by the artists themselves, bonus
tracks, and so forth ("More Than Just Re-Issues" 1996).

This is a lesson that must be heeded in an era when recordings are
seemingly more and more accessible and now dominate the media
market. This is particularly the case with mainstream cinema, whose
business is, like the music industry today, increasingly dependent on
the sale of recordings and finds illicit duplication increasingly a threat.
It is in this context that we are simultaneously treated to and threatened by films that seemingly never go away. And like popular music,
our cinema seems to flow from site to site, medium to medium, and in
every case we are offered a number of chances to invest in their textual
pleasures. Movies that we had once convinced ourselves were forever
dead now walk among us in ever-popular (and sometimes "limited")
DVD editions. For example, take the restoration of a few but celebrated
films Hollywood has recently offered, such as *Spartacus* (Kubrick 1960)
in 1991, *My Fair Lady* (Cukor 1964) in 1994, and *Vertigo* (Hitchcock 1958)
in 1996. Rereleased in major markets throughout the United States, each

restoration garnered widespread attention and rejuvenated an interest in these films, their directors, and actors. Immaculately researched and rehabilitated by James C. Katz and Robert A. Harris, each film brings with it its own specific set of difficult circumstances that only an interested investor can help ease.

In the case of *My Fair Lady*, the frame-by-frame restoration of the text was financed by Sony, which had acquired Columbia's recording properties in an earlier transaction. Taking nearly a year and expending close to $750,000, Katz and Harris worked the film materials, which had been acquired from Warner Brothers Studios in 1971 by CBS, into a film for theatrical rerelease, along with a restored video and laserdisc version. Each of these versions boasted generally better aesthetic properties and some newfound archival materials that the restorers had discovered (Grimes 1994, 9). While the "limited edition" laserdisc included additional memorabilia such as reproductions of Cecil Beaton's detailed costume sketches, the box of the videotape simply claimed that this restoration was "now more loverly than ever" and would allow one to "see and hear [the film] as it was meant to be experienced" (Cukor 1964). Two years later another version of the film featuring a soundtrack reengineered through George Lucas's THX process appeared on VHS and laserdisc formats.

While the original goal was to restore a negative through which any number of "masters" would be struck, there was no greater shock than the discovery of Audrey Hepburn's voice. Intentionally "lost" but now "found" in *My Fair Lady*'s alternate soundtracks, what was once dubbed over in the original had been unearthed in a never-before-seen version. Almost thirty years after Hepburn's renditions of "Wouldn't It Be Loverly" and "Show Me" were recorded, versions of each were exhibited to the public. While the Hepburn version of "Wouldn't It Be Loverly" was played as the final credits rolled in a New York benefit screening (Grimes 1994, 9), "Show Me" found its way onto the commemorative laserdisc version of the film. Yet none of these tracks were culled from one continuous, mistake-free track. Rather, each version of "Show Me" and "Wouldn't It Be Loverly" was a restoration in itself. By piecing together the best portions of each track to make an entire song, newfound digital technologies became the medicine through which Audrey found her voice (Grimes 1994, 12).

One should not be surprised to find *My Fair Lady* appear in yet another format in the future. Coinciding with the rerelease of the film, Columbia rereleased, again, the film sound track (this time with never-before-released material extending the length of the disc to seventy-two minutes) and the original-cast record. Digitally remastered, given new liner notes, and pressed on a twenty-four-karat gold disc, this version of the original-cast record proudly proclaimed on its jacket to be the "definitive version" of the release. If you pay close attention, the disc does provide a never-before-heard clarity. But is it really the definitive version? If you pay even closer attention, you can hear the voice of Eliza Doolittle scream "Not bloody likely!"

PART III

Stereo, Hi-Fi, and the
Modern Pleasures of Easy Listening

5

A Tale of Two Ears

The Concert Hall Aesthetic and Stereo

> Earlier much futile thought had been devoted to the question of
> whether photography is an art. The primary question—whether
> the very invention of photography had not transformed the entire
> nature of art—was not raised.
>
> —Walter Benjamin, "Art in the Age
> of Mechanical Reproduction"

THE MOST PRESSING QUESTIONS IN THIS BOOK ARE THOSE THAT
investigate the nature and our understanding of recordings. Institutionally, the record is created through an assortment of concerns. We have
seen how the record industry shaped the recording as a unit whose success is predicated on its exchange. Broadcasters, on the other hand, positioned the record as an essential facet in scheduling programming, a
position the industry shows no intent of altering. In other activities we
may notice how musicians form recordings for exchange, education, and
archiving. The utility of recordings for scholars of music is unprecedented. And historians of all types seek recordings *not* because they are simply the "residue" of specific activities but because they so often exist as
premeditated aesthetic formations founded by and placed into particular systems of production and exchange. Yet despite our commonsense

understanding, recordings are not merely reproductions that reflect events in audiovisual terms. Rather, we need to conceive of recordings as heterogeneous technologies whose expectations and functions vary from logic to logic, period to period.

Let's begin with Benjamin's assertion regarding the questions posed about photography. Photography is a technology whose basis is typically asserted as an ur-method in unmediated recording; Benjamin argues the need for a different line of questioning in order to understand the art of the medium. This is not shocking for many of us. For many, the question of whether photography is an art is not worth asking. And, of course, the same goes for music, as well as recording: many of us understand these areas as spaces of aesthetic expertise. What distinguishes Benjamin's question is that it forces us to think of the medium as a component with a distinct aesthetic impact. Even when we admit that the recording process is an artistic process—and most of us do—when we listen to our favorite MP3s, CDs, and LPs, recognizing the processes that go into creating these compositions is not part of our everyday experience. By moving our attention away from a commonsense understanding of the record as a historical document and toward new considerations of its aesthetic composition, Benjamin's assertion brings not only the technique and craft behind the record's arrangement to the fore but also the medium's impact on how we perceive the aesthetic domain. Benjamin's question about photography specifically reveals that inside the techniques and craft of photography another important history of aesthetic experience lies.

The proposal that technological change could alter not only our creative processes but also the manner in which we perceive the world is tricky, to be sure. This section of *Making Easy Listening* submits that an aesthetic inquiry regarding the high-fidelity technologies of the postwar period is needed precisely because I feel that such an ambitious claim about perception and technology is not beyond reason. More ambitiously, I suggest throughout this section that the initial wave of high-fidelity products, listeners, and musicians was appealing to listeners because they enchanted them with the possibilities of listening to music, as well as the new, modern, and more convenient possibilities of listening in general. Specifically, I argue that a good portion of these possibilities can be teased out through an understanding of the general discourse surrounding the issue of stereo sound. While stereo is commonly perceived as a realist technology, this section asserts that stereo's promise for a more "realistic" reproduction of music was also accompanied by a definite impact on issues of recorded music and sound production that had little to do with realism in the naive sense of the word. These perceptual alterations not only influenced the production of popular musical genres but also affected the perception and representation of more conservative musical genres such as those involving the Western classical repertoire.

Many readers may sense that I am primarily focused on the act of listening. For a moment we need to understand that the focus on the listener is fundamental to the questions surrounding high-fidelity technologies. These technologies are designed for better, more pleasurable experiences, but they are terribly underappreciated on a number of fronts by listeners and theorists alike for their influence on the act of listening. As I have been suggesting throughout, the listening act is neither passive nor simpleminded. For example, while it is true that some of the more pleasurable aspects of listening may seem calming and even submissive, these states of idle bliss and comfort require a significant amount of preparation. The relaxed listener has often sought a moment, a space, and a technology in which the act of "easy listening" can be fostered. The conditions may vary from finding the time in one's daily schedule to fit in a light operetta to choosing and designing a sound system; from exploring a number of record stores looking for the record that will certainly fit the evening's bill, to understanding when a "moment of ease" has turned into an annoyance and should be terminated. The listening act is always an act of resolve, intent manifested at a particular level of understanding that may vary from subject to subject, time to time, space to space; it is never passive in the true sense of the word.

Perhaps a weightier criticism that readers may posit exists in the potential suggestion that I am not addressing issues directly related to the music—more precisely, that any analysis of listening has little relevance to an understanding of musical production. Yet as ethnomusicologist John Blacking argues, since musicians and listeners alike must recognize any true transformation in musical production, sound exists as a critical category for production (1977). Following Blacking's assertion, Paul Théberge argues that the idea that an identifiable "sound" could become a marketable feature by which musicians, critics, record companies, and listeners differentiate recordings was well under way by the 1960s. Although Théberge draws from William Ivey's work on the production of the "Nashville sound" vis-à-vis "traditional" country music (1982), Théberge's point concerns no one singular genre but a larger organization of musical manufacturing. He writes, "It should be made clear, however, especially for this [postwar period] in the development of sound technology, that the concept of 'sound' was not simply a 'technical' phenomenon in the limited sense of the term; recording technology must be understood as a complete 'system' of production involving the organization of musical, social and technical means" (193). It is precisely because the sound of music became more and more an indispensable condition for the production and consumption of recordings from the 1950s to the 1960s that we need to do a better job of understanding why both listeners and musicians began their widespread contemplation of recorded audio. A better understanding would offer us not only a greater grasp of audio history but also a greater potential to discern how audio decisions are made in conjunction with the promotion and distribution of musical recordings to specific marketplace segments.

Of course, I do not want to suggest that somehow sound was always separated from "musical" concerns until the rise of high-fidelity technologies. This has never been the case. As Théberge points out,

> Many cultures do not recognize a clear distinction between musical instruments, sounds, and musical theory, often making it difficult for outside observers to understand native musical concepts and practices. The problem is further compounded in cultures where there exists little difference between playing music and dancing to it, or a clear division between spoken and sung speech.

But Théberge also notes that Western minds have often gone to great lengths to make the two categories distinct from one another:

> In the West, the scientific development of physics and acoustics and, equally important, the development of a precise form of musical notation have led to a series of distinctions that separate, conceptually if not always practically, sound from music and performance from composition. One of the legacies of the eighteenth and nineteenth centuries was the growing separation between the score, as musical text, and performance, as mere execution and virtuosic display. (188–89)

By construing this separation as a framework wherein the typical Western understanding of music is gained, Théberge does not propose that this frame is no longer employed or that it collapsed during any historical period. Rather, he wants to hold this framework up for a thorough critique through which he can make an argument concerning how new music technologies continue to blur the borders between the performer and composer, sound and music.

Théberge's critique is not without precedent, a fact he openly acknowledges. In fact, his critique parallels a particular claim of many Western avant-garde and experimental musicians and composers who have spent significant energies addressing this division. Possibly the most celebrated example of this work exists in the figure of John Cage, who, as Allen Weiss observes, works in a tradition that follows from the stylings of Varèse and Russolo in its attention to dissolving the lines between instrumentation and effects, music and sound, writing and performance (Weiss 1995, 49). While much of Cage's work in the 1930s and 1940s was, as Weiss notes, "created for dance (especially that of Merce Cunningham)" (1995, 48), Cage also spent considerable time exploring the sonic relationships between mechanical/electronic technologies and traditional musical elements. This tendency is perhaps best illustrated in his *Imaginary Landscape* compositions, pieces designed to incorporate items such as microphones, radios, and record players as musical instruments. Cage's best expression of his desire to find new aesthetic possibilities through unorthodox instrumentation exists in his 1942 essay "For More New Sounds":

> Many objects not originally intended for musical purposes, such as automobile parts, pipe lengths, and sheets of metal have been used. In some cases, the word percussion has become something of a misnomer, the sound being produced through other means than hitting. Shells and whistles are blown; dials turned and buttons pushed; needles lowered onto records. (Cage 1991, 64)

It is important to understand that Cage's comments indicate his desire for not only a new compositional palette but also a liberated auditor. That is, Cage hopes for a listener who is allowed and aspires to recognize the genius of sonic musication before written composition:

These instruments are by no means the ultimate ones dreamed of, but they are available and useful and constitute at least a step into the "hitherto unheard or even unimagined." It is possible, but with some difficulty, to transplant them from the radio studio to the concert hall. Loudspeakers, amplifiers, and turntables must be set up in the midst of a fantastic assemblage of wires and electrical connections. In using this material for musical purposes it would be easier and more natural to do so in radio studios where the material has been developed. Organizations of sound effects, with their expressive rather than representational qualities in mind, can be made. Such compositions could be presented by themselves as "experimental radio music," or for the purpose of heightening dramatic effects in connection with the use of sounds recorded on film, film phonographs, and organizations of such material for the moving picture. In writing for these sounds, as in writing for percussion instruments alone, the composer is dealing with material that does not fit into the orthodox scales and harmonies. It is therefore necessary to find some other means than those in use for symphonic instruments. These sounds cannot be organized through reference to an underlying fundamental tone since such a tone does not exist. (66)

I include this lengthy passage from Cage's essay because of the rather optimistic wartime vision it provides. Cage was not alone in his convictions. By 1957 this search for new sonic territories would lead Christian Wolff to claim that Morton Feldman, Earle Brown, Karlheinz Stockhausen, Pierre Boulez, Bo Nilsson, Henri Pousseur, and the already-mentioned Edgard Varèse were involved in the production of musical combinations through "simply the sounds we hear." For Wolff it was perhaps more interesting that these "composers" proposed compositions that were "indifferent to motive, originating in no psychology nor in dramatic pretensions, nor in literary or pictorial purposes" (Wolff 1993, 85). Wolff's point is interesting not simply because it identifies an interesting collective characteristic but also because it isolates a desire to produce aural objects that lack a traditional sense of musical intent or origin. Wolff sees and separates these objects from their "everydayness," a quotidian aspect that is sequestered and examined for the momentous aesthetic potentials it contains. Yet the employment of these objects, as Wolff notes, was predicated on significant electronic improvements, and thus the genre was dubbed "electronic music." As a genre, electronic music was produced from synthetic or reproduced sounds, involved no proper instruments, and found its "only final realization [in] a record or tape of series of tapes (in stereophonic presentation)" (Wolff 1993, 89).

Although Wolff's allusion to stereophonic presentation is parenthetical, it should not be ignored. While Wolff's oblique reference to stereo may be read as a sardonic comment on the ubiquity of high-fidelity merchandise and promotions during the late 1950s, it is also possible to view this digression as both a simple observation and an ideal request. It is discerning in the respect that, by 1957, the promise of in-home stereo technology had become widely anticipated by musicians and serious listeners alike and was viewed as a model audio technique that had (and continues to have) a significant relationship with musical recording and reproduction. In an avant-garde context, mentioning the term "stereophonic" places these artists in an interesting, perhaps unexpected and fascinating, relationship to another context of fashionable consumer technologies, industrial demands, and popular listening practices of the period—unexpected, given the hermetic, insulated nature within which many audiences typically envision avant-garde movements as working. And fascinating because the statement deposits this set of international avant-garde artists into a dynamic, industrial structure that more mainstream postwar American musical genres, musicians, and audiences immersed themselves in, confronted, and encountered.

I argued earlier that the results of the 1948 recording ban afforded a confidence to the music industry that its future would rest firmly in recordings and electronic reproducing technologies rather than live performances. As the American public began to engage a collection of innovative audio technologies, these devices not only influenced the listening experience but also altered what listeners came to expect and desire from musicians and audio objects alike. Indeed, the variety of postwar innovations in audio engineering is legendary. Long-play 10-inch and 12-inch $33\frac{1}{3}$ rpm as well as 7-inch 45 rpm records, new forms of styli, tone arms, magnetic tape, a variety of turntables, speakers, and reel-to-reel decks, two-track tape recording and multiple-track, nonlinear editing techniques, "non-breakable" vinyl discs with reduced static surfaces, and the general increase in frequency range among recordings and dynamic response among playback equipment were all significant audio developments in the decade following the end of the war. In addition to these novel technologies, older prewar technologies such as FM radio, "Muzak," other forms of FM multiplexing, and storecasting found a much more enthusiastic (and in some cases lucrative) acceptance in the prosperous postwar climate. Add to these the graphic rise in sales and the recording industry's strength, and it takes a relatively short leap to assume that a good portion of the American public took a specific interest in the act of listening, particularly when it involved recordings.

This is the basis on which I want to draw two lines of argumentation about high-fidelity aesthetics in general and stereo in particular. The first assertion revolves around issues of authority, "the original" and the recording. As James Kraft argues in his study of the American Federation of Musicians (AFM) and musical laborers, the introduction of sound-reproduction technologies has engaged a logic aimed at converting "diffused, labor-intensive job markets and workplaces into more centralized and mechanized ones" (Kraft 1996, 193). By aligning the two AFM recording bans with general labor concerns and unrest, Kraft recognizes an affinity between the general anxieties of many industrial workers and musicians, with each group protesting increased mechanization at the expense of jobs. I make a similar point in chapters 1 and 2, but unlike Kraft, I invoke the work of Jacques Attali and claim that the losses of the AFM were both predicated on and necessary to creating a larger shift in the industrial process of American music making from a performative economy to a repetitive economy based on recordings. The combination of a rapidly growing recorded music industry and the diminished power of musicians to control their fate and the fate and effect of the properties they produce assembled the foundational logic for an industry that continues today, often to the detriment of the musicians it employs. This commercial turning point signaled a crisis manifested as an anxiety regarding a lack in the authority of music production. Specifically, this lack involved a deficiency of "liveness," the presence of a musician in the production of music. With recordings now the dominant means through which the public would enjoy music, the industry was forced to respond to the fact that recordings were, historically speaking, drastically inadequate compared to live music performances. While recordings could not (and may never) equal musicians for on-the-spot flexibility, another aesthetic characteristic, the issue of the recording's sound quality, was viewed as an attribute of the sound recording that could and should be improved. It is this aesthetic lack that many postwar audio technologies aimed at fulfilling, and it is within this ambition that I would like to place stereophonic technologies. Out of this desire come two prongs of aesthetic legitimation. The first is best represented in discussions of stereo as it acted as a source of legitimation in the recording of canonical works, whether made in the studio or in the spaces where classical musicians traditionally perform, and their representation through recordings. It is this prong that I will explore in this chapter.

The other prong of my argument is mobilized in chapter 6 and positions stereo as something qualitatively different from an aesthetic form of representational realism. I argue that throughout its development, stereo was *also* part of an investment in an effort to assemble records and playback systems that produced musical and sonic possibilities that were distinct from live musical spaces and occasions. In this sense, with tools like stereo, the record producer could act as a "musical" functionary since the producer is the most responsible for creating a record's "sound." Unlike the discussion of realist representation in more canonical pieces, this aesthetic branch positions stereo as a productive musical element that is best represented in the creation of "popular" music, particularly when these pieces fall into genres as seemingly undistinguished as "light jazz," "novelty/comedy," or "pop and rock" records. Rather than define stereo's effects in each genre, chapter 6 concentrates on a small number of labels and artists who specialized in utilizing stereophonic sound technologies in a distinctly "musical" manner. Moreover, the chapter will illustrate that though the use of so-called effects may appear to be simply means for product differentiation (and to some extent they are), effects also signaled an interest in listening to musical reproductions that go beyond fulfilling "realistic" criteria.

It is important to recognize that these two threads are not so much contradictions as they are separate narratives in the fabrication of a larger high-fidelity narrative wherein the terms of audio realism and spectacle were constantly reconsidered and negotiated. In other words, unlike film studies that have traditionally offered analytical narratives posing binary distinctions between conflicting issues of realism and spectacle, this type of two-sided conflict is *not* the discursive basis through which high-fidelity technologies were initially established. Whereas the rock, rhythm and blues, post-bop, and free jazz movements of the 1950s and 1960s positioned their musicians and recordings as real, authentic alternatives to massified, synthetic, overly determined popular productions, high fidelity offered a version of "the real" as a realizable fantasy. In this sense, high fidelity was always already positioned as a celebrated form of artifice and spectacle that, through the union of science and the arts, would provide listeners with sensational renditions of the real. Thus high-fidelity recordings provided, in many cases, what could be termed a more "cinematic" form of music. Indeed, I am using the term "cinematic" as it relates to the French term *cinématique*. Referring to the geometry of motion, "cinematic"'s derivation from *cinématique* allows the issue of sonic motility, a vital one to understanding stereo even at its most basic terms, to become even more prominent. It also allows us to better visualize how the encounter of music with these technologies, much like visual culture's encounters with the earliest machines of cinema, opened the preexisting art form to a number of innovations, aesthetic possibilities, and social scenarios involving elements of musical exhibition and language. Just as Tom Gunning has argued that at its birth "cinema was often referred to as 'animated pictures'" because, " [it] seemed to add the surplus of life like movement to images previously experienced as static" (Gunning 1995, 468), the narrative behind high fidelity positioned the technology as bringing not only a real representation of musical performances but also a surplus of "the real." In this sense, as composers yielded new sounds, high fidelity brought forth a modern listening experience, seasoned by a newfound palette of frequencies with a sense of audible motility. As David Tardy writes in his 1959 guide to stereo, the high-fidelity movement did not just offer realistic music, but music that was *"REALER than real"* (Tardy 1959, 15).

Finally, as I have already hinted, throughout this chapter I want to underline the activities of the listener. To be sure, the main concerns of the high-fidelity movement were focused on providing better listening technologies. This is a meaningful distinction, for with this framework the demands of the listener remained paramount and, most significantly, productive. Whereas recordings are seen as musical productions created by musicians and engineers, it is important to remember that they are made to satisfy the demands of an audience. Unlike past audiences, the postwar, high-fidelity public was equipped with better playback equipment, a greater ability to participate in consumer culture, and an interest in the effects of scientific research at the popular level. In some ways the call for music and sounds that were "REALER than real" was a twofold negotiation between record producers and audiences. Out of this negotiation flowed a reconception and re-production of what the terms of audible realism, no matter how apparently contradictory, would be.[1]

One of the more interesting and, oddly enough, underresearched historical problems concerning the recording industry has been the continual need to convince the public that musical recordings are, at best, either accurate reproductions of sonic events or, at least, representations sufficient enough to stand as a satisfactory musical substitute for live performances. The most conspicuous expression of this creed is the Memorex blank tape slogan of the 1980s that asked, "Is it real, or is it Memorex?" The catchphrase's emphasis on the inaudible distinction between the performer and recording displays an interest in what Mary Ann Doane argues is the search for lifelike "presence," "a standard to measure quality in the sound industry as a whole" (Doane 1985, 163). Doane asserts that the music industry's overall emphasis on its products' ability to reproduce presence indicates a conscious strategy to perpetually assemble and maintain the connection between the mechanically reproduced product and the unique item it has recorded: "[Thus,] while the desire to bring things closer is certainly exploited in making sound marketable, the qualities of uniqueness and authenticity are not sacrificed—it is not any voice which the tape brings to the consumer but the voice of Ella Fitzgerald. The voice is not detachable from a body which is quite specific—that of the star" (164). Doane fashions her argument to underscore a particular element regarding Hollywood's use of postsynchronous sound techniques to match the proper voice to the "proper body," but her other suggestions concerning audible presence and the star should not be overlooked. As Doane points out, while "cult value and aura resurface in the star system," the strategies "of the sound recording industry offer evidence which supports Walter Benjamin's linking of mechanical reproduction as a phenomenon to contemporary society's destruction of 'aura' (which he defines as 'the unique phenomenon of distance, however close it may be')" (164).

Doane's invocation of Benjamin is astute, if only because she is able to find in issues of production a common connection between the mainstream film and music industries. According to Doane, each industry hopes to imbue each of its products, whose success is measured by their ubiquity, with an "aura" of unique distance. For Benjamin, the auratic nature of any work of art is contingent on its authenticity—its unique existence in time and space. Locating the origins of the arts and artistic objects in religious rituals, Benjamin views an artistic object as a unique, sacred item that is essentially nonreproducible. But as art has become more and more secularized and reproducible, the auratic element shrivels as a product becomes more and more pervasive. Benjamin argues that "film responds to [this deterioration in aura] with an artificial build-up of the 'personality' outside the studio," that is, the development of the star system (1968, 231). In some fashion, the reproducible object of the film or the recording exerts a similar dilemma for actors and musicians. In each case, the record and the film transport the players' essential abilities away from their bodies, reproduces their labors, and places them into a system of public exhibition far beyond their control. Indeed, one manner in which film dealt with this trauma, Benjamin argues, was through a form of denial particular to cinema's development in the West. Instead of being concerned with how to fulfill and satisfy modern man's claim in being to the power of reproduction, the West "[tried] hard to spur the interest of the masses through illusion-promoting spectacles and dubious speculations" (1968, 232).

Workers' traumatic loss of control over their actions in film or musical recordings is an important issue for both artists and audiences. As "liveness" is lost, both industries consistently smooth over and disavow this fact by celebrating the victories made through technological "advances," the organization of the product, or the magnificence of the star. Certainly the specific methods of disavowal and promotion utilized by American record and film industries are substantially different, and to compare a film studio to a recording label is simply inappropriate. And indeed there are similarities between each system of production. At one point in time, both record labels and film studios have relied on rosters of stars, producers, and engineers, and each has made major attempts to create a vertically integrated industry of production, distribution, and "presentation."[2] Yet the differences between the two systems are significant. Not only does the film studio require substantially more in available capital assets to produce the typical feature film than what it takes to produce even the most expensive pop CD; the record label and the film studio negotiate significantly different histories of production, development, success, and failure.

But perhaps most important is the fact that film scholars typically view the cinema as a "modern" technology while music scholars have made comparatively few attempts to address the aesthetic influence of recording on the production of music. In other words, modern film scholarship has tended to define the cinema as a modern art form whose conditions and aesthetic language are, despite noticeable similarities, significantly different from those of the theater, the novel, the camera obscura, or the photograph. With few exceptions, the majority of scholarship pertaining to music or the music industry has yet to wholeheartedly question how the recording process negotiates both the production and experience of music.

While I argue that the rise of postwar record industry practices involved a number of significant differences, I do not want to suggest that this involved a wholesale break with past musical practices. The modern American record industry has negotiated, and must continue to do so, the traditions cultivated throughout music history from both its prominent prerecorded and precapitalist pasts. This issue recurs throughout this book, but it can never be easily reduced to a set of axioms. The nature of each musical recording scenario cannot be accounted for through a uniform set of rules or practices. Each musical recording engages a variety of questions, each of which is posed to involve the peculiarities of each scenario. It is this fact that has led practitioners of musical genres to consider and prefer numerous sets of recording practices, producers, and spaces. To be sure, the issues surrounding the history of musical reproductions and high fidelity are no different, with a heterogeneous set of issues existing in the development and application of stereophonic sound.

One of the issues influencing the postwar development of stereophonic sound was that this audio technology held a significant prewar past, a past that accommodated a diversified set of aesthetic trajectories. According to Russell Sanjek, experiments with two-channel sound began as early as the 1930s by British EMI, who also secured a patent for a "practical two-channel disk, using both hill-and-dale and lateral recording [techniques]."[3] Sanjek also notes that, although the sound track for Walt Disney's 1940 release of *Fantasia* offered film audiences "what stereophonic music could sound like" (1988, 359), it was not until April 1940, at New York City's Carnegie Hall, that the public would hear a demonstration of "practical true stereophonic recording." Presented by laboratory technicians of Western Electric–Bell Laboratories,

Two hours of stereo music had come over three speakers, hidden as was all the equipment on stage, behind an immense screen. Music by Leoppold [sic] Stokowski and the Philadelphia Orchestra and the Mormon Tabernacle Choir, and the dramatic presentation of a scene from Eugene O'Neill's *Emperor Jones*, starring Paul Robeson, had been recorded on three different tracks on a single continuous reel of film tape, with a fourth track to regulate volume in order to avoid distortion. The three tracks were fed through separate amplifiers to the speakers, which were spread across the stage to provide width and depth to the music, lending the illusion that the sound actually traveled just as it did when performed by live musicians. (1988, 358–59)

As elaborate and spectacular as this event was, it is not clear whether it was the first demonstration of a working, true stereo recording. In his entry in *The Audio Dictionary*, Glenn White claims that a similar large-scale stereo test probably took place under the guidance of "Harvey Fletcher and his co-workers at the Bell Telephone Labs in 1933." Playing in Philadelphia, the Philadelphia Orchestra was picked up by three microphones placed in front of the proscenium. Amplified and transmitted over telephone lines, the signal was sent to Constitution Hall in Washington, D.C., "where [it was] further amplified and sent to three specially designed high-power loudspeaker systems on the stage." Stokowski's presence in Constitution Hall rather than Philadelphia was designed to proclaim his position as a conductor. But instead of directing his orchestra's performance, White notes, Stokowski's authority was visible only as he controlled the volume of the three channels from the Hall's stage. The obstacles involved in the demonstration were as immense as the amplifiers and loudspeakers, for the setup did not exist and needed to be designed and constructed specifically for the occasion. As an experiment, the event proved "that three independent microphones, amplifiers, and loudspeakers [were] sufficient to provide a convincing illusion of spatial perspective" (White 1987, 318–19).

These accounts may seem more or less obsessed with details, given that this chapter is not a chronological history of stereo recording but a historical-theoretical piece that hopes to make a point about how stereo was envisioned. Nevertheless, each of these demonstrations underscores two distinct technological ambitions of stereo. The first ambition addresses the issue of audio-spatial aesthetics. By conjoining theatrical spaces with electrical reproduction devices, these demonstrations under-lined a fascination not only with reproduced sound but also with a spe-cific sound definition. As events, their status as spectacular occasions was based not simply on producing a sense of "realism" but also on the distinctive sensation of a clear and adequate theatrical sound. While the combination of film soundtracks and musical recordings may involve an interdisciplinary set of desires, the fact remains that each engages the specific audio space of the theater. It is important that we understand that this identification and preoccupation is with a specific type of *audio space*. The consequence of this appreciation is that we can move our understanding of stereo beyond a realism that embraces the strict obses-sion with the perfect reproduction and representation of any particular audio event. It should be clear that I am not claiming that these events omitted an underlying promise of "fidelity," an "accurate" representa-tion of an event or performance. In fact, I assume the wish for a realistic, unblemished representation of audio events exists as a basic desire be-hind the production of almost all recordings. Rather, I want to underline that these demonstrations, perhaps more than anything else, aspire to electronically match the space. It is most likely that in these demonstra-tions listeners greatly anticipated the prospects of hearing Paul Robeson or the Philadelphia Orchestra (or even Deems Taylor), but they must have been equally impressed by the fact that an electronic system could pro-vide these extensive spaces a fulfilling, satisfactory sound.

Second, these events provide exceptional illustrations of a particular aesthetic desire for the seemingly "solid reproduction" of music. In an age when the word "stereo" has become synonymous for modern sound sys-tems or general dual-loudspeaker arrangements, it is helpful to remem-ber that, as a term, it comes from the ancient Greek word *stereós*, mean-ing "solid." These demonstrations manifested an anxiety, an uneasiness that every musical recording must confront at the act or reproduction: that the lack of a live performer would constitute a substantial aesthetic gap. While the Carnegie and Constitutional Hall demonstrations impli-cated the present-absence of a symphonic orchestra, the case of *Fantasia* (Sharpsteen et al. 1940) submitted a different scenario. If each hall pre-sentation was marked through its reference to the concert hall tradition of orchestral performance, then what are we to make of an animated film whose title is taken from the spectacular sound system it employed?

True, the "fantasound" sound system must have wrested forth a sub-stantial sound improvement, but its very name has a dubious ring if only because it alludes to a fictional domain of sound. Fantasound suggests a particular sphere of sonic imagination adept at displaying desire-laden fabrications that are all too often excluded in day-to-day discussions of electronic sound reproduction. For example, Deems Taylor, the revered musicologist and popular critic, opens the film with "an explanation that [Fantasia] will visually interpret music that tells a story, music that paints a picture, an *absolute music,* music for music's sake" (Peary 1981, 90; emphasis added). This promise of an absolute music is somewhat confusing given that it exists as a distinct counterdefinition to program music, music that is deliberately composed with an illustrative or nar-rative purpose (Kennedy 1980, 506). On the other hand, absolute music is composed to provide purely "musical," nonmimetic experiences that neither support nor rely on narrative foundations. It is not clear what exactly one can make of Taylor's proclamation when one considers that the film consists of a number of fifteen-to-twenty-minute animated vi-gnettes accompanied by passages from famous compositions. Yet one might infer that part of *Fantasia*'s project was to present a stridently non-subordinate music that elevated selections from *The Nutcracker Suite,* Beethoven's *Pastoral Symphony,* and Stravinsky's *The Rite of Spring* to a clear prominence above the images of dancing mushrooms, a "jolly" Bacchus and his mule, and the extinction of the dinosaurs. In this con-text it becomes apparent that these animations are little more than ec-centric escorts for these spectacularly sounding musical performances. As an example of this intentional spectacle, out of practicality Disney initially showed the version of *Fantasia* with the fantasound system in only six cities. The reason for this was clear: the installation of fanta-sound systems was, in itself, quite remarkable. According to Stephen Handzo, "For the Los Angeles premiere [of *Fantasia*], Disney added a primitive 'surround' channel of 96 small speakers to pick up sound from one or more of the main channels, e.g., the choir singing 'Ave Maria' was heard throughout the theater" (Handzo 1985, 418–19). It was not until the film was rereleased in 1956 with magnetic sound that a substantially larger number of theaters throughout the United Stated would hear an electronic surround sound effect, an effect that could never be approxi-mated by a live orchestra In fact, one manner of understanding *Fantasia* is as something of a fantastic wish: a dream that for one evening the onscreen text will become subordinate and act as an aesthetic support for sonically extraordinary musical passages.[4] No doubt this possibility warrants rigorous historical investigation into *Fantasia*'s production and reception.

Yet if box office is any measure of aesthetic success, then one might gather that Disney's goal of musical "absoluteness" was either not achieved or well received or both. Danny Peary speculates that *Fantasia*'s initial failure owed to the fact that Disney lost out on substantial foreign markets during the tumultuous events of World War II, as well as poor distribution by RKO. Peary also claims that the film's profitable rerelease was the result of audiences hip enough not to be overly inflamed by the popularization of classics, something that antagonized many critics and reviewers during its initial release (Peary 1981, 93). These assertions may be true, but each of *Fantasia*'s subsequent rereleases, beginning in the late 1950s, has taken advantage of the significant improvements in theatrical sound systems. These technical refinements range from improved amplification and loudspeaker arrangements to projection booths equipped with THX digital processes. Because of these improvements, the musical fictions and sonic fantasies could finally be presented in such a fashion that they could aesthetically eclipse Disney's onscreen animations. Through these systems, audiences across the nation can enjoy modern cinema's extravagant audio perspectives. In the case of *Fantasia*, this included a positively lush and full musical fabrication, a wonderful vision of how modern technologies could render the classics.

By comparing the concert hall and the cinematic visions of stereo we begin to glean how each conception of stereo draws on two specific convictions behind the production of sound reproductions: the realistic and the melocentric. The realistic is conservative and proposes an audio perspective based on replicating the perspective that an ideal, stable auditor (and mode of audition) would maintain throughout the ideal live performance. *Fantasia*'s more cinematic line proposes a competing vision. Through its exhibition and text, the film puts forth a melocentric conception of musical sound. In this sense, fantasound, with its early form of surround sound, released an ultra-solid reproduction of these fragmented classics into the filmhouse in such a substantial fashion that sound could be intentionally molded, shifted, and moved through the reproduction process. The result was that *Fantasia* could avoid the rigidity of the concert hall and its accompanying aesthetics and could explore the music's meanings through a dialogical relationship with onscreen images that have little to do with the intents of each piece's original composer. Unlike the concert hall aesthetic, *Fantasia*'s primitive surround sound effects illustrated that traditional sonic perspectives could never provide the revolutionary possibilities that even the most rudimentary forms of high fidelity and stereo renditions could deliver.

Again, it is important to recognize that within these early attempts at stereo reproduction a heterogeneous set of demands make themselves felt. To be sure, this heterogeneity of desires was sustained from stereo's prewar roots and developed along with high fidelity's postwar curiosities. A portion of North America's curiosity and interest in the postwar high-fidelity industry is deeply embedded in stereo's technological history. This historical interest included not only *Fantasia* and the above demonstrations but also an invocation of Thomas Edison. Mentioning Edison's patent for the "multiplex graphaphone grand" in an article for *High Fidelity*, Herbert Reid argued that the machine suggested yet another idea of what this early recording technology foresaw. According to Reid, the case of the multiplex graphaphone grand heralded "some surprisingly modern studio techniques" such as the use of separate channels for separate musical voices and, most interestingly, stereo (Reid 1959).[5] Reid's supposition is interesting not so much because he details yet another past for stereo but because his speculation involves the nature of Edison's intents and genius.

The association with Edison entails a specifically willful interpretation of the intentions of America's most heralded inventor. More importantly, the nature of the speculation advances one specific narrative regarding the motives behind sound-reproduction technologies. As equipment in the ever-ongoing search for the undiminished and uncompromised representation of presence, high-fidelity technologies are often portrayed as aesthetic armament in the fight to establish greater and greater degrees of realism. The most apparent problem with this commonsensical notion of how realistic sound can be achieved exists in the fact that at any moment there are a variety of competing "realisms." That is, by simply discussing a desire for a "realistic" style, one does not point to a singular, definitive form or method of artistic production. Without entering into a comparative discussion concerning the numerous methodological and metaphysical bases for every form of realism, I believe we can assume that every form of realism proposes a set of tenets that demand a reference to *the* real as it is constituted through a specific set of concrete details.[6] Certainly, what is at stake behind competing realisms are competing methodologies of access to the plane of pure representation. It is the manner in which this plane is uncovered that is at the base of many elaborate theoretical debates.[7]

To quote Barthes, "The 'real' is supposed to be self-sufficient, that is strong enough to belie any notion of 'function,' that its 'speech-act' has no need to be integrated into a structure and that the *having-been-there* of things is a sufficient principle of speech" (1989, 147). The real is the captured not "narrated" event. For film enthusiasts and cinema scholars the paradigmatic example of realist discussion is Jacques Bazin's *What Is Cinema?* (1967), regarding the ontological nature of the photographic image. For Bazin,

> Originality in photography as distinct from originality in painting lies in the essentially objective character of photography. For the first time, between the originating object and its reproduction there intervenes only the instrumentality of a nonliving agent. For the first time an image of the world is formed automatically, without the creative intervention of man. The personality of the photographer enters into the proceedings only in his selection of the object to be photographed and by way of the purpose he has in mind. (13)

The fascinating advantage of the photographic image for Bazin lies not in the expression of the artist's presence but "from his absence" (13). No matter how stylized a set, how intricate a director's use of mise-en-scène, or how subtle an actor's gestures, the photographic basis of the classical cinema encounters a pure event, a happening that may be edited to convey a unity of time that is not real but whose basis exists through a combination of "real" events.

The concept of the "captured event" is crucial to understanding a number of issues surrounding both the reception and production of recorded music.[8] In his discussion of rock aesthetics, Theodore Gracyk asserts, "One complication [in thinking about recording technologies aesthetic and economic effects] is that in musical traditions predating rock, recordings are basically byproducts of singular live performances. To be sure, for many musics performance remains the basic medium" (Gracyk 1996, 38). One can assume that Gracyk is invoking a general understanding of pre-rock musics by drawing on evidence such as Simon Frith's declaration that "recording was, in its early days, simply that: the direct recording onto a cylinder or disc. What record buyers heard was the sound of the *original performance*" (quoted in Gracyk 1996, 38; emphasis added). Thus, Gracyk argues, the limitations of early recording technologies involved a specific ontological principle whereby these productions could act only as depictions of live events.

To some extent this is true. Before the use of magnetic tape in American recording studios became widespread throughout the late 1940s and 1950s, records were the result of live-to-disc performances. In essence, these records *were* representations of real-time events, without the support of overdubs, complete with the performer's mistakes and/or spot-on improvisations. Yet Gracyk's thesis that rock music somehow entails a more complicated relationship to the recorded medium than previous popular musics is certainly debatable. For Gracyk, rock is unlike previous popular musics because it is involved in "a tradition of popular music whose creation and dissemination centers on recording technology," whereas previous popular and serious musics' encounters were organized around other technologies such as publishing and the complicated social traditions involved in theatrical and music hall presentations. I am tempted to agree with Gracyk's proposition,[9] but I also believe that his thesis exerts several historical distortions vis-à-vis early rock music and postwar popular music in general. For example, the rise of American rock and roll music is typically portrayed as a mid-1950s phenomenon beginning with the emergence of Elvis Presley out of Sam Phillips's Sun Studios in Memphis, Tennessee. Yet even after the genre's initial commercial successes and major-label acceptance of Presley, many considered rock and roll music a sonic fad, a stylish sound among a panapoly of other sounds that waxed and waned over time (for example, the bossa nova, the "twist," rhythm blues, doo-wop, bebop, post-bop jazz, Owen Bradley's "Nashville" sound, etc.). When framing this period of popular music history it is important to continually remind ourselves that between 1955 and 1964 rock music shared, rather than dominated, the popular musical landscape. This is not only true of live performance circuits; it is particularly true when one considers that rock recordings were often mixed in record bins and radio charts with other popular genres such as rhythm and blues, country and western, comedic performances, jazz, and showtunes (particularly original Broadway recordings). In fact, I would argue that it is only with the Beatles-led "British Invasion" of pop and rock acts in the early and mid-1960s that rock music becomes a truly dominant genre, and even this is questionable.[10]

Given the variety of popular music genres, it is an unlikely suggestion that none of these genres (or the industry as a whole) would have developed an extensive recording vocabulary. Indeed, the assertion that pre-rock musical forms have failed to generate a complicated posture in relation to recording processes begs for detailed historical investigation. In many ways this investigation is already underway. Beginning in the late 1980s and peaking at the end of the 1990s, record enthusiasts throughout North America began to work their ways through the record collections of generations before them, with a particular attention paid to the pre-rock tastes of their grandparents' generation. In avoiding the more well-known and classic items such as the LPs of The Beatles, The Rolling Stones, and others, many pop music fans found a set of unexpected surprises in the more excessive terrain of so-called easy listening. To many readers this generic designation is perhaps best remembered and parodied because of its fantastic embrace of the "swinging bachelor" and his urban and ultramodern "pad." Designed to avoid conjugal commitments, the space sheltered the hedonistic conveniences of mood lighting, the wet bar, and, of course, a hi-fi accompanied by an astute record collection.

But as memorable as this scene is, it is also a set of blinders obscuring an important portion of high-fidelity culture that should not be forgotten. To be sure, in one sense there exists a resolutely strong sense of musical fun bordering on hi-fi "camp" in popular artists such as Esquivel, Martin Denny, Jackie Gleason's orchestra, and the entirety of Enoch Light's Command label, which included the likes of Tony Mottola and Doc Severinsen. All these artists resided within a resolutely masculine segment of culture, thereby providing an amusing stereotype that can be easily dismissed and/or parodied.[11] Unfortunately, the use of this stereotype has tended to conceal those elements of the high-fidelity movement that included earnest middlebrow (as well as highbrow) interests in raising the cultural aspects of the nation.[12]

Despite this fact, it is the campy, excessive aspects of the hi-fi movement that have received the attention of record companies that have responded to demand for reissuing those titles most embraced by a somewhat-underground "lounge" movement. I pay far more attention to the issue of excess in chapter 6. Yet I should note here that one of the results of the lounge movement is that it has conveniently obscured high fidelity's more serious and critical aspirations for its own purpose of "ironic" commentary and nostalgia.[13] While this is in no way an attempt to censure this movement (indeed, in some ways my affection for these records and elements of style makes me something of a member), I would like to rescue from the demands of the nostalgic a memory of some of high fidelity's more interesting ambitions. I would like to consider stereo and high fidelity's mutual relationship with what is generally deemed the most conservative of all musical genres: Western classical music.

As mentioned earlier, throughout the postwar period a number of technologies were devoted to the aesthetic improvement of recordings. Most of these improvements in frequency range and dynamic response records and playback devices were ostensibly devoted to expanded opportunities to access music. But it is also clear that what drove high fidelity was not simply a devotion to musical realism but a drive to better "democratize" the basic Western repertoire of "good music." This desire to receive a "clearer music" may seem nothing more than a common-sense desire, but we should not ignore the fact that much of the initiative pushing this goal was a desire to bring Beethoven, Bach, and Brahms to the listening masses. In many ways this desire is best exemplified by the postwar rise of a specific high-fidelity technology throughout the United States: FM radio as a "good music" medium. Unlike postwar television, which used the concept of "liveness" to promote its medium, and AM radio, a medium that stepped away from live performers to use recordings for a new order of economic efficiency, FM found another, less financially lucrative pathway to success. Instead of embracing more conventional, commercially proven methods, on-network, independent FMers emphasized the medium's tonal "clarity" in a manner that tended to supersede the musical content of both its live performances and recordings. It is true that both AM and FM broadcasters utilized recordings as a dominant means of programming throughout this period. But while independent AMers wrought forth the rise of the disc jockey and on-air personalities to the accompaniment of recorded music, independent FMers began to promote themselves as "concert stations" with facilities and programming particularly tuned and prepared for the refined and sensitive transmission of high fidelity and, in some cases, stereo recordings.

The "feel" of FM's progress cannot be underestimated. The sound of FM was dramatic if for no other reason than that most Americans throughout the 1920s or early 1930s could not have envisioned this level of electromagnetic improvement. According to Christopher Sterling, "prior to the early 1930s, there seemed to be no method of eliminating static in AM radio telephony reception." But Edwin Armstrong's research resulted in a new method that reportedly utilized "frequency modulated radio waves to which static did not adhere" (Sterling 1975, 132). Even if we were to assume early radio audiences forged such a fantasy of a static-free medium, it is unlikely that such a vision could imagine that radio would fabricate such a close association with recordings. Given the prewar limitations of shellac (its brittle nature, density, limited playing time, narrow frequency range, and inability to remain scratch free), wire, and the lack of anything closely resembling a modern "tape" medium, broadcasters "looked down upon [recordings] as inherently weak pro-gramming" (Ganzert 1992, 203). But with the postwar arrival of new, full frequency and audio technologies such as the long-play microgroove re-cord and magnetic tape, many of these restrictions and concerns were rendered moot. Thus, while the "concert station" designation may elicit connotations of live performance, many of these FM stations aimed to present an "ideal" musical rather than a theatrical experience. This ideal experience would intend to eliminate the unwanted aspects of concert while emphasizing its more democratic aspects. Accordingly, these sta-tions eliminated "the theatre-like auditorium, designed to accommodate an immense and hilarious audience, in favor of a small, acoustically correct studio for live programs such as chamber music and soloists" ("Music on the Air" 1951). While an auditorium's architecture valued acoustic clarity, the concert station that emphasized recordings had to ensure similarly top-notch standards involving its equipment:

> Great attention is given to [the concert station's] equipment. (Sometimes too much attention! Engineers occasionally get out of hand and add so much noise suppressing, equalizing, and range-expanding equipment that the same record sounds better played over home equipment!). Generally speaking, station managers are audio-philes and are as interested in providing you with maximum realism as you are in receiving it. ("Music on the Air" 1951, 16).

Issues of acoustic realism and fantasy aside, I want to focus for a moment on the enthusiastic attention given to suppressing noise and "unmediation."[14] Not simply a technical preference, this is part of a never-ending pursuit to eliminate noise and thereby thoroughly reproduce signal. But it is also a quest for "presence." In the ideal scenario of pure reproduction, the reproduced object would be rendered complete, without any loss of detail. Yet as Walter Benjamin argues, "even the most perfect reproduction of a work of art is lacking in one element: its presence in time and space, its unique existence at the place where it happens to be" (1968, 220). While the mechanical reproduction of a sculpture or a painting may always lack the authenticity of the original (that is, the original's position in time and space), we need to heed Benjamin's observations with regard to what he calls "process reproduction" and how this better serves our understanding of musical recordings and some of the general desires involving Western music.

Benjamin's observations specifically concentrate on how the mode of production is differentiated from manual reproduction. Whereas manual reproductions of artworks fall into the rubric of forgeries, process reproductions utilize mechanical methods that provide a heretofore impossible independence for the artwork that allows copies to enter "into situations which would be out of reach for the original itself" (220). Benjamin continues, "Above all, it enables the original to meet the beholder halfway, be it in the form of a photograph or a phonograph record. The cathedral leaves its locale to be received in the studio of a lover of art; the choral production, performed in an auditorium or in the open air, resounds in the drawing room" (220–21). The conditions of a mechanically reproduced artwork deliver a number of advantages, including convenience and accessibility. Yet, for Benjamin, the "quality of [the reproduced object's] presence is always depreciated" given the object's lack of authenticity—its lack of a substance that speaks to the terms of its production (221). Given music's essential reliance on temporality, the ephemeral moment of the live musical event, no matter the context, is viewed as the most elevated manner in which to enjoy a composition.

But as already indicated, one of the aesthetic hopes for the concert station was a purer, more ideal musical experience that strained undesirable elements out of the concert-going experience. Specifically these elements included noisy audience members and inconsistent acoustic spaces. These sentiments are best expressed in Glenn Gould's controversial publication of "On the Prospects of Recording" in an April 1966 edition of *High Fidelity*. Gould's essay is organized around numerous quotes from prominent composers, producers, and record executives including Milton Babbitt, Aaron Copland, Goddard Lieberson, and Enoch Light that are aimed to echo (or confront) his own opinions and arguments regarding recordings. As interesting as these topics are, none is more important than the status of the musical concert in the face of advancing technologies. "In an unguarded moment some months ago," Gould begins, "I predicted that the public concert as we know it today would no longer exist a century hence, that its functions would have been entirely taken over by electronic media" (47). Gould continues: "It had not occurred to me that this statement represented a particularly radical pronouncement. Indeed, I regarded it almost as self-evident truth and, in any case, as defining only one of the peripheral effects occasioned by developments in the electronic age. But never has a statement of mine been so widely quoted—or so hotly disputed" (47). While a number of voices disagreed with Gould's sentiments (typically citing the loss of each performance's unique and unpredictable nature), other notable figures concurred. Resonating with Gould's opinion, Goddard Lieberson claimed that the concert was "an antique form" and he implied that recordings and radio offered a democratic option for communities, many of which could never "afford the best concert artists" and would be forced to accept second-rate performers, an option Lieberson found completely unacceptable. Milton Babbitt proclaimed, "I can't believe that people really prefer to go to the concert hall under intellectually trying conditions, unable to repeat something they have missed, when they can sit home under the most comfortable circumstances and hear it as they want to hear it. I can't believe what would happen to literature today if one was forced to congregate in an unpleasant hall and read novels projected on a screen" (1966, 47). It is interesting that such esteemed dignitaries of the music world would feel free to voice these opinions. Yet any sense of peculiarity that these statements might hold for the reader must be countered with a reminder that they were in concert with the goal of the high-fidelity movement. As a 1953 *Life* article contended, high fidelity and its enthusiasts hoped to "transport the listener to the concert hall." Indeed, other magazines and journals, such as *Fortune* and *High Fidelity,* acknowledged that quality hi-fi equipment—from turntable to transistor amplifier—should provide the perspective that one may have in an ideal concert hall seat (Keightley 1996, 153). For the most part, rather than bemoaning the loss of aura, each proponent of electronic media recognized that better technology could produce an ideal auditor who would not suffer through the many blemishes of live performances.

Although concert spaces remain an important portion of contemporary musical experience, FM's ability to accurately reproduce and transmit the live and recorded performances from these spaces was seen as a detriment as well as a benefit: a benefit if one heard the music, a detriment if one heard the hall. In short, the ideal concert hall experience was one that would render the materiality of that hall inaudible. In a letter to the editors of *High Fidelity*, Otto R. Wormer, a listener from Oak Park, Illinois, expressed this concern and hope to surpass the concert hall: "The ultimate goal of music reproduction is no longer 'to approach the values of the concert hall' but to render to the truest and fullest the production of the performers, so as to bring out the best of the music." And though there was "no absolute standard for what [was considered to be] best," Mr. Wormer confessed to more than once preferring an FM broadcast over "the real thing" of hearing a concert in a live setting (Wormer 1962). Mr. Wormer most likely listened to a number of these radio concerts on WFMT, Chicago's most heralded FM outlet and a station that took great pride in its ability to deliver broadcasts with "concert hall realism." In a statement published in a 1957 edition of WFMT's fine arts guide, a guide subscribed to by many of the station's listeners, the editor declared, "WFMT adheres to the highest possible standards of broadcast fidelity and has, ever since its inception, pioneered the art of high fidelity broadcasting. The music lover with high fidelity equipment receives this transmission with reproduction that is as close to concert hall realism as present broadcast development permits" ("WFMT Broadcasted from the Show" 1957).

Although many believed FM could bring radio into the realm of "concert hall realism," and music beyond bad acoustics and unappreciative audiences, others fancied the medium for less theoretical reasons. One pragmatic motivation rested in the desire to record live concert performances broadcast over FM, a practice praised for preserving great performers and performances. With the introduction of relatively low-cost high-fidelity tape recorders in the 1950s, a good FM receiver could provide the serious collector with opportunities to make recordings of performances either not printed on or deleted from disc formats. Although most of these recordings were illegal, that certainly did not hinder a collector from taping an FM broadcast if it offered the occasional musical treasure that had been buried or would never be released by the recording industry (Canby 1963; M**r 1963). With praiseworthy facilities, a quality FM station could wrest music from collections and the problems of interference, and freely transmit works from Bach to Berg, Paganini to Palestrina, or even Armstrong to Brubeck, into households in a fashion that could never have been imagined through AM.

Despite the protestations about the seemingly outdated concert hall, the wish of independent FM broadcasters to eliminate aural "impurities" through technological advances, whether ruggedly pragmatic or obliquely abstract, is part of a long-standing effort to approach an ideal "concert hall" aesthetic. As an architectural form, the Western concert hall space encloses a public sphere of aural pleasures somewhat akin to the opera house but distinct from the music hall, a working-class space where the presence of a collective enjoying itself *as a collective* is essential to the musical event. But, as noted earlier, the presence of a mass consciousness is continually denigrated in Western thought for deterring the individuated appreciation that the concert hall engenders. Michael Chanan (1994) points out that the Western concert hall is part of a larger historical undertaking in the development of bourgeois aesthetic spaces that, much like the refined theater or the art museum, endorse and sanction individuated, reflective contemplation rather than the mass appreciation of its preferred aesthetic object, the music.[15]

Throughout, the general ambition of the ideal concert hall is to engineer a spatial process that acoustically balances and separates "music" from any imperfections resulting from an inadequate room, and to present works to a well-behaved audience distinct from the players. As part of a nineteenth-century project, the processes of the concert hall emerged from a desire to establish a site where, unlike the variety of sites where music was located before, the focus was on the audience's behaviors and the presentation of music:

> In the days when concerts were held in assorted venues—taverns, theatres, entertainment gardens and homes—they did not differ greatly in their social manners from other kinds of socializing and entertainment which took place in those locales. As the superior heroine of Fanny Burney's late-eighteenth-century novel *Evelina* remarked, "indeed I am quite astonished to find how little music is attended to in silence; for though everybody seems to admire, hardly anybody listens." (Chanan 1994, 156–57)

To be sure, in response to the history of negative sentiments long associated with live musical performances, the bourgeois concert hall submitted an idealized venue for uniform acoustics, serious renditions, and sober audiences. To achieve these goals, seating arrangements began to be organized with the audience now directly facing the orchestra to suppress unruly behaviors "in the auditorium, and [thereby displacing them] to corridors, bars and salons" (Chanan 1994, 157). In the concert hall, audiences are separated and distinguished from the music and its interpretation. Following the aesthetic aims of the romantic-era symphony, Chanan argues that while the symphony orchestra hoped to cultivate "a more attentive relationship with the *music*," many of the great European concert halls of the nineteenth century strove to proliferate and enable reflective attentiveness in a much more democratic fashion. Whereas these compositions previously existed in the chambers of the aristocracy, the great size of the concert hall embodied "the ideals of bourgeois democracy" that promised greater access to culture in general. According to Chanan, the size of the concert hall housed a wide variety of patrons, "[who] inside . . . share a uniformly warm and responsive acoustical state of being" (157–58). One should not gloss over Chanan's emphasis on aesthetic issues. The acoustic uniformity of the ideal concert hall allows every member of the audience, whether sitting in the priciest seats or forced to use a pair of opera glasses to see the conductor, to access a consistent sound perspective.

These two objectives remain ideal goals for music presentation in a number of genres whereby the audience establishes a demand for "serious" listening. And like all ideals, aesthetic or otherwise, they are very rarely met but oft invoked for a number of objectives and purposes. In the case of FM radio, its technical advantages conveniently dovetailed with a number of historical demands to promise an uplifting tone for American mass media in general. Indeed, both FM's graphic improvements in audio and the aims of the concert hall aesthetic fit within the bourgeois desire to wrest forth music for clear contemplation. This particular desire to eliminate noise and interference is a wish to escape what Kristin Ross argues is the "nightmare" of production. While Ross offers Barthes's critique of the new Citroen as a specifically French example of a popular postwar, bourgeois phenomenon that celebrated seamless continuity (Ross 1995, 147),[16] the hi-fi movement, as noted above, participated in an atmosphere of American popularity brought on primarily by upper-middle-class men who hoped for perfect audio reproduction. This "hi-fi" quest continues today with the fevered intensities and blessings of hobbyists and the electronics industry alike. While audio technologies frame each new discovery as an improvement in the modern and perpetual move toward better and clearer "music" and "sound," the drive belongs to a long-standing ambition of Western musicology to realize musical devices that force music above and beyond the influence of its context, out of which the concert hall, FM concert stations, and hi-fi machinery were designed and participate. John Corbett asserts that the long line of audiophilic devices and technologies created by the music industry participates in this continual attack on the "enemies of 'fidelity'" (surface noise, scratch, hum, and hiss) that impede the production of an "autonomous music" (Corbett 1994, 41).[17] This aim for an unmediated and transparent art whose truth and beauty are clearly sensible, according to Leonard Meyer, is a desire firmly ensconced in a romantic ideology that demands "natural" forms of expression, "free from calculation and contrivance" (Meyer 1996, 175).

The desire for an unmediated, autonomous music has become a basic driving element of the transnational music industry. Therefore, it should come as no surprise that the music industry has combined an interest in "serious" music and listening with a scientific fervor for research and progress. When we look at the last ten years of digital dominance within the music industry we see an interesting union between a scientific rhetoric of improved sound reproduction and "serious" (read "classic" or "canonical") musical works. According to John Corbett "it is no mere coincidence, then, that compact discs [the latest in audiophilic technologies] experienced their first wholesale takeover in classical music" (41). As Simon Frith notes, the compact disc's embrace of classic catalogues is simply a continuation of the fact that, "all hi-fi inventions have been marketed, at first, on the assumption that the consumers most concerned about sound quality and a permanent record library are 'serious' consumers, consuming 'serious' music" (1988, 21), hence the tendency to emphasize "classic" music.[18]

Indeed, there is a continuum onto which the aesthetic advantages of postwar high-fidelity technology can be positioned. These feats of acoustic engineering were as greatly sought after as the bourgeois concert hall was in its day. And it should be clear that the generally improved audio systems were viewed as designs with a particular set of aesthetic prospects. These "prospects of recording," as Gould notes, existed as achievements through which musicians and audiences could encounter once unimaginable musical and sonic opportunities. Even the culture industries' most heralded critic, Theodor Adorno, viewed the high-fidelity development of the long-play record as truly remarkable progress and a much anticipated advance. In his 1994 essay "The Curves of the Needle," Adorno argued that among many of the gramophone's more glaring problems were the constrictions it engendered in the reproduction process. Most wearisome for Adorno were the limits it placed on accurately reproducing female voices and, consequently, forcing some musical genres to make significant aesthetic compromises to accommodate the recording process. With the high-fidelity LP record, many of these problems were eliminated, a fact that Adorno believed was potentially transformative: "the term 'revolution' is hardly an exaggeration with regard to the long-playing record. The entire musical literature could now become available in quite-authentic form to listeners desirous of auditioning and studying such works at a time convenient to them" (1990, 63).

A greater adaptability of recorded music production and the improved representation of musical performance accompanied this newfound flexibility of audition. Much of this was brought about by new materials yielded during wartime. Replacing the natural resin essential to the production of shellac, new artificial polymers became the dominant means of producing records in the postwar period, thereby assigning another order of predictability to the manufacturing process.[19] On the other hand, the evolving in-studio use of another technological prize obtained from wartime, magnetic tape, throughout the late 1940s and 1950s permitted recordings to be made that were substantially longer, and of greater fidelity, than ever before.[20] With these technologies American record companies quickly began to reap the rewards that tape recording's relatively lightweight systems could afford them. For a few thousand dollars record companies could purchase a quality tape recorder, go out into the field, and build seemingly ad hoc recording spaces. As a result, with magnetic tape these entrepreneurs could exert novel technical abilities by creating high-quality recordings of music and performers in a variety of places. As a material for field recordings, tape not only stood in marked contrast to magnetic wire, acetates, and shellac, each of which could be easily marred or destroyed, but also offered an economic alternative to transporting artists to expensive soundstages or assembling difficult and inconvenient machinery for on-site transcription (Chanan 1995, 96–98). The implications of this new production scenario were profound. This flexibility effectively decentered a portion of the production process and allowed independent labels specializing in underserviced audio and musical genres typically ignored by major labels that specialized in established stars, proven scores, and prudent methods of song production to find greater foothold in the marketplace. In other words, the altered mode of production not only made the recording process more efficient in terms of profits and losses; decentralization likewise affected the received wisdom about what could be recorded, where the recording could be made, and how the recording could be received.

This flexibility allowed recording companies to stake out additional claims on authenticity as musicians and musical genres could now be recorded in the local communities that fostered them. Conversely, such flexibility brought a newfound malleability to recordings that also threatened the object's claim on authenticity.[21] For example, magnetic tape provided musicians and engineers the first recording medium that could be easily edited in a nonlinear fashion. Multiple performances could be spliced together to create an ideal rendition from many recordings, a fact that, as I discussed in chapters 3 and 4 with regard to the film version of *My Fair Lady*, a large portion of the listening audience understood. Further, magnetic tape technologies eventually developed to the point that the typical musical recording began to incorporate distinct yet multiple channels of sound, whose aesthetic techniques were to become well developed and commonplace throughout the 1960s and 1970s. As the popular consciousness of these studio arrangements grew, by 1965 *Time* could claim that the architect of many recordings was "no longer the conductor but the producer [in his studio]" (quoted in Chanan 1995, 131). Indeed, it must have been difficult for many listeners to accept that the authority of any particular performance was commonly usurped in the search for the ideal recording. But to suggest that a "gadgeteer," a fellow trained in knobs and wires, could surpass the most symbolic icon of performative authority in the Western musical tradition, the conductor, must have been even more disturbing. To paraphrase Theodore Gracyk, to the stubborn realist, all the in-studio production techniques, effects, edits, and remixing capabilities in the world are nothing more than gimmicks, contrivances that, like a cheap sauce that is used to conceal the true character of a lesser cut of meat, often obscure rather than enhance musical performances (1996, 40). Although many in-studio techniques were viewed, as noted above with reference to Glenn Gould, as modern tools that could deliver musical productions into a variety of virtual and ideal scenarios, we need to remember that many of these scenarios included "realist" promises.

By the early fifties it was evident that magnetic tape could support at least two distinct audio tracks, a fact that would serve as the basis for many stereo recording and reproducing techniques. Although the term "stereo" denotes solidity, the word's association continues to be anchored to "duality" in day-to-day, commonsense language. Used by many North Americans, the phrase "in stereo" almost always connotes audio separated by and interacting through two channels. Still, despite stereo's conspicuous artifice, its relationship with standards of audio realism remains its most overdetermined affiliation. But stereo simultaneously connotes a search for the real in the opulent vibrancy of the entire sonic spectrum. High fidelity's cultivation of simulations was embedded in the studied, detailed re-creation of dynamic, colorful experiences that accompany live performance. In essence, through the physical sciences one could grasp the material contingencies of particular sonic events in order to reproduce them in detail. The goal of the high-fidelity crusade was to define aesthetic issues as sonic details that could be resolved through mathematics and engineering. Writing in one of the earliest editions of *High Fidelity*, John W. Campbell argues that the movement has more in common with the player piano and player violin than with the excessive electronic gimmicks that seemingly dominated the field. Campbell suggests, "The thing we're seeking is a method of packaging human experience in such a fashion that we can unpackage it anywhere, anytime, and enjoy it." Admitting that "canned peas are not as good as fresh spring peas," Campbell asserts that as "modern frozen peas are getting hard to distinguish" from the fresh variety, so too are high-fidelity systems when compared to live performances (Campbell 1953, 27). The proof came from various sources, some of them scientific, others anecdotal. One of these anecdotes appeared in a 1957 *Time* article, in which it was noted that a stereo tape system had recently been used to dub over stage actors who walked through the staging of Mozart's *Marriage of Figaro* at the San Francisco Opera House. According to the article, the achievement was so grand that "few in the audience guessed that they were listening to canned music" ("And Now, Stereo" 1957).

Yet Campbell's article goes on to make an important distinction between high-fidelity systems and player instruments. According to Campbell, the player instrument tried to simulate a performance. On the other hand, instruments of high fidelity, beginning with Edison's first phonograph, "attempted to duplicate the sensation-of-hearing." Comprehending where this logic would eventually lead his argument, Campbell noted,

> Man himself is the ultimate high fidelity instrument; it took billions of years of engineering field-trials to develop the magnificent sensory and correlative system we have—and we can stop trying to fool that system right now and save a lot of effort. Instead, let's work with it. The modern recorded music approach works with it, instead of trying to fool it. (1953, 28).

Campbell's interest in relocating music's artistic emphases is not simply a political maneuver wherein the listener usurps the position of the musician as the determinant aesthetic force. Campbell is also interested and involved with the physiological domain. While "player" instrumentation simulated the administration of aesthetic commands, high fidelity was, from its inception, a techno-aesthetic architecture focused on reception. Many readers, particularly musicians and composers, may argue that this is nothing more than a false distinction since reception is *always* envisioned in the production and exhibition of musical pieces. No doubt this is the case. But there also exists a more profound difference between the two systems. Whereas the musician and composer work through a tradition of musical tropes and principles that they assume their audience will recognize, understand, and/or be affected by, the high-fidelity system is explicitly devoted to the physical sciences as a basis through which it conceives aesthetic reception. Thus Campbell's article has a pronounced physiological component. Titled "Hearing Is Believing?," it locates the musical experience within the organs involved in the listening process, including both eyes and skin. Campbell maintains that we should remember that the listener does not perceive simply music but a "precise point in space and time, the sense of orientation with respect to the whole system of the world and life" (1953, 28).

Interestingly, the dominance of the science of acoustics in many popular hi-fi discussions was bound up with specific lack of technical authority. Although not every critic portrayed the high-fidelity movement as a scientific endeavor, as a whole the prominent search for technical standards was also a search for each system's legitimacy. In many ways the movement was decidedly unorganized, with some of this disorder resulting from a lack of any agreed-on standards regarding which systems did and did not produce high-fidelity sound. As Campbell's comments indicate, many hi-fi enthusiasts spent the better portion of their efforts on capturing and accurately reproducing the full range of frequencies audible to the average person.[22] While some critics explained that high-fidelity equipment should ensure "a high degree of faithfulness in the reproduction" (Canby 1958, 13), others claimed that the goal was not to be simply faithful but, as mentioned earlier, "realer than real" (Tardy 1959, 15). Predictably, the lack of fixed standards furthered the movement's disarray, thus allowing any audio system manufacturer to claim that their equipment was "hi-fi." To paraphrase one *Playboy* critic, this lack of limits not only introduced shoddy machinery but also submitted equipment whose excellence was all too often lost on audiences. In many cases, it was not that these audiences were inadequate listeners but that the systems reproduced frequencies far beyond the average listener's auditory capabilities (Lavely 1954, 12). Perhaps the most interesting admission of the term's arbitrary nature came from J. Gordon Holt, who, in writing about this problem vis-à-vis the process of purchasing a sound system, noted, "If we are defining high fidelity, then 'as faithfulness to the original sound,' it becomes obvious that what is fidelity to one listener may not be fidelity to another, which will not come as a surprise to anybody" (1956, 47). Another hypothesis for why high fidelity lacked a set of standards held that the movement involved "the integration of scientific knowledge and technological skill with a sensitive understanding of aesthetic values, to the end that an artistic experience may be communicated. It is in itself a creative act." This creativity led to, among other things, the continual shift of standards for which a system's distortion level might be considered acceptable ("High Fidelity Ill Defined" 1963).

High fidelity's inability to define a set of criteria for its equipment placed greater and greater emphasis on the listener and the listening experience as the analytical site where the movement's explorations should

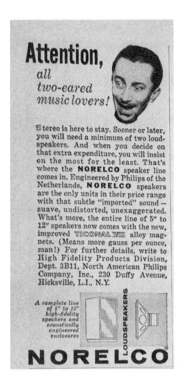

Alternately comic and serious, this Norelco advertisement demands that the serious music lover consider the necessity of purchasing a modern stereo system.

be conducted. As a result, much of the popular high-fidelity research and dialogue consisted of identifying those characteristics that could realistically reproduce not music but the listening experience. To boast improvements among concepts such as frequency responses, dynamic ranges, signal-to-noise ratios, and other abstractions depicted through mathematical equations is one thing. It is quite another to enthusiastically produce and market stereo and hi-fi equipment because it reproduces senses of sonic direction, placement, and a variety of aural fields. This is a claim that, unlike any formulaic representation of acoustics, could invoke a fact basic to the average listener: we listen with not one but two ears. By appealing to the well-known flattening effects of mono-ocularity on vision, stereo emphasized its ability to solicit both ears through two-tracked recordings. Indeed, stereo's claim that its petition of both ears (one for each track) would render an improved perception of music and sonic spaces became a continually deployed trope in explaining how the system worked and establishing its legitimacy as an aesthetic technique. Again, the binaural aspect of stereo not only echoed the makeup of a typical system's two speakers but also literally invoked the listener's physical condition. In the words of one 1954 *High Fidelity* article, "'Two ears' showing up as part of a title in a publication of this nature can mean but one thing: binaural reproduction—or, if you prefer, stereophony" (Cohen 1954, 28). By 1957 stereo-related advertisements such as Norelco's "Attention, all two-eared music lovers" were de rigueur ("Norelco Loudspeakers" 1958).

The result throughout the 1950s was that the potential to reproduce precise, concrete simulations of specific audio spaces from two-channel systems gained a sense of both notoriety and destiny for much of the record industry. Two years before the widespread introduction of commercially produced stereophonic tapes and six years before the release of the disc equivalent onto the market, the noted audio researcher Emory Cook declared that the creation of a successful binaural disc was inevitable. By 1952, the advances made in binaural tape had gained a certain amount of celebrity as a rumored source of superior sound. According to Cook, "Coming from a binaural system, the simplest things in music take on a new and vivid life, making even the best wide range, low distortion mono-aural reproducer sound dry and harsh." Most impressive was the simplicity with which the binaural method could render such brilliant results. By placing two considerably separate, equidistant microphones from a sound source, the audio engineer could produce a two-track recording. When played back through two separated speakers (one for each of the two channels), the recording would result in "the aural equivalent of the visual three-dimensional effect produced by a stereoscope—a lively illusion of space and perspective. [Thus], a recorded orchestra no longer sounds either Lilliputian or as if it were being heard through a port hole." As Cook noted, listening to binaural recordings, "[the orchestra] actually seems to extend across the end of the listening room" (Cook 1952, 33).

In another 1952 issue, *High Fidelity*'s editorial staff continued to draw on a correlation between binaural listening systems and stereoscopic photography but made an important distinction between stereophonic and binaural sound systems. In reviewing a New York audio fair, the article stated that each system gave sound new "dimensions" and a purpose: "to add a new factor of realism to music, voices, and sound effects by enabling listeners to hear them at home as they would be heard at the studio." Continuing, the review asserted that binaural listening was simply "natural," a process made by "listening with two ears." But in making this definition, the review also noted that,

> at the Audio Fair, there was much argument over the correct term to describe two-channel sound. Strictly speaking, [the experts] said, binaural reproduction requires the use of two microphones spaced six inches apart, the same as our ears, and that listening be done with earphones instead of loudspeakers. Those who favor this point of view claim that sound reproduced through two channels over loudspeakers should be called stereophonic. But others maintained that stereophonic reproduction requires *three* channels, two for position and one for depth. The dictionary says binaural means "of, with, or for both ears."
> With the support of that rather loose definition, we shall probably continue to call two-channel sound binaural, and reserve stereophonic for three-channel sound.

Again, the situation was further complicated by "rather loose definitions" and also the introduction of other trade names, such as "stereosonic" (Fowler 1953, 47). Four years later *High Fidelity* backed up its definition by positing a convenient equation of "binaural [sound] is stereo with earphones; stereo is with loudspeakers" ("Noted with Interest" 1957).

As stereo and binaural listening continued to focus attention on the listener's physical makeup, it also engaged another aesthetic issue: perspective. A newfound excitement in headphone listening was one manifestation resulting from an interest in reproducing audio perspectives. To quote one Columbia Records advertisement, one of the aims of stereo was to put "you in *the Center of Sound*" ("Let's Talk Stereo" 1958), a fact literalized by the listener who would find great pleasure in wearing headphones. Because headphones literally center the listener between two sound sources, both binaural and stereo's separated sound sources become even more exaggerated, which fact provoked Hans Fantel to note in a 1959 *HiFi Review* article that the headphone, a "practically extinct" technology from the 1920s, had, in the wake of stereo, become stylish once again. Unlike earlier forms of headphone listening (the initial means through which radio broadcasts were heard), these new stereo and binaural headphone experiences forced the listener to reach "for his pate and assure himself that, despite the intracranial orchestra, his hat-size stayed the same" (Fantel 1959, 36). Positioning an entire orchestra within the six-inch span of an auditor's skull may seem an extreme example. Still, one should consider that, as a 1964 *High Fidelity* article noted, the acoustic contours produced by headphones revealed a "super-terrestial place" (Steding 1964, 52). For example, the incredible acoustic terrain that headphones provided was often viewed as an extraordinary technological graft onto the auditory nerves. As one writer noted, in an almost McLuhanesque manner, binaural headphone listening provides the listener "with electronic 'extensions' for his ears, much as if he were fitted with a pair of hearing aids, connected by cables to a pair of closely spaced microphones at a remote location" (Garner 1958, 47).

Locating the listener in such a fashion raises numerous issues, most of which involve questions surrounding microphone placement, volume, and the recording's "mix." Unfortunately, popular music scholars have posed few questions concerning how the listener is "placed" or "located" by recordings. On the other hand, film scholars have tended to look on the question of how spectators are positioned by cinematic processes as one of the more fertile fields of investigation.[23] There are a number of reasons for this, ranging from film studies' history of close association and affinity with the study of literature, theater, and art history, to the fact that, as a discipline, film studies has tended to focus on issues of narrative and narration. Thus narrative film processes have always considered "how" and "where" a viewer is positioned in relation to a set of filmic techniques. In fact, in most cases film studies positions issues of narrative space and visual perspective as fundamental to any quality textual analysis. Because of this active interest in perspective, as David Bordwell has illustrated, film studies has been able to draw from a considerable and lengthy past of investigations into questions of perspective, particularly those investigations from other visual arts, whether they be mimetic or narrative in nature (Bordwell 1985, 3–15).

Bordwell also reminds us that perspective means "'seeing through'— a handy way to recognize that both the object (the depicted world) and the subject (the viewer) are bound together through the picture plane" (5).[24] Though it is not necessarily at the forefront of film studies, there exists a significant collection of film scholarship that investigates how film soundtracks provide perspectival-like information through audible renditions of narrative spaces. Though diverse in their sentiments and theoretical moorings, scholars wrestle with film sound as an aesthetic component that conveys important narrative information. This research has, for the most part, evolved out of an interest in understanding various narrative cinemas' (particularly the classical Hollywood cinema) use and development of audio aesthetics.[25] While the fashioning of film audio perspectives predated America's hi-fi movement by almost twenty years, the movements contained similar concerns. In both cases, the development of "audio perspective" paralleled the formation of perspectival principles in past graphic arts, specifically painting and theater. For as in the case of the graphic arts, audio perspectives consist of a combination of creative and scientific demands that are designed to engage the auditor.

Though the systemization of acoustic distances and acoustic mise-èn-scene organize sonic perspectives with reference to acoustic principles and aesthetic priorities, it is important to remember that these arrangements are conceived only to provide an ideal auditor with the illusion of a specific space. The calculated definition and utilization of space in musical performances is nothing new. As mentioned earlier, the space of the concert hall was viewed as engendering democratic and aesthetic possibilities that were not possible in private aristocratic settings. The immense spaces of eighteenth- and nineteenth-century concert halls were filled not only with larger, more heterogeneous audiences but a new musical phenomenon: the symphonic orchestra. Producing louder volumes, the symphonic orchestra's sounds were architecturally distributed by these halls in such a manner that those in the upper galleries were privy to the same audible details as those in the best seats (Chanan 1994, 156–61).

As the ideal concert hall perspective liberally amplified musical compositions, it also provided opportunities for other forms of aesthetic manipulation. Offering an example of perspectival manipulation of music, Cohen notes that Beethoven took advantage of the concert hall space in his *Leonore Overture No. 3*:

> Beethoven saw fit to write a trumpet passage in the distance, not just a quiet passage, mind you, that would sound as if it were far away, but actually a *distantly placed* sound. In its performance the trumpeter is usually located somewhere in the wings of the

auditorium, so that the concert hall listener hears, not imagines, the master's idea. He hears two physically separated sources of sound, the orchestra nearer to him, and the distant trumpeter. (1954, 30)

Cohen proposes that Beethoven's use of audio space and distance is part of the composition's distinct appeal, but most importantly, Beethoven's overture generates the perception of a sonic expanse that acts as both an attraction and a narrative device. "If Beethoven saw fit to use an *acoustic artifice* to accomplish his artistic ends in the concert hall, then there is every reason today to use *technological devices* to bring these same legitimate concert hall effects into the home," Cohen argues (30; emphasis added). He furthers his point by proposing that the sense of sound moving through space is as essential to the musical experience as perceiving a wide range of dynamics:

A similar but subtler problem is that of the apparent and inherent motion of orchestral themes in symphonic music. The *physical* thematic motion I like to call musical kinetics in preference to dynamics, since in conventional orchestral parlance, dynamics refers to the loudness-spread between pianissimos and fortissimos. By kinetics I mean the movement of the musical themes *physically* before our eyes as well as tonally before our ears. Perhaps an unconscious appreciation of just this sort of kinetics and motility draws us to the concert hall. The point is that the concertgoer is immersed in more than just musical sounds. He is immersed in musical motion as well. The man at home misses this motion, this depth, unless the musical technicians take the necessary steps to bring it to him. (78, 80)

In this conception, concert hall space is not a static arena but a radically liberating sonic space. Listeners may hear "equally," but they also witness various renditions of space through the physical energies of the hall's acoustics and orchestral arrangements. In its specific display of sound's ethereal tangibility, the concert hall acts as a curious palette, a distinctive arrangement of materials that simultaneously exhibit and mark every harmony and lyric.

Recognizing the space-specific nature of the listening experience is a holistic and radical proposition that challenges traditional text-based studies of music. As a rule, the study of music has tended to place its greatest focus on written scores and has spent little time in systematically evaluating the listening experience. Indeed, the common objects of music studies remain performance, composition, and music history. For the most part, the study of listening is viewed as a scientific endeavor best embodied by the discipline of audiology. What is interesting about advocates of high fidelity is that they pose at least an ad hoc movement and moment of energetic inquiry, an extremely vocal community that throughout the 1950s and 1960s examined at least one aspect of music listening. Still concerned with the quality of the musical performance, this community's primary object of criticism lies in inadequate reproductions of musical performances. High-fidelity backers embraced stereo techniques because they provided an attentive simulation of what it would *sound like to listen to a musical performance* (Burstein 1960, 54).

This emphasis on stereo's ability to yield sonic space is best evidenced in early stereo "demonstration" discs. Ostensibly, demonstration discs acted as samples of stereo and, as *High Fidelity* put it, were designed "to sell a whole new listening medium" (Smith 1959, 45). One manner of doing this was to explain how the new recording medium works by displaying a variety of sonic possibilities. The key word is "variety," since, with rare exception, the quality demonstration disc is prized because it verifies a system's capabilities by skillfully exhibiting several musical genres, sonic events, audible locations, and individual styles. One typical

The figure of a man seated at leisure while surrounded by audio technology and its accompanying pleasures is a visual trope still seen in high-fidelity advertisements.

example is the RCA Victor/Breck Cosmetics coproduction that included one side of Red Seal classical artists and the other of popular acts that celebrated a "New Golden Age of Sound Albums" (*Beautiful Hair Breck* 1959).[26] The aim of this variety, as the promotion of Capitol's 1958 demonstration release, *The Stereo Disc*, suggested, was to capture "the full spectrum of sound" ("Capitol Stereo Records Capture" 1958). It should be noted that through these musical varieties both discs illustrate how stereo could deliver assorted spatial contexts. For example, while RCA Victor's "Living Stereo" included the Boston Pops and the Chicago Symphony Orchestra, it also featured Harry Belafonte at Carnegie Hall (*Beautiful Hair Breck* 1959). On the other hand, the Capitol disc contained a more emphatic consideration of spatial representations. In addition to representatives from Capitol's stable of artists such as Stan Kenton, Nat "King" Cole, and the Pittsburgh Symphony, *The Stereo Disc* championed

> common sounds, in uncommonly lifelike reproduction: New Year's Eve at midnight in Times Square; a ball rolling down the alley and blasting the pins; traffic on a rainy day; the Staten Island ferry in a storm; children scampering along a picket fence; the roar of a New York subway train; a thrilling sequence at a crossing as a train approaches from afar, thunders past, and speeds into the distance. ("Capitol Stereo Records Capture" 1958).[27]

Included in the same sampler was "a 'balance track' of castanet sounds to help you in equalizing speaker levels" ("Capitol Stereo Records Capture" 1958), making the demonstration record something of a regulator for improved spatial definition. As *High Fidelity* put it, "Spatial perspective describes, perhaps better than any other term, the quality added to reproduced sound by a good stereo system." More importantly, the system needed to be properly assembled. If the system worked, "listening to the sound reproduced through such an installation, one [would need only to] close his eyes and the sense of 'being there' takes over" (Garner 1958, 47). As noted earlier, the recognition and promise of spatial presence certainly exists as a continuing promise of all high-fidelity technologies. Despite stereo's affiliation with this tradition, it is important to understand the technology as a system with a significant difference. Whereas the promise of presence is usually predicated on an authentic object, stereo space promised not only the presentation of spatial simulations (for example, the acoustic dimension of Carnegie Hall, the Hollywood Bowl) but also a technique for producing the sensation of sonic space. Stereo reveals spatial dimensions through the acoustic principles that constitute the audio sensation of space, namely, reverberation, echo, and source separation. Indeed, when Capitol advertised that its stereo records provided "the full spectrum of sound," this claim included the spatial dimension as well. With its stereo slogan, "Music swirls around you," Capitol reinforced this sense of a visceral, exotic space with the passionate image of a woman being caressed in flowing, silken fabrics, a visual equivalent for the supposed wondrous audio that promised to surround the listener and fill the room ("Music Swirls around You" 1958).

Capitol's advertisement for its stereo records promises the reproduction of a visceral space of exotic, luxurious sonic textures that are here represented by a woman caressed by flowing silks.

The concept of filling a room with a particular form of acoustic space may feel awkward, but it is a discourse that still lingers in consumer technologies that promise appropriate tone settings for specific genres of music. Still, the matter of being able to place a particular spatial perspective within another distinctive acoustic space reflected several concerns about the problems stereo posed for the typical listener. The most common complication was the typical domestic interior, which presented difficulties beyond microphone placement or loudspeaker capacities. "Most good sound-installation men regard modern house styling as deplorable," opened *High Fidelity*'s 1959 article on domestic interiors and hi-fi listening. While admitting that the modern house "may let in lots of sunlight and afford an economy of footwork to the housewife," the feature piece bemoaned an interior geometry that benefited domesticity at the expense of acoustic precision. This particular problem was most evident in the living room:

> usually symmetrically rectilinear, picture-windowed, smooth-walled, and sparsely furnished, [the living room is] all too likely to be echoic, slow in treble decay time, and generative of standing waves. The housewife may view it with delight. The high-fidelity outfitter, entering, may shrink as if he had had a glimpse of Gehenna. In truth, there probably are some modernistic living rooms in which good reproduction of music is impossible, without extensive remodeling. ("Designed for Music in the Modern Manner" 1959, 41).

Oliver P. Ferrell, editor of *HiFi & Stereo Review*, succinctly summed up the problem by noting that "in small living rooms stereo is fighting a space problem" (Ferrell 1960). To be sure, the intent of a quality stereo system and recording was to grant listeners "a gracious sonic vista" by conjoining "the area of the concert hall with that of your listening room" ("Balderdash for People with Two Ears" 1959). Although the competent recording engineer would "take into account the probable acoustic surroundings—the average living room in the average home—in which the recording [would] probably be heard," not surprisingly, a certain amount of responsibility needed to be placed on the listener. Accordingly, the competent listener would feel compelled to "make certain that their particular rooms complement rather than frustrate the sonic effect which has been provided in advance" (Eisenman 1963, 50).

Most listeners also understood that even the most complex system or efficient listening space could only act as a temporary substitute for hearing a symphony in a concert hall. Still, in a busy world, the active professional could use his or her stereo system, as in the case with one profiled physician, "as a direct substitute for 'live' listening sessions at Carnegie Hall" and help postpone the desire to visit one's favorite "musical habitat" ("Installation of the Month" 1961).

No matter how common, the presumption that one would continue to favor live performances and performance spaces over even the most excellent forms of in-home listening betrays at least two tenets basic to much of the hi-fi movement. The first principle holds that orchestral, operatic, and chamber spaces would continue to operate as the primary arenas in which music would be produced. This belief is born out of a "realist" aspiration that is promoted and championed throughout the pages of listener-oriented magazines such as *High Fidelity* and *HiFi & Stereo Review*. For example, in his article "Towards the Stereophonic Orchestra," Eric Salzman states that "every company making stereo records has said that its principal aim in life is to reproduce the sound of the symphony orchestra *as it really is*." In at least one case, the Mercury record company posted an explicit "policy of recording orchestras in the halls in which they normally play and with their usual seating arrangements" (Salzman 1959, 48; emphasis added). Notwithstanding that it often resulted in acoustic conflict rather than sonic unity, offering the in-home listener a concert-hall sensation, as the renowned inventor of the long-play 33⅓ rpm record, Dr. Peter Goldmark, noted in a 1960 interview, should remain high fidelity's greatest ambition. Goldmark's logic flowed from a staunch belief in authorial intent:

> The composer of chamber music meant his music to be played in a small chamberlike listening area. We haven't much opportunity to hear it played that way today. But we could enjoy that opportunity through records that aim at *true* realism. Similarly symphonies and operas were written to be heard in a large hall or auditorium. When listening to them in the home, we should have the sense of being in a large hall. This is the kind of realism that should be our goal. (Freas 1960, 47).

As an objective, a stereo record could only hope to equal live performances. Moving this logic forward, in some cases stereo enthusiasts argued that record companies had nothing less than a "moral obligation" to record their best talents performing the basic repertoire in great concert halls. Most importantly, stereo techniques needed to be used to take advantage of these halls' sonic "warmth" and "richness," to bring to the listener the concert hall sensation as well as the Western canon (Bookspan 1959, 34).[28]

Finally, the second principle underpinning the high-fidelity movement's acceptance of stereo techniques is that these methods would be continually invoked as complex simulations. Despite their roots in scientific research, stereo technologies were continually considered illusions that only mediated the "real" domains of musical production. Furthermore, stereo's illusory nature could only be discerned by the seasoned public of hi-fi listeners, whose "infinite capacity for taking things apart" could "easily rupture" the aural apparition. For some, this type of rigorous listening was seen as something of a parlor game; listeners should focus on musical performance rather than stereo's inadequacies. These listeners, according to *High Fidelity*, would "likely find that going stereo amply justifies the expense and effort [of finding an acceptable system]" (Burstein 1957, 53). And this was the point of the high-fidelity game: while stereo provided an adequate approximation of the concert hall, it was to be understood that it provided simply a simulation through which listeners could attain a new level of listening ease. Whether these simulations were considered woefully deceptive or adequately representative, almost every critic agreed that stereo furnished "a more effortless perception of beauty than monophony can yield" ("Balderdash for People with Two Ears" 1959, 41).[29] Indeed, it is this attention to the average listener, the audience with two ears, that marks the high-fidelity movement as a particularly listener-oriented faction. By smoothing away the inconveniences of the concert hall, this loose-knit group of enthusiasts demanded and enabled an affordable, modern convenience: "easy listening."

6

Space, the Pliable Frontier

Stereo as the New Spatial Palette of Audio

In opening this chapter I want to return to the beginning of this study and recall the rather extraordinary example given in the introduction, "There's a New Sound." Not quite the smash single, the record still holds novelty if only because of the composition's status as a pop-music experiment. Popular music is replete with sonic experiments, a fact that is borne out in simple reflection. Ask yourself how many of your favorite recent pop records are flush with samples, studio effects, and so on. How few modern vocalists record unadorned, steadfastly avoiding a dash of echo or chorus? For the informed listener, the producer and the engineer can be just as much part of the music-making process as the musicians. The quest for a new sound is part of popular music's need to be always ever more in fashion. The new sound, its novelty, is just as necessary for breaking a pop song as a pop record, often conflated in the mind of the listener.

But this continual search for novelty should never be reduced to a simple outgrowth of a never-satiated capitalist music industry. Part of this search involves a legitimate artistic pursuit for new sonic vistas, new worlds that cannot be envisioned but can be heard. The move to building new high-fidelity technologies was one part conservative and one part exploratory. Chapter 5 documents the former; the latter involves both a pioneering and a sometimes freewheeling spirit, a spirit that is just as important for understanding the demands of the high-fidelity enthusiast as well as those of the more typical popular music fan. To be whisked away to a new world, a sonic landscape that provides a brief respite from the all-too-pervasive audio world of everyday experience, is a promise that can never be underestimated, no matter how frightening, bizarre, religious, humorous, openly illusory and artificial that world is. And what has led us through these experiments? To paraphrase Michael Jarrett, it's not clear: "Chicken or egg? Aristotle or Plato? Marx or Hegel? Did the acoustic properties of medieval cathedrals give rise to antiphonal chanting, or were cathedrals erected in order to manufacture the echoes and reverberations that suggest transcendence?" (1998, 72). Whether the spaces be "psychedelic" or sonic samples, the experience of multiple "exotic audio spaces" is now part of our everyday life. That instant exotic audio spaces can reside in radios, cinemas, and in-home stereo systems as multifaceted musical ornaments that we may enjoy at will is the promise of modern audio technologies.

The power to create the illusions of sonic spaces has significant precedents, pasts that are filled with persistent cultural and aesthetic forces. As mentioned earlier, the processes behind these illusions became so intricate throughout the postwar period that a new third party between the composer and the performer evolved: the recording director or producer. According to a *High Fidelity* article, "The Search for a Third Dimension," the recording director moved the craft of recorded audio to the point that recordings could become more and more aesthetically convincing (Solomon 1959, 37). But the article also testified that these records, no matter how aesthetically accurate or imaginative, consisted of skillful fabrications rather than the unmediated representation of "real" events. The persistent editorial comments of Hans Fantel in periodicals such as *HiFi Review* best expressed this form of skepticism. Writing in 1959, Fantel noted that "[though] philosophers may question whether an imagined space can be called an illusion as long as its counterpoint in reality exists in the studio . . . , when the 'studio space' appears to you in your head [when listening with headphones], some sort of psychological hokus-pokus is evidently involved" (1959, 36). Still, the recording skills and perspectival techniques employed by the record producer were simply too exciting to either ignore or wholeheartedly dismiss. Of these methods, the most basic addressed the dilemma posed by recording a symphonic orchestra in a studio rather than in an orchestral hall. The solutions, dependent on the effects the recording director wished to produce, simply involved rearranging the players in patterns completely distinct from their seating in live performances. These studio orchestrations resulted in specific acoustic relationships through which the audible space could be organized and molded (Salzman 1959, 164).

To create ever more visceral spatial impressions, record producers began to advocate the use of new electronic means of audio enhancement both inside the home and outside the studio. The most important method was the use of personal reverberation units. As an audio effect, reverberation units have always been framed as somewhat duplicitous tools. Because reverb units utilize the simple principle of playback delay to split off, suspend, and reintroduce a portion of a signal to the original signal, once-flat audio can be presented to the audience as if it is swaddled in space without the trouble of actually moving through the space it intends to represent (Salzman 1959, 126). In other words, while the reverb unit may have closed the gap between the sound in the living room and the sound of the concert hall, its presence widened the gap between the modern recording and its primary spatial referent. Still, critics continued to assert that if "concert hall realism [could not be] achieved in the living room," then a reverb unit should be used "on the premise that, without it, what the listener hears [would lack] a final touch of *realism*" (Gorman 1960, 42; emphasis added). These touches aimed, according to another critic, "to create the illusion that the performance is taking place in a large hall instead of the typical living room." As the same author later explained, "The enhanced aesthetic appeal obtained from an auditory-perspective reproduction of an orchestra is not due so much to an accurate localization of the various sounds as to a general effect of space distribution, which adds a fullness to the over-all effect" (Burstein 1960, 54).

Burstein's article was concerned primarily with stereo's creation of audible "spaciousness." The search for sensible space created, in addition to stereo and reverb units, devices such as the "stereophoner," the "duophonic inductor," and the "xophonic." Each device was produced and marketed to a public interested in gaining a more spacious sound from their systems. In some cases these contraptions were simply variations on reverb techniques, while others concentrated in splitting and separating monophonic signals to create a "pseudo-stereo" aspect impressive enough to shroud older monophonic LPs in the reality effect of space (Ferrell 1959; Fantel 1960). This abundance of stereo products, pseudo or otherwise, was impressive, to be sure. Even as high-fidelity connoisseurs like Oliver Ferrell, editor of *HiFi Review,* emphatically asserted that "NO ENHANCING DEVICE, HOWEVER EXCELLENT, IS A SUBSTITUTE FOR GENUINE MULTI-CHANNEL STEREOPHONIC REPRODUCTION," it was apparent that by the late 1950s the taste for audible space had become a widespread phenomenon (Ferrell 1958, 56). For example, the use of reverb units was by no means limited to in-home accessories and the "classical repertoire" of recordings. As Ferrell points out, while recordings made in "acoustically 'tight' surroundings" benefited from the judicious use of electronic reverb, pop records had begun to utilize reverb techniques to bring a "sense of life" to the voices of many rock and roll, rhythm and blues, and jazz singers. For Ferrell, "the addition of a barrel-like echo [was now a] standard practice for pop records [in order] to give the singer's voice whatever qualities of sultriness, hollow mystery or smoldering passion please our teenagers" (55). Exactly what significance the addition of reverb held for popular music records of this period is uncertain. What is certain is that by 1956 the use, if not flat-out abuse, of reverb in doo-wop, rhythm and blues, and rock and roll genre records had become an acceptable convention. Each of these genres produced popular, chart-topping records wherein voices were audibly enveloped in artificial spaces produced by in-studio reverb units, sometimes in manners that seem excessive today.[1]

What could be considered excessive was simply a matter of personal taste since none of these pop records broke any hard and fast rules about recording or stereo reproduction—and, indeed, no rules were broken at the time because when it came to the issue of stereo or reverb conventions, there were few to none to break. Despite the involved discussion between recording professionals and critics early in the "stereo revolution," stereo was considered, by at least one prominent hi-fi authority, to be "too young to have settled down to [a] normative [set of] rules" (Fantel 1959, 62). This lack of hard-and-fast conventions only strengthened the objections of stereo detractors, many of whom believed that this effect was little more than a callow gadget, a trick that often distracted a lesser hi-fi enthusiast from the merits of the "music." In many cases these critics were more than willing to take their complaints to print in the popular high-fidelity and stereo journals of the day. "The man who hates stereo, oddly enough, seems often to be a *real* music lover. The man who has become an out-and-out devotee is likely, at least in my experience, to be one who knows relatively little about music itself," Edward Tatnall Canby opens his 1961 article, "Stereo for the Man Who Hates Stereo" (Canby 1961, 48; emphasis added). Unlike the general tone of those who disavowed stereo as being little more than an effective simulation, Canby's critique rests on the assumption that stereo was simply a fad, the latest craze in a long line of hi-fi contrivances. While Canby chides those stereo systems that deliberately took "on the character of a status symbol" (49), Charles Sinclair follows this line by claiming that the man whose interest in hi-fi was much more active than his interest in musical performance "really wasn't a musical connoisseur; he just makes people think he is one." For Sinclair, this individual is involved in a game of "Stereomanship," whereby the hi-fi fanatic maintains his authority by creating an "aura of knowledge" most often achieved through a dense, foggy, technical vocabulary that the fanatic often did not understand himself (Sinclair 1962, 43).

Other critics considered the stereo effect a distraction, little more than a gimmick that had an annoying tendency to beget stunts, audio tricks, and noisy exhibitions rather than music. In the words of an ardent defender of monophonic recordings, "while record companies big and little vied with one another to release ever glossier *Scheherazades* and *1812s* in the exciting new medium [of stereo], the more esoteric music was shunned." Worse yet, fine mono recordings of more unfamiliar pieces were deleted from catalogues to make room for new stereo records (Silverberg 1961, 50). For some it seemed that the propensity to release stereo recordings of an already-recorded piece, no matter how superior the monophonic version, was, for the most part, motivated by the need to insert one's product into the stereo marketplace before others did. Stereo took part in, as one of the editors of *High Fidelity* admitted, "one of the less fortunate results" of the high fidelity movement: "the belief that high quality sound is in itself a justification for recording" (Osborne 1962, 43).

While one critical faction framed stereo as little more than a specious strategy of planned obsolescence and extraneous gimmicks, another viewed the rerecording process as availing novel opportunities and conditions for aesthetic uplift. Attempting to gain a spot on the rerelease and recording of "stereo versions" of past catalogue items, the editors of *High Fidelity* demanded, "If everything is to be recorded afresh, let us have some of what our hearts desire" ("As the Editors See It" 1958). Of course, these desires engaged ambitions far beyond simply producing better-sounding records. Certainly, while improved sound remained a goal, some critics saw it as simply a step in legitimating and defining the recorded object as something greater than an acoustic mirror. As head of the Vanguard Recording Society, a society dedicated to exploring and using "all the main routes to realism in stereophonic sound reproduction," Seymour Solomon avowed that recordings contained values far beyond their reflective capacities. As Solomon argued in 1959, the boon in recording technology supplied a clear difference between the manner that those generations before and after these developments experienced and interpreted music:

> Whatever their limitations, recordings stand on their own as a valid means of reproducing the printed music page. They have created what can now be perceived as a revolutionary change in the sound of music in performance. Further, an entire new generation of music lovers is being conditioned to Mozart and Beethoven with the musical balances unlike those which their fathers heard before them. And since for every person who attends a live concert there are hundreds who gain their musical experience from records, the revolution is the more significant. Each new generation reinterprets the masterworks of music in light of its own needs and experience. In our electronic age we are *developing our own sound* in music as well. (Solomon 1959, 130–32; emphasis added).

Solomon's argument is interesting for a number of reasons. For some, Solomon's note regarding the generational rearticulation of sound may hold substantial analytical purchase. I, however, am interested in the manner that Solomon simply divines a bright-line distinction between music and sound. Indeed, the category of what can be considered a "musical sound" exists as an interesting classification, a grouping whose semiotic boundaries are in constant dialogue and fluctuation. Still, while the division between musical sound and nonmusical noise may seem obvious, a basic comparative consideration of what one social group considers to be "musical" when compared to others reveals that once-clear dividing lines are arbitrary and socially determined. For example, one of the reasons that Michael Chanan values Schoenberg's investigations into dissonance is that these aesthetic experiments highlight a specific dividing line between the "musical" and the "nonmusical" sound, hold that line up for analysis, and thereby attempt to redefine timbre. Chanan argues that Schoenberg's specifically modern genius led to an understanding of music and noise as simply sonic categories that exist at opposing ends of a singular continuum, rather than expressly antithetical divisions. The result for Chanan is that "the whole palette of sounds, including the nosiest instrumental timbres, opened up" (1994, 241). It is important to remember that this "opening up" process is never simply initiated through the work of a genius composer but also through the social dialogue that ensues from the reception of one group of musical pieces or a specific aesthetic movement. Along with Luigi Russolo's demand to make music out of noise (a demand that certainly anticipated Pierre Schaeffer's *musique concrète*), Schoenberg's experiments in twelve-tone compositional methods are certainly among the most celebrated and debated moments in the Western classical tradition of musical composition and performance (241–49). For this chapter, it is not so much the substance of Schoenberg's or Russolo's challenges to Western tonality that is most interesting but the fact that they were issued vis-à-vis a specific system of musical production with roots firmly entrenched in nineteenth-century notions of romanticism as well as more classical notions of tonality. Thus the general narrative of music history notes how in the late nineteenth and throughout the twentieth century the emphasis on measures of tonality gives way to modern, and ever-more controversial, experiments in atonality. The seed of these controversies has much to do with what is considered both normal and just in music. Because of their deliberate avoidance of basic, deeply held principles of musical harmony, experiments in atonality were both viewed with suspicion and celebrated because these challenges contested traditional conceptions of natural order and the hierarchy of things as well as modern man's ability to exceed past limits. While these challenges are often the most remembered, it is helpful to remind ourselves that other controversial aesthetic challenges take place in less rarefied, more popular contexts. Thus any collective opposition to (or the proposed definition of) a "sound" tends to be one of the more prominent points of interest for most popular music fans and producers. Examples of these debates are diverse. They include the "new school" versus "old school" debates in North Atlantic hip-hop culture of the late 1980s and early 1990s and the 1970s country and western music debate between the "Nashville sound" and the "new outlaw" movement, each of which took place through a widespread genre terrain composed of many social and industrial arenas.

Ultimately these processes produce not only a new group of listeners that includes other musicians, critics, and audiences but also new standards of listening. To understand this process is, in the words of Steven Feld, to understand a dialectical aspect to listening:

> What happens in the process of listening? First, one makes some attention shifts and adjustments within the dialectic of musical and extramusical features. As one listens, one works through the dialectics in a series of "interpretive moves," developing choices and juxtaposing background knowledge. Interpretive moves involve the discovery of patterns as our experience is organized by juxtapositions, interactions, or choices in time when we engage symbolic objects or performances. Interpretive moves—regardless of complexity, variety, intensity, involvement—emerge dialectically from the human social encounter with a sound object or event. (1994, 86)

While Feld represents his speculations graphically through an intricate system of social and categorical interactions, the key to his conception of listening is to understand that it is categorized as an interactive cultural system, wherein listeners are conditionally albeit never completely fixed. This particular understanding offers an explanation for why a listener is able to (and often does) move from one set of musical preferences to others as he or she moves from one social group to another.

It is fundamental to understand that the exorbitant amounts of criticism regarding stereo sound I have already cited are discursive snippets indicative of a widespread interest in new sound systems. Given the general interest in these developments, it is not surprising to discover that the contents of the two leading popular American journals for stereo and hi-fi listening, *High Fidelity* and *HiFi & Stereo Review*, contained occasional, ancillary remarks from and about those composers who actively worked with new sound-generating methods and machinery. These articles not only mentioned those musicians, composers, and producers who produced innovative arrangements of more traditional instruments but also accommodated a reflexivity that embraced the use of "nonmusical" devices, such as records and radios, in the pursuit of novel musical inventions. As one *High Fidelity* critic states in a 1953 column, this search for new sounds, whether it came from radio broadcasts or cloud chambers, was simply a natural portion of music's evolution:

> This process has been repeated in every age; composers have never been satisfied with the laws laid down by earlier composers, or with the sounds available to them. Always they have fought for new effects, new instruments, new compositional procedures. Critical hazards never seem to bother them.
>
> Sometimes they find new sounds they want by imposing mutations on existing instruments; sometimes they invent or, by criticizing, help invent new instruments; sometimes they are presented with a new sound source through accident; sometimes they just go out to the junk heap and rummage around until they find a resonating body that suits their purposes. Twentieth-century composers have frequently adapted to their musical uses objects that were never intended for such combat—brake drums, engines, boards, sirens, Mason jars, wash tubs, whips, vacuum tubes, and so on. (Hinton 1953, 49)

The critic further noted that while this process may seem obvious, each new musical progression was inevitably accompanied with the emphatic declaration "That is *not* music!"

If a middlebrow journal such as *High Fidelity* can present a discussion that closely echoes John Cage's call for new sounds, then it seems to me we need to reposition any vision of the high-fidelity movement that holds it as simply a conservative bastion of high-tech realists. Of course, I want to make it clear that not every audience member, musician, or record or stereo company consciously engaged high fidelity as an aesthetic explorer in search of new musical possibilities. As I indicate in the previous chapter, stereo speaker systems, along with other components of the hi-fi movement, valued the stereo recording for its ability to reflect and represent a concert hall perspective. With this in mind it is interesting to note that stereo was involved in another, more fantastic discussion regarding possible musical futures. Throughout this conversation the desire to explore new musical and aural prospects *through* stereo and hi-fi techniques is continually exposed and highlighted. As melocentric ingredients in the production of new musical experiences, both the reverberation of once-unrepresentable spaces and other unimaginable sounds radiated forth as

Ralph Bellamy, starring in "Sunrise At Campobello", listens to stereo on his Collaro changer and Goodmans Triaxonal Speaker System.

Collaro—your _silent_ partner for Stereo

Silence is the requirement — and *silent* performance is what you get when you select the new Collaro stereo changer for your stereo system. Collaro engineers have designed the high fidelity changer precision-engineered to meet stereo's rigid quality demands. Collaro's *silent* operation assures flawless reproduction of the exciting new stereo records every time. Here is why Collaro is your best buy.

Five-terminal plug-in head: Exclusive with Collaro. Provides two completely independent circuits thus guaranteeing the ultimate in noise-reduction circuitry.

Transcription-type tone arm: Another Collaro exclusive. As records pile up on a changer, tracking pressure tends to increase. Result may be damage to records or sensitive stereo cartridge. This can't happen with Collaro's counter-balanced arm, which varies less than 1 gram in pressure between the top and bottom of a stack of records. The arm accepts any standard stereo or monaural cartridge.

Velocity trip mechanism: Unique design of this sensitive mechanism insures that the Collaro changer will trip at extraordinarily light tracking pressures — a requirement of many stereo cartridges.

FEBRUARY 1959

New Collaro changers include *all* of the best features which have made Collaro the largest manufacturer of record changers in the world — as well as important new features vital for superb stereo as well as monaural performance. There are three Collaro changers: The Conquest, $38.50; The Coronation, $42.50 and The Continental (illustrated), $49.50.

For full information on the new Collaro stereo changers, write to Dept. HF-2, Rockbar Corp., Mamaroneck, N. Y.

ROCKBAR
Corporation

American sales representative for Collaro Ltd. and other fine companies. RC-9

As conservative as the high-fidelity movement may seem, the promises of this new technology went far beyond realistic reproduction of music. In many cases, as in this Collaro advertisement featuring Ralph Bellamy, the promise of hi-fi technology suggests the listener will be surrounded by an exotic sonic landscape.

novel aesthetic foundations. Through this new aesthetic infrastructure record producers and musicians alike responded to the opportunities posed by the prima facie contradiction of merging the uncompromising reproduction of realistic sound with never-before-heard timbres or once-impossible orchestrations.

Contradictions tend to beg for resolution, or at least an attempt to resolve uncooperative differences in a search for harmony. In some ways it was this search for resolution that shaped and fashioned the movement. It is undeniable that some of this artistic and scientific experimentation generated a listening vogue for a popular "sound for sound's sake" aesthetic that had multiple impacts on American audiences. One forum through which this aesthetic contradiction was best expressed was in the growing popularity of "exotic" music. John Ball Jr. of *HiFi & Stereo Review* noted that the exotic music category arose from recording technologies that could make even "the triangle in the Lizst First Concerto ring with a new clarity" (Ball 1960, 63). With "the fresh world of stereo waiting in the wings," artists such as Les Baxter, Martin Denny, Arthur Lyman, and Alfred Apaka could capitalize on the twofold desire to produce and hear strange music that was founded on colorful instrumentation and vibrant arrangements that sounded both foreign and unusual (63–65). Explaining his own popularity, Martin Denny admitted to an interviewer in 1993 that "part of the reason [his] records caught on [with the public in this period] was that *stereo* had just appeared on the market, with its amazing separation into right and left channels. People were interested in sound *per se*—and that included the so-called 'exotic' sound" (Vale and Juno 1993, 147).[2]

Recently, cultural discussions have grouped many of these artists under the generic banner of "exotica." This category operates on the basis that the genre is twice removed from the dominant set of present-day pop musical genres. Unlike most Western popular music, the genre of exotica is primarily instrumental and employs instruments typically omitted in contemporary, blues-based popular music. Instead, the genre is noted for its invocation of non-Western (typically Southeast Asian or Pacific) instruments that represent musical cultures deemed "exotic" in the West. Further, the genre arises from a recent resuscitation of exotic music based on the artists and recordings mentioned in the previous paragraph. The best confirmation of this interest in 1950s and 1960s exotic music is the multitude of these once-forgotten records finding their way onto reissue labels and gaining greater prominence among record collectors. Yet the reborn interest in this past recording genre is, for many contemporary listeners, also an exotic pleasure—these records exist as strange forces that lie distinctly outside the standard rock or pop music canon. In other words, these recordings have reemerged because they contain a double fascination: they are intriguing as both a musically unique genre and a set of lost documents that has maintained a strange existence distinct from the familiar constellation of popular, youth-oriented musical pleasures. I note this to clarify one point about these records: their reappearance in recent popular culture should not be downplayed through accounts that attribute their acceptance in strictly musicological terms. While it may be true that some musicians and fans are interested in musical arrangements and compositional techniques, these records manifest not only exotic musical techniques but also recording methods and aesthetic sensibilities that appear exotic to today's audiences. For the present-day listener these elements are odd antiquities, archaic materials that act as reminders of an age when stereo and high fidelity were young and held yet-to-be-forgotten futures. Of course, these recordings also reflect a past wherein the sensation of exotic "nonmusical" audio curiosities existed as the basis for their popularity. Consider the prominence accorded to the sound of the renowned Henry J. Kaiser Aluminum Dome occupied in some of Arthur Lyman's, Alfred Apaka's, and Martin Denny's releases. For these artists, the recordings they made in Kaiser's Hawaiian Village were not simply recordings of their *music*. Instead, their "exoticism" also rested in an audience's ability to listen to this music as it reflected off and around a geodesic-dome auditorium created out of the modern "wonder material" of aluminum. In other words, many of these records promised audiences unique, imported timbres as well as exotic music.[3]

While audio-spatial novelties such as the Henry J. Kaiser Aluminum Dome were recorded with a keen interest, they existed alongside a previously impossible instrumental vividness. Perhaps those records produced by the Command Records label best evidence this fact. While not initially considered "exotic music," much of the Command record catalogue has been caught up in the exotica's recent recycling of hi-fi oriented records of the same period (Dorling 1997). Given Command's fascination with outlandish stereo-produced sounds, it is not difficult to see why these records have found popularity within this context. Although one of its promotional phrases boasted "Stereo didn't make Command; Command made Stereo" ("The Man Behind Command" 1962, 75), Command was not simply an enterprise of superior engineering. Managed by the conductor and leader of a popular dance band of the 1930s, Enoch Light, the label recorded and released recordings by such significant popular instrumentalists, groups, singers, and celebrities as Doc Severinsen, Tony Mottola, Dick Hyman, the Ray Charles Singers, and Dick Van Dyke. Yet, as a record producer, Light maintained a considerable curiosity for the potential that records and the recording process possessed, particularly stereophony. According to one of the label's own advertisements, "when stereo came along, [Light] soon realized that the full potential of this field was scarcely tapped" ("The Man behind Command" 1962, 74). This potential is noted in the liner notes of the 1959 Command release *Persuasive Percussion*, featuring Terry Snyder and the All Stars. According to the notes, Command Records is "the result of a concentrated effort by a dedicated group of world-renowned artists and sound scientists, an effort which represents years of painstaking research in all phases of the recording field." Indeed, the *Persuasive Percussion* record possesses an aura all its own. Its cover art is by Josef Albers, a member of the famous German Bauhaus movement and school; its liner notes promise "the most unusual record you have ever put on your turntable . . . [It is] a unique mixture of entertainment, excitement, beauty and practicality" (Stars 1959).

Positioned in the liner notes as "*the definitive record* for checking out all aspects of your stereo system," *Persuasive Percussion* is pitched as a product beyond novelty (Stars 1959). Unlike the typical stereo demonstration record, *Persuasive Percussion* maintains that it consists of "*music—* not sound effects—but music. Brilliantly recorded music, played on fascinating percussion instruments with *new and exciting tone textures*; music planned and arranged to bring out the whole spectrum of sound on your stereo equipment even while it puts your system through a series of acoustical alignment tests" ("The Greatest Advance," 81; emphasis added). While the *Atlantic Monthly* claimed that the record would revolutionize the record industry (quoted in "The Man Behind," 75), *Persuasive Percussion* garnered both critical and economic success on its release. Its financial accomplishment heralded a number of "sequel" records such as *Provocative Percussion* (a series which included a number of volumes after the original), as well as encouraged competing companies to release their own records emphasizing percussion.

For the most part, these percussion records highlighted distinct forms of stereo separation, but they also included the explicit, well-defined textures of various instruments. Given the West's long-standing view of percussion instruments as exotic, nonmelodic elements of music, the popularity of an entire album's worth of percussive textures and accents must have generated an eccentric aura. But there was certainly no more eccentric an emphasis on novel sounds and odd aural grains than the many comedy records that emphasized strange and peculiar sounds. For example, take the promotion of Spike Jones's 1960 Warner Brothers release *Spike Jones in Stereo*, buried deep in the April 1960 edition of *High Fidelity*:

BURP!

Beg pardon for being impolite, but Spike Jones does burp . . . in stereo, too! Hear a pistol shot race across the room! The most spectacular stereo sounds ever in one album. And there's Spike Jones' humor too—for all the family. ("Spike Jones in Stereo" 1960)

A case could be made that, much like RCA Victor's *Bob and Ray Throw a Stereo Spectacular*, the music was given second billing to the more spectacular sound-effect elements of the record. The stereo record was a follow-up release to *Spike Jones in Hi-Fi*, a record that features Paul Frees, one of Hollywood's more famous voice-over talents whose credits included Francis the Mule, Tom and Jerry, and "the voice of suspense" (Jones 1959). Still, depositing Jones's work into the spectacle of stereo and high fidelity was justified by a career established on the conspicuous incorporation of sonic novelties in musical performances and recordings. Fans of these Warner Brothers albums were expected to understand that Spike Jones and his City Slickers' performances and arrangements consisted of combining the "classic" repertoire and popular standards with the outlandish noises ranging from birdcalls to breaking glass. But the technical improvements afforded by high fidelity rendered these noises into new dimensions where they could be made even more pronounced throughout the aural space of the record. Indeed, Jones had released a popular LP for MGM records, *Dinner Music for People Who Aren't Very Hungry*, whose subtitle, *Spike Jones Demonstrates Your Hi-Fi*, made Jones's interest in capitalizing on the vogue apparent to all. On the record, the voice of a narrator who acts as a straightman makes connections from one humorous piece to another, continually highlighting and mocking high fidelity for its effect on the listening experience as a whole. Effects such as "barking dogs in Hi-Fido" assert a dominance within the record's sonic space. For an artist whose live show boasted an entire railroad car for his entourage's "props," stereo and high fidelity were sonic boons.[4] In his liner notes for *Dinner Music,* the Academy Award winning film composer Dmitri Tiomkin wrote,

> Spike is a perfectionist and will go to any length in time and expense to get authenticity. A case in point is the following item that appeared in the Chicago Daily News, August 30, 1956. Tony Weitzel, the Town Crier wrote, "Spike Jones got into the Michigan Boulevard repair act Wednesday. Turned up on a curbstone at 7:00 a.m. with Bill Putnam of Universal Recording, plus one tape recorder; gravely recorded the noise of a pneumatic drill to be added to a Spike Jones Dinner Music Album."

While the sound of the "Pneumatic Pile-driver breaking Pavement" is listed in the liner notes, so are "Glugs," "Phrts," "Skks," variations of a "Garbage Disposal," a "Klaxon," and various other sounds under the title of "Spike Jones' Legitimate Instruments Heard In This Album" (Jones 1957). Jones's exploitation of high-fidelity and stereo recordings featured a continuation of his interest in sonic novelties from his days as a comedic live performer.

While the visceral friction between music and noise provoked a variety of comedic possibilities, it did resolve the seeming contradiction between recording sonic realities and producing fantastic sounds. One solution that seemed to consolidate the antagonistic pair of music and noise appeared in the new cultural figure of the record producer. Take, for example, Emory Cook, a figure whose status as an innovative recording engineer is firmly established in American history through the preservation of his records by the Smithsonian.[5] As a man of science, Cook promoted his Cook Laboratories and Sounds of Our Times labels as producers and distributors of recordings that captured a "stark realism." At the same time Cook alternately championed the search for the wondrous tones, "dramatic new horizons in recorded sound—cataclysmic forces of nature, weird noises from outer space; exotic, primitive, enchanting music from distant lands," and, in general, *out-of-this world* sounds"

("New Horizons in Sound" 1956). This interest in the exotic/exploitative real has a significant foothold in Western culture. In early-nineteenth-century Europe it was most apparent in the institution of the museum. As Tony Bennett points out, the museum was born out of (and continues to embrace) the seemingly contradictory, exploitative logic of the fair in order to kindle curiosities and wonder for the sake of knowledge (Bennett 1995).[6]

To be sure, Cook may have framed his documents through advertising that his records would provide a scientific antidote to distorted sound, but the same recordings also included an adequate measure of the medicine show. While Emory Cook consistently voiced an ardent belief in the empirical obligations of documenting sound,[7] his recordings were often tendered as dramatic novelties. The sound of these long-play recordings was carefully tailored, and as early as 1954 the Cook catalogue listed both mono and binaural versions of every recording, no matter how classic or low the product was. Indeed, producing records in two formats would not become widespread among major labels until the late 1950s and it certainly distinguished Cook's wares from their counterparts. Also distinguishing both labels was the sheer variety of sounds his records accommodated, ranging from sounds of the wild, theater organs, rail engines, and music boxes to more straightforward symphonic orchestras (Conly 1954, 128, 130, 132). Unlike most major labels, whose catalogues are celebrated for the quality of the musical artists and performances they include, the Cook catalogue will forever be associated with the spectacular sounds it contains. Typical of the Cook inventory is a 1954 recording devoted to capturing and representing "the voice of the storm." According to Cook, the record distinguished itself by presenting the sounds of thunderbolts and the part of the storm "you usually don't hear, unless it's too damn close for appreciation." As one critic noted, "the thunder in [this release] is not ordinary, down in the valley thunder. It is special *Emory Cook thunder*, as heard by eagles, complete with high-frequency sizzle and tape-edited for maximum dramatics." Even Cook had to admit, "Al [sic] right, maybe I do make it into the composition. I just don't want to get too heady about it" (Conly 1954, 50; emphasis added).

While Cook somewhat mildly calls into question the realist impulse of his sonic spectacles, demonstrations that often outstripped any "real" musical or audio event, his critical interviewer would probably agree

SPACE, THE PLIABLE FRONTIER

that a Cook recording of a thunderbolt was an acceptable reproduction of a real thunderbolt. Stereo's ability to vividly recreate spatial sensations and expand the palette of frequencies allowed some high-fidelity fans, as Frank Jacobs notes, to not only hear an opera, chamber music, a symphony orchestra, or a hot jazz quartet but also to simply "listen for the joy of just 'hearing' sounds not likely to be found in the average living room." That an author could assume that the sound of an orchestra was now an unexceptional living room sound is one thing; it is another to observe that listeners could now attest that a thousand snapping shrimp sound like "subterranean static," or that the drum fish sounds like "an erratic riveter" (Jacobs 1958, 33).

Because these sounds were so vibrant and novel, record producers such as Moses Asch, co-founder and dominant force behind Folkways Records, could take great pride in their contribution to the sciences. Asch openly claimed that his label's science records were so accurate and realistic that he regularly received written testimonials from experts attesting to their authenticity and scientific benefit (Jacobs 1958, 35).[8] Still, it would be difficult not to attribute these recordings' successes to their position as sonic novelties. As one minor label after another jumped into the fray of the stereo craze, the production of recordings composed solely of genuinely unique and unconventional sounds grew proportionately. A good portion of the stereo phenomenon was staged through the success of records produced by major labels. But while these major label productions included a variety of artists, genres, and styles, minor labels frequently made their mark by selling sound-oriented records as relatively cheap, marketable alternatives to expensive name artists. By far the most ballyhooed and one of the most successful of these independent labels was Sidney Frey's Audio Fidelity label. As an independent label, Frey decided early on to establish his company with recordings of "ideas and situations." Frey began his business as Audio Varieties, distributing recordings such as "Parakeet Lessons," an album devoted to teaching speech to birds. Finding himself annoyed by the audio quality of these records and enthused by the fact that the general public was investing greater amounts of leisure time and money into sound equipment, Frey decided to enter the stereo record market in 1957. Beating the majors to the punch in terms of stereo productions by almost a year, Frey's first two releases, *Railroad Sounds* and a music record, *The Dukes of Dixieland*, represented a continued interest in sonic varieties. By 1959 the company grossed close to $5 million and was exploring the possibility of signing a few name acts. The most prominent of these was Louis Armstrong, who received $40,000 in advance royalties to record two stereo recordings ("Records: Woofers and Tweeters" 1959).

Still, Frey's specialty remained records whose primary emphasis involved novel sounds or odd musical acts like those of the midget-led act Johnny Puleo and his Harmonica Gang. By 1961 the independent label claimed to have moved more than four million records. And as such impressive growth continued, so did the extravagance and drama of the acoustic scenarios. Speaking in 1961 about how stereo sound's horizons are only limited "by the present state of public taste," a *Time* magazine article noted that Frey had

> recently abandoned the sound of a belching baby for fear that it might offend potential customers and he ruled out frying bacon and tooth brushing as not sufficiently dramatic. But he hopes soon to record an aerial dogfight between two World War I relics, the crash of a sprung gallows trap, the wack of a guillotine blade against the block. And his enduring dream is to catch on his own high-fidelity equipment the mid-century ultimate sound—an exploding hydrogen bomb. ("Music: Noise Merchant" 1961)

The voyeuristic fascination with perspectives into large-scale sonic demolitions and combat scenarios are prima facie fantasies, fictive sonic vistas whose purchase on our collective attention is more exploitative than it is educational. As attractions, these sounds not only outflanked any "musical" demands placed on their arrangement and position within the recordings but also asserted an authority through their location as the most striking, emphatic elements in the recording.[9] Stereo's importance in this process cannot be understated: reproduction of these sonic events was predicated precisely on recreating their physical unfolding through a particular sonic space. To recreate these events, the illusion of space that stereo provided was not so much a notable sonic improvement but an element necessary to completing the audio trick.

As spectacular displays of technique and invention, these recordings were often produced to be contrasted with and distinguish themselves from musical recordings. Yet, as I have insinuated throughout this chapter, unlike classical genres of music, popular music has historically had fewer reservations when it comes to the incorporation of audio effects into its recordings. As mentioned in chapter 5, the sonic goal of classical music records (and their employment) has typically been to replicate a "concert hall" aesthetic. But as Bruce Swedien, a recording engineer with such pop music credits as recording Michael Jackson and Quincy Jones, testifies, the recording palette for pop music is far more expansive than that for classical music. Swedien should know. As an engineer he spent a number of years recording symphonic orchestras and decided to make the switch to pop music because of the greater creative possibilities it held in the recording process:

> When I started recording classical music, in a big way (I worked for RCA in Chicago, my gig was recording the Chicago Orchestra) I soon began to feel as if I was taking dictation, or something. In other words, the most that I could do in recording classical music was to re-create the original sound field. On the other hand, in pop music (all types, rock, R&B, etc.), the only thing that limits the sound image that we create is our own imagination. Mix up those reverb formats, get crazy, don't try to rationalize anything. (Quoted in Jones 1992, 173)

In recorded popular music, producers and musicians alike take greater liberties with sound effects. Yet, despite their freedoms, their use of effects is always adjudicated through their availability and the adherence of producers to generic conventions. This dialogue of studio possibilities is always contained within distinctive social, industrial, and aesthetic debates.[10]

While present-day popular music productions integrate any number of recording effects, it is impressive, and notable, that early stereo-effects records held a significant popularity with the general public. Effects recordings are still profitable ventures, although today they tend to find their customers in industrial rather than popular settings. Despite the outstanding quality of some of Audio Fidelity's musical catalogue, the label garnered most of its praise for its sound-effect productions. Certainly, most of these records comprised sounds far more common and banal than the seemingly absurd sonic engagement of atomic weaponry. For the most part, these records ostensibly presented the "sounds we live by," sounds such as

> rasping, blasting, roaring, hissing, shrieking, crackling, ringing, blurping, bubbling, rattling sounds . . . buzzing, clicking,

rumbling, popping, gurgling, humming, moaning, grating sounds . . . crashing, zooming, squaking, whining, thundering, gushing, tinkling, humming, slamming, fizzing, steaming sounds . . . sounds all around us, all day, every day . . . but sounds we don't really listen to because we're apt to take them for granted. (Frey 1960)

According to Frey's *Sound Effects, Volume 1,* the primary reason that these sounds had not come to our attention earlier was that sound was "not really born until the coming of high fidelity recording." Even more significant was Frey's claim that "[sound] did not come of age" until the Audio Fidelity label applied high-fidelity and stereophonic techniques to the recording. For Frey, the result of the label's application made the long-play record "doctored for super sound" or "super stereo." In publicizing the technological aspects of these processes, these records often fixed an illustration of a hypodermic needle in the cover art that was angled and apparently readied to inoculate the sound register with the benefits of science. The implication of this scientific discourse was that, by listening to an Audio Fidelity record, one could hear "sound effects people hear everyday, but never really listen to either because they are taken for granted or are distilled by a thousand and one things that contribute to their impurity" (Frey 1960).

The most important facet of this unsullied listening process was the ability of a recording to capture, cultivate, and reproduce spectacular, stereophonic sound. Though Frey openly professed that listening to such doctored effects satisfied a "basic craving for listening stereophonically," it was not clear if this "base" need was more psychological or physiological, or both ("Music: Noise Merchant" 1961). Still, what is clear is that high-fidelity technologies offer listeners the ability to recognize and alter the reproduction of music at its most basic: the sonic spectrum. For the most part, a good portion of the appeal of the superior sound system resides in the possible sonic adjustments it allows one to make. These adjustments can be as simple as tweaking a system's treble knob to gain a closer control of the spectrum through a simple equalizing unit.[11] For the high-fidelity movement, extending the ability to significantly amplify signals with an increased dynamic response and minimal distortion stood as its most important achievement. The effect of this on the perception of sound is something akin to the effect that modern optical

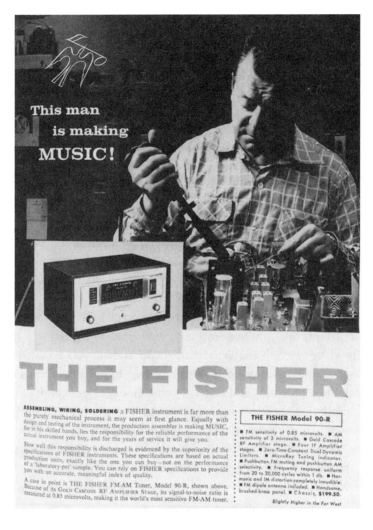

This Fisher advertisement deliberately conflates the creation of music with the science and technological proficiency of precise sound reproduction.

instruments had on our sense of what could be "visualized." As modern scopic technologies have fostered visual scenarios that thrill audiences and scientists alike, we need to remember that these technologies have imparted new perspectives on familiar materials. And like high fidelity's claims on the sonic spectrum, modern visual devices existed because their processes of magnification, coloration, spectral division, and separation were based on scientific research. High-fidelity enthusiasts constantly made this comparison and argued that their research responded to a general set of underdeveloped listening faculties. Through scientific investigations there existed a resolute hope to uncover once unnoticeable processes:

> The camera's eye, the microscope lens, the telescope's probing mirror—through these and countless other devices modern man focuses his perception on the universe around him.
>   In the realm of sound, stereophonic recording makes it possible for the first time to capture sounds, the noises, the tones, the breath of human activity and experience in the *fullest* realism. The simplest everyday sounds take on new freshness, new clarity and meaning for us when heard through this medium of stereophonic recording. We *revel* in a heightened awareness of the world in which we live. (Cunningham and Jordan 1956; emphasis added)

In the case of *Sound in the Round,* the producers claimed that the record did not simply take you to events but made you *"participate"* in a "pell-mell mixture of event and sensation" (Cunningham and Jordan 1956). Through amplification one could literally magnify the mixture, thereby making these processes and materials much more evident to the ear. In fact, amplifying these records could bring listeners into "unsettling" sensations. Thus, "when played at top volume, the fizz of a freshly opened soda bottle on an [Audio Fidelity sound effect] album *explodes* into a fury of a hurricane-whipped ocean; the gurgle of water washing down a drain becomes the belch of some prehistoric monster" ("Music: Noise Merchant" 1961; emphasis added).

The suggestion that stereo systems and records could facilitate a sonic object's playful transgression of audio categories is one of the movement's most important fantasies. The melocentric aspect of stereo technology is skillfully expressed in the productions of Juan Garcia Esquivel and his impressive use of stereo separation as a compositional device. Amid a general excitement for postwar hi-fi spectaculars, Esquivel's recordings have recently been rereleased by major and independent labels alike to considerable success. Along with a penchant for large orchestral arrangements with a wide variety of instruments, most of these albums include a famous "signature" Esquivel effect: the "zoom-zoom-zoom" singers. Composed of a chorus of mixed voices, this effect was created by intoning "nonsense" words that would then be mixed for the illusion of rapid movement, as audio would appear to move left to right and back again, over and over. Although Esquivel was an accomplished musician, his "straightforward" interpretations were quickly rejected in favor of his more fascinating orchestral and stereo arrangements. This is best illustrated in the case of Esquivel's first commercial failure, a simple, small combo record titled *Four Corners of the World*:

> I made a mistake [in recording this record]: having recorded an album with a big orchestra and dazzling stereo effects, the audience didn't expect the next album to be a small combo. *Other Worlds, Other Sounds* got a wonderful reception; at Music City on Hollywood and Vine it was Number One for 12 weeks. But *Four Corners of the World* didn't get that acceptance. (Juno and Vale 1994, 154–55)

Actually the title of his earlier success, *Other Worlds, Other Sounds,* was something of an afterthought. The project was recorded under the working title of *Beguine for Beginners* and changed only later when RCA Victor decided that the working title had nothing to do with the way the album sounded (Juno and Vale 1994, 155). After realizing that the public wanted a larger, hi-fi, effect-laden sound, Esquivel soon produced *Exploring New Sounds: Esquivel in Hi-Fi, Infinity in Sound Vol. 1* and *Vol. 2, Strings Aflame* (in "Living Stereo"), and *More Other Worlds, Other Sounds* (155–59). While each of these LPs varied in its popularity, Esquivel's fame as a composer/arranger was predicated on his explorations of studio recording techniques. His stereo experiments strove to cultivate an assortment of high-fidelity methods and tricks for new compositional possibilities, or, as he would later disclose, "I was always trying to produce amazing sounds, different sounds—sounds that would attract attention." Of course, what distinguished these sounds from those of the more popular American composers of the day was the fact that they were the product of recording advancements and were dependent on the recording medium. Consider Esquivel's response to a question concerning what he thought was his favorite track on *Latin-esque*:

> *Stereo-wise,* "La Raspa." It starts with the sound of a "scratcher" (a gourd with grooves cut in it) jumping from left to the right. To me it was an interesting challenge to record a "conversation"

between a scratcher and trumpet—the scratcher would make scratching sounds, and on the other channel the trumpet would answer. (Juno and Vale 1994, 159–60)

In each case, Esquivel's musical use of stereo effects—the perceptible transformation of one sound into another form through amplification through the melocentric application of stereo and high-fidelity recording techniques—should not be shrugged aside as mere gimmickry. Rather, these seemingly bizarre applications point to another high-fidelity vision that is interested in creating another distinctly modern terrain of listening dealing with distinctly fantastic possibilities. Indeed, one of the reasons I find this supposed movement between sonic categories— music/noise, household appliance/prehistoric animal, drum-fish sounds/ erratic riveting, and so forth—interesting is that these shifts entail the clear, distinctive application of modern sound processes. Rather than gaining new frequencies, it is their magnification or their movement that alters not only our perception of them but also their potential to be subsequently categorized. These operations disfigure our auditory sensations, positioning them into new classificatory possibilities. High-fidelity techniques provided the key to effecting these audible transformations of seemingly unremarkable tones into extravagant reverberations. Thus, the hi-fi listener/producer could easily make once distinctive boundaries nebulous and flimsy under the weight of their willful exaggerations, something that cannot and should not be simply dismissed. Instead, I would like to deposit one portion of high fidelity's fantasies firmly within a modern imagination that envisions art works (and acts) beyond the realm of realist representations. Rather, I believe that a significant parcel of the hi-fi movement, despite the phrase's intimations of accuracy and truth, was not invested in accurately representing audio materials but in their radical alteration.[12] This is a difficult argument to make, one that would require another significant quantity of research that I am not prepared to take on at this time.[13] One of the reasons for the degree of difficulty is that, in comparison to the visual arts, the ambitions and techniques of the recording artist are nowhere as grounded or policed by self-reflexive institutions of tradition. That is, traditionally there have been no structural equivalents to art schools or fine art departments in the United States or Europe for the recording artist. If anything, the most evident influence, both formally and informally, exists in institutions devoted to musical performance. Thus the history of the visual arts, whether taught in film schools or fine arts programs, is designed to provide an understanding of stylistic movements as they relate to the specific material and cultural conditions of the actors therein. In general, visual culture is cultivated through institutions and organizations that emphasize modernist styles of painting, sculpture, photography, and filmmaking. In part, this organization hopes to foster a self-consciousness among visual artists that, at the very minimum, understands the debate between the politics of representation and aesthetics of experience.

I also want to make it clear that I am not calling for the academic institutionalization of recording arts departments. Rather, I am interested in identifying those moments and social organizations in which recording materials are identified, discussed, debated, and categorized as ingredients for new, modern listening possibilities. Key to understanding the promise of modern recordings, whether this is the radical transformation of sound or an exacting representation of a sonic space, is that the power of rendition moves from the musician to the listener. Consequently, the responsibilities of the listener have increased radically. Representations of these responsibilities took many forms. Some stereo manufacturers, for example, often framed the ear as an underserviced organ that, with the right amount of attention, could gain from the advancements of high fidelity. Through these techniques audiences could finally hear "everything" they needed to hear when they had heard a stereo version of their favorite composition or artist. Rather than alienating the listener from the production of music, hi-fi technologies promised raw sonic materials for the listener to investigate, enlarge, exaggerate, and pick apart. Throughout this discourse the material advancements in recordings and recording technologies were positioned as redemptive formations whose capabilities could save the listener from the limits of the facsimile and usher in a new order of listening.

But, as is the case in all rhetoric of deliverance, the listener had to move responsibly to deliver her ears to the graces of greater audio pleasures. Under this new order the listener was given a new proximity that warranted at least a modicum of control. Ads during this period continually frame domestic scenarios reaffirming this new position of power. Not surprisingly, such scenarios are often aligned with conservative gender conventions that place the man in a position of activity while women passively listen. Yet even the supposedly passive organ of the ear

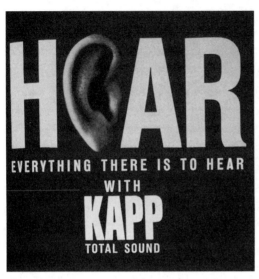

THE EAR THAT HAS HEARD EVERYTHING, HAS HEARD NOTHING UNTIL IT HEARS

"JOSE MELIS AT CHRISTMAS"

Dazzling, superlative, swirling scintillating and kaleideoscopic, could all be used to describe the music of Jose Melis... You will discover that his technique, whether displayed in monophonic or stereo recording, is a listening experience of rare pleasure, deserving inclusion in every record library.

Available both in Stereo and Monaural

HI-FIDELITY

STEREOPHONIC RECORDS

CHRISTMAS WITH MELIS

CELP 423

SEECO RECORDS, 39 W. 60 ST., N.Y.C.

The image of the ear in these advertisements recalls nineteenth-century experiments with phonautography, where, as Jonathan Sterne points out, the ear was seen as the primary instrument for the precise, scientific reproduction of sound.

is accorded a new position. Witness Knapp Records' incorporation of the ear in a 1958 advertising campaign. Whereas other companies may have simply included a drawing or photograph of an ear in their advertising text, Knapp changes the ear into a vowel. Forcing an iconic connection between the ear and the letter "E," the image is inserted into the initial "HEAR" portion of the copy that reads, "Hear everything there is to hear with Knapp total sound" ("Hear Everything There Is to Hear" 1958).

Again, within this discourse, the activities and responsibilities of the listener (and the listener's ear) are only possible because of recordings' graphic improvements. Full-frequency stereo LPs, 45s, and tapes contained hyperreal aspects that promised musical renditions better than live performances, realizations unhindered by the noise and pollution of inadequate architectures and audiences that "originals" often encounter.[14] These techniques provided a reality that was a complete, organic extension of the so-called real.[15] This belief in the recording's potential to illuminate the old order of listening and to bring forth a new era in which the workings of science and a technician's artistry could evoke greater brilliance from its subjects continues to be a dominant rhetoric for the recording industry. But if this discursive motif appears obvious to today's listeners (indeed, almost comical, if today's kitschy celebration of "high-fidelity" records is any indication), then one must keep in mind that one of the driving forces behind stereo and other high-fidelity techniques was to convince listeners that they not only heard "reality" or a realistic representation but also that the material act of listening had become much more sensitive—and, most important, that as listeners they had been significantly altered in the process. Sometimes this opinion was expressed in an almost folksy fashion by liner notes that pleasantly inquired, "Checked your sound sensitivity lately? No . . . we're not being facetious. Everybody is *exposed* to sound. Most folks *hear* it from one end of day to the other. But how many actually *listen*?" (Frey 1960).

"How many actually listen?" This question reflects an interesting motivational basis, one that I feel stands firmly behind the development of many modern musical experiences. But most important is the modern experience of listening that is more attentive, spectacular, and democratic. That listening, particularly modern listening, is continually framed by critics, listeners, and the audio industry as a passive activity is significant and should not be forgotten.[16] Assuredly, the charms of passivity spring from the id of "easy listening" as guilty pleasures that more discriminating sensibilities are supposed to keep in check. But while the passive subject may find pleasures in submitting to stimuli with or without his or her consent, we need to recognize those moments when listening is brought to the fore and the subject of technological change. The listening subject is not uniform. It is the heterogeneity of listening activities and skills that makes the listener. While the high-fidelity movement promoted a generally more active, self-consciously engaged perception of sound and its material contingencies, stereo both revealed and reveled in the obscene possibilities of sonic representation. I am using "obscene" in its most literal sense: as indicative of a representation that breaks out of both the concert hall and, in some cases, the audio arrangements of the theater. Stereo technologies not only rendered new pieces of domestic furniture but also a once-unthinkable proximity to audio spaces.[17]

Of course, common sense tells us that listening to stereo has more to do with the former than the latter. In our collective imagination "the stereo" is a technological entity that is completely distinct from the listener. The stereo is the active musical source and we do little more than take heed of its aural emanations. When the stereo becomes too loud, too strident, too obscene, the responsibilities of the listener are automatically invoked. In the worst cases these can involve litigation. Neighbors can call the police and legislators can write laws, but, for the most part, these measures need not be taken if only the listener conducts himself responsibly and turns down the volume. Yet we need to recognize that this investment in the obscene potentials of the stereo also contain seeds of a new democratic aesthetic. Music and musical spaces can now be projected into and forged in once-unimaginable arenas. That these recordings and stereo apparati contain the possibilities to beautify as well as disturb or ease one's existence should not be too surprising for they, too, are essentially the same promises that any democratic society contains for its public. Indeed, the recorded music object can not be turned off when it disturbs others, but it can be turned on to annoy or placate oneself with the tones of Carnegie Hall or Lincoln Center. This is as true for listeners in New York or Washington, DC, as it is for those in Phoenix, St. Petersburg, or Sydney. Stereo space may be a virtual space, but this is its appeal. As a virtual space, stereo space contains a space of great potential, great promise that can reproduce these spaces across the globe and for listeners of every kind, no matter how widespread and scattered these spaces and ears may be.

Conclusion

The Flip Side
(and a Few Concluding Thoughts)

"The flip side of the record" is one of the more roman-
tic phrases in record culture. Placing the long-play or 45-rpm record between your hands, turning it over, and finding that "side," that song
or performance hidden to the casual listener but imminently accessible
to anyone who chooses to look for it, are actions that neatly sum up all
that I find delightfully intriguing about these objects. Records are hardly
simple objects. Inside these sides are grooves, the common spaces, the
topoi, of many aesthetic renditions and offerings. They can be flipped,
spun backward, scratched; they can gather dust, be traded, sampled, and
sold. Records record history and can be historical objects. They can act
as objects of great passion. In a sense, with every record purchased and
played comes an unspoken guarantee of connection and common spaces,
for when we play a record we avail ourselves to the possibilities of a
common experience, even if the distances of generations or cultures separate us from one another.

That said, records can, as in the case of Lou Reed's *Metal Machine Music*,
also be awfully annoying:

> I have heard this record [*Metal Machine Music*] characterized as
> "anti-human" and "anti-emotional." That it is, in a sense, since it

is music made more by tape recorders, amps, speakers, micro-phones, and ring modulators than any set of human hands and emotions. But so what? Almost *all* music today is anti-emotional and made by machines too. At least Lou is upfront about it, which makes him *more* human than the rest of those MOR dicknoses. Besides which, any record that sends listeners fleeing the room screaming for surcease of aural flagellation, or alternately, getting physical and disturbing your medications to the point of *breaking* the damn thing, can hardly be accused, at least in results if not original creative man-hours, of lacking emotional content. (Bangs 1988, 196)

As Lester Bangs celebrates "any record that sends listeners fleeing the room screaming for surcease of aural flagellation, or alternately, get-ting physical and disturbing your medications to the point of *breaking* the damn thing," his words take on an interesting force. Bangs's asser-tion, in writing about *Metal Machine Music,* that a record may cause an across-the-board need to eliminate these common spaces of irritation is, in itself, a celebration of an object of abjection. At sixty-four minutes, the double-sided long-play record is as great a statement of "uneasy listen-ing" as has ever been produced. A record such as *Metal Machine Music* has most certainly earned its antihuman reputation, but this palette of "inhumane audio" is also a humorous reductio ad absurdum of the au-dible horrors of machines in general. The record hums, wheezes, and screams through magnetically generated feedback loops. It contains no rhythmic structure, no melodies, no human voices or any of the other aspects that we consider essential to a humanistic conception of music. And as interest in the record has slowly grown over the last twenty-five or so years, a number of odd adulations and rumors have grown around the recordings, the most fantastic being that sides three and four consist simply of the tapes of sides one and two reversed and played backwards. In the words of the rock critic Chuck Eddy, the record is "almost undeni-ably the most dauntless 'fuck-you'move/hype/tour de force/sham in the history of history, but that's only to say that this is real nice to *own,* not necessarily to *listen* to" (Eddy 1991, 101).

But Reed's creation of a machine-made *machine music* arrived only after close to a quarter century in which the American experience of music was becoming one of recordings and playback systems rather than primarily consisting of performances. Reed's recording of oscillators, amplifiers, reverb units, and modulators also has all the telltale signs of an experiment gone wrong (or terribly right!). And the experiments, as I have detailed, were manifold and grand. The new science of audio, or modern machinery, whose powers can be harnessed by the likes of Lou Reed, a self-proclaimed musical illiterate, to power his own solo career and the avant-garde ambitions of his band, the Velvet Underground, was if anything founded on popular science as much as popular music. The power of recorded music, tapes, and high-fidelity systems was not simply the power to strip music from musicians but the power to make the science of music far more available to the general population.

It was now possible to generate and produce a relatively widespread interest in the production, distribution, and exhibition of music in more facets of our lives than one could have imagined before. As Leopold Stokowski noted in 1943, the experiments surrounding recordings often spilled into discussions of the living room space: "There are those who would like to hear orchestral music recorded and reproduced exactly as it sounds in the concert hall. Others realize that their living room is much smaller than a concert hall, and would like to reduce the volume range of the records proportionately. Is either of the methods of recording possible—or desirable?" (Stokowski 1943, 233).

The desirability of such audio experiments continues to this day. But as Americans began to enjoy the musical pleasures of Horowitz and Brubeck in their own homes, these concerns were as new as the plethora of other audio pleasures such as amplifiers and transistor radios that were finding places as diverse as the living room, the kitchen, the den, the garages, and even the park and the beach. This new mobility of musical and sonic enjoyments has certainly affected the history of musical production and our understanding of music in general. For example, if given a detailed account of how postwar advancements in electric technologies were necessary to the development of modern amplification and musical instruments, most mainstream rock historians and critics would quickly begin to grasp how important the development of the transistor and modern recording materials have been to changing the musical vernacular of this country. A persona such as Lou Reed, with his emphasis on layering amplified sonorities produced through lengthy experiments in feedback over extremely simple musical structures, is perhaps a good place to begin the discussion. After all, along with other popular American musicians, artists such as Reed have convinced so many young people that they, too, can make wonderful noises, noises previously unimaginable. That, in and of itself, is something of a grand dream of democratic access and production or musical experiments. Perhaps simply envisioning the tremendous scale of this postwar combination of new instrumentation and new instrumentalists comes closest to Stokowski's 1943 vision of the future of music: "In the future there will be no limits—everything will be possible in the realm of sound—and music will reach new heights of tonal quality, power, delicacy, beauty" (1943, 229).

Of course, Lou Reed's career of tonal power and delicacies began at the end of the mid-1960s, right where this book ends. Reed, much like Hendrix, Dylan, and his other American contemporaries, emerges at a period of time when rock and roll music goes from its status as a genre among many other genres of popular music (in fact, some would claim a novelty genre) to become the dominant genre of American popular music until the early 1990s. Part of the purpose of this book is to supply an alternative history about postwar American popular music, one where rock and all the genres that came to forge that genre (blues, rhythm and blues, country, hillbilly, etc.) are simply bracketed off to the side in order to ask a set of questions that are all too often forgotten. For as much as I love these genres (and I do), if one were to read the many pages written by those historians and writers who take this period of American popular music seriously, one may come to believe that the cultural-material issues I detail in this book were of little importance to American music during the postwar period and that understanding them is of little importance to readers today. Put simply, to make sense of the past sometimes we need to look at what we, as writers, have moved to the margins. In the case of postwar American popular music, histories are written that all too often ignore the importance of these mainstream American struggles about popular technologies and everyday pleasures. But worse yet, by ignoring these mainstream concerns, we make the mistake of intellectual hubris by either assuming that we understand all we need to understand about such issues or, worse yet, that these pleasures simply do not merit our attention. One of the small goals of this book is to continue a small but nascent interest in these pleasures by writers, musicians, and scholars who are beginning to rethink and reinterpret this period of pop music history.

To be sure, this work is taking place. From semipopular artists such as Stereolab to the recent interest in postwar exotic music, the postwar period of mainstream American pop music has gained a new appreciation for its experimental ethos. The most recent expression of this in the academy comes in the form of Timothy Taylor's study *Strange Sounds: Music, Technology, and Culture* (2001). Taylor establishes his study in a larger, more international and global debate about how new modes of music technology affect the production and consumption of music in the Western tradition (hence his dedicated interest in "exotic" music and the "modern music" of Boulez and Schaeffer). Taylor's theoretical work is one manner in which the debate can be forwarded. But so is close, detailed historical research that makes use of existing archives and creates new ones in its demands. One of the issues I have tried to underline throughout my research is just how little we actually know about our popular music past simply because we have all too often failed to question what we take for granted. This period of time is ripe for exploration by scholars, each of whom will have decidedly different and intelligent observations and arguments to make. More specifically, I hope that the cases I have decided to present, in concert with those of Timothy Taylor, Keir Keightley, Rebecca Leydon, and others, will spark a wholesale reconsideration of this oft-unmentioned terrain of popular music production, distribution, and consumption. I have organized each chapter of this book around the premise that the conditions affecting the production, exhibition, and reception of music are primary conditions we need to understand if we are to better understand what it means to be "popular." Popular recorded music and sounds exist as specific sets of material, aesthetic logics, and cultural contingencies, a perpetually changing framework that affects an object's material status as a cultural force. If the reader has felt confused by the recorded object's prominence and cultural influence as it shifts from chapter to chapter, this is understandable. In every case it should be clear that I believe the study of recordings should always posit an understanding of any recording's relationship to a media industry. And in this examination, the recording can often possess histories that include, but are not limited to, programmed and sometimes accidental intertextual opportunities and openings. In fact, it may be that the history of the record industry cannot and should not be written as if the music industry is an autonomous entity among other industries. Like the film and broadcast industries, its history has been intertwined with other forms of media and media capital.

The belief that the recorded music industry processes its products through a heterogeneity of aesthetic procedures, institutional desires, and systems of manufacturing may not be new. But I would hope that the study of the popular music recording becomes just as much a study that involves issues pertinent to broadcasters, film producers, labor unions, and listeners. As such, any scholarly understanding of modern popular music in America must comprehend that these aesthetic objects have a basic interdependence on various mass media, using *basic* in the most literal sense of the word. Thus, much as the mass appreciation of popular music is never simply only about "the music," perhaps the research on popular music should never only be about popular music. In all cases we should always remember that there are specific ideological consequences that result when the material necessary for musical production remains unacknowledged. In particular, this lack of attention given to the expressive energies of materials removes music from the systems out of which our everyday pleasures are produced.

Taking this principle as a guiding energy means that we cannot ignore movements such as musician strikes. While labor is all too often separated from "music," it cannot be separated from the musician and, subsequently, serious questions of culture. This is particularly the case when we consider contests regarding the effects of modern modes of entertainment. Perhaps the greatest benefit that mass media industries have provided listeners and scholars is the huge set of recorded music catalogues and inventories that we enjoy, exchange, and debate every day of our lives. Of course, this catalogue has structural similarities to the catalogues of popular songs amassed by music publishers. But the catalogue of recordings does not need musicians for their continual rendering. Instead, these recordings provide us with a new form of listening, most often referred to throughout popular literature as "easy listening." Rendered only once, the object can be repetitively auditioned through mechanical and electronic means by the listener herself—an elaborate dream, if not actually unimaginable, until the advent of the recording.

This political-economic focus might be seen as less than aesthetic. But culture is not simply the discussion of ideas; it also includes the objects, procedures, and professions that constitute taste and artistic processes. The point of my argument is that the very elements of modern musical production *cannot* be separated from the economic scenarios and material arrangements that affect our production and perception of these objects.

Recordings have a material basis, a basis that musicians, producers, and the general public simultaneously must acknowledge and disavow to produce the aesthetic consequences for which they hope.

These hopes persist. In fact they are part of the cultural ambitions that are embedded in automobile and in-home sound systems. Specific recorded objects such as the long-play high-fidelity record and magnetic tape are not simply technological innovations but exceptional mediums that can engender any number of concert-hall musical experiences. As "media of distinction," they embody a number of aesthetic techniques designed to create virtual in-home concerts. The combination hi-fi playback machinery and improved recordings brought a widespread sense of aesthetic "uplift" that the country has rarely experienced vis-à-vis American mass media.

By no means, needless to say, have I offered an exhaustive account of how recordings are utilized and informed. The musical recording's composition is a site that not only foresees its own placement within spaces of pleasure but inscribes an audible set of spaces. By detailing this long-term investment by recording companies and research labs, we begin to understand how specific high-fidelity techniques, particularly stereo, construct and conceptualize a variety of musical and listening opportunities. Thus the emphasis is on listening systems, an important distinction since it identifies the material arrangements that have distinctive effects on both the production and reception of recordings.

Finally, by placing an emphasis on these systems, we begin to reveal some (although not all) of the demands of musical audiences. If we continue to investigate the role of "the listener," both real and conceptual, we gain a new understanding of the complexities that both enable and plague popular music production. As I argue that what occurs throughout the postwar period is an emergence of two dominant types of audio aesthetics, I am arguing for two lines of logic rather than two sets of practices. Thus a "realist" approach that emphasizes a reproduction of exact audio presence and a "hyperrealist" approach that stresses the production of once-unaudible spaces and spatial arrangements are simply identifiable modes through which we could begin to identify multiple practices and experiments. Each aesthetic line contains particular ideological implications. The realist approach follows in a long tradition of audio engineering principles that celebrate the ability of specific material organizations to obscure their existence and produce an idealized music or audio space. Because these arrangements artificially produce a great variety of spatial simulations, these techniques allowed studio producers to combine and arrange fantastic spatial presences that had no precendent in recording history. Frequently producers of popular music openly embraced the possibilities provided by these recording and studio techniques, thereby establishing a culturally informed aesthetic binary: those recordings and genres that embrace a "realist" aesthetic gain an upper hand in terms of cultural capital; popular productions that revel in their artifice are considered "pop" and are treated as such. To be sure, exceptions exist, but recognizing the establishment of this culturally informed aesthetic binary begins a conversation through which we can begin to see when, where, and why popular music recordings embrace and spurn these techniques.

My argument comes down to this: The expert contribution of mass media scholarship *exists* in the identification of the material aspects involved in the process of communication. If we were to understand this aspect correctly, perhaps we would begin to rethink even some of the most well-known popular musicians and producers and their influence on music history. For example, perhaps we could begin to understand a figure such as Phil Spector not simply as a well-regarded producer of pop music hits but as someone who was involved in a watershed moment of technological ambitions and musical experiments that attempted to renegotiate our understanding of the popular. Thus his patented "wall of sound" or Owen Bradley's contribution to a "Nashville sound" or Berry Gordy's "Sound of Young America" all become particular postwar American aesthetic expressions. As such, each presents us with a challenge, a demand that we rethink what goes into the creation of a popular sound and why particular records and recording processes are the primary, indeed the only, mediums through which this kind of aesthetic expression can be staged.

But no doubt Spector's staging was something special. More so than for Bradley or Gordy, there is a real impetus to bestow on Spector the status of *auteur*. No doubt it may be well deserved. As for all great media auteurs, stories of his eccentricities are only outstripped by his oeuvre. As David Hinckley points out in the liner notes of the 1991 ABKCO box set commemorating the period of Spector's most highly regarded work, *Back to Mono (1958–1969)*,

When it comes to assessing great artists, Americans have a bad habit of mistrusting the art. We acknowledge its value, then start poking around its creator's dark corners for the "real story." It's as if Renaissance Italians told Michaelangelo that the Sistine Chapel was nice, but say, wasn't he feuding with a major marble importer while he worked on the Pieta? Fascination with trivia—some of it, granted, good trivia—has colored our thinking about Phil Spector for three decades. What we have here now then is the counterbalance.

This music is the real point. It is why we care about Phil Spector, and why we should.

Anyone who likes these records, from "To Know Him Is To Love Him" through "Black Pearl" and "Love Is All I Have To Give," likes Phil Spector. (Spector 1991, liner notes)

Phil Spector's career is one of the pop legends. His love of that great American vernacular known to listeners as rhythm and blues was unparalleled, as was his influence on how we heard it. But, to paraphrase one of his most famous songs, to know Phil Spector's records is to love him. The eccentric behind the Raybans, the genius behind his patented "wall of sound" is not revealed in his personal associates but rather in his chosen form of thinking: his medium, his recordings.

Spector the producer, the recording mogul, the arranger, the musician—to which are we to listen? Artists like Spector, Bradley, and Gordy pose as much a challenge to mass media scholars as they do to musicologists. In fact, their existence as active interdisciplinarians makes our claim on popular music studies that much more essential, for we have a methodological bounty that draws from the preexisting work on radio, television, and film to offer. I would hope that we could generate a multiplicity of methods and questions that recasts modern popular music as a mass media system. Through this rethinking we gain not only material insights but insight into those specific aesthetic debates such as the "sound" of a record or a specific production style that all too often elude more traditional means of studying music. This discipline should not be limited to the recording but extended to the analysis of sites of mass-mediated musical production such as the concert tour, amplified instrumentation, or music video programming and production, to name but a few. In each case, the strengths of quality media scholarship should be exerted on popular music studies by devising discussions that continually expose musical materials. The trick is to understand that, although sound is ephemeral, it is also always a material process. As fleeting and momentary as sound may be, we should never let the processes that go into its production elude us. For it is through these processes that we ultimately experience and produce our musical culture. And it is through understanding these processes that we ultimately begin to understand who we are and why we sound the way we sound.

NOTES

Introduction

1. I want to make it clear that there exist many above-average studies that trace out a technological history of recorded object. Both Roland Gelatt and the duo of Oliver Read and Walter Welch offer fine general histories of the phonograph. Still, both volumes more or less focus on the technical rather than musical influences of the sound machine. See Gelatt (1977) and Read and Welch (1977). Andre Millard's recent work, *America on Record: A History of Recorded Sound* (1995), is a more gracious attempt to detail more of the cultural impacts that recorded music and sound have made at the musical level, but as a whole it remains a general history that provides little theoretical leverage. From a more global perspective, the most significant work of late is Michael Chanan's recent work on the recording (1995). As scholarship, Chanan's work is invaluable as it provides more analytical and theoretical insights and questions regarding the effects that both the recording studio and the object have had on music than perhaps any other source. Chanan's work criss-crosses the apparent limits of genre and national borders in order to frame the record as an aesthetic force deserving of our attention. As a history its reach is grand, as it attempts to attend to recording formations from cylinders to compact discs. What we gain is a general rather than specific insight, yet Chanan provides us with a set of questions regarding how music is mediated through specific industrial arrangements and technological formations. In this sense, Chanan's significance rests in the fact that his work begins to sketch out a cultural materialist stance.

2. One recent move in cultural and social media histories has occurred in the field of television studies. The methodological emphasis on the social terrain of television has provided a particular inspiration for this study. Indeed, many of these studies detail the reception of television throughout the postwar period. As such, these authors explore and deduce their insights from a diverse set of nontraditional data sources such as advertisements, housing policies, advice columns, handbooks, and others that are seemingly tangential to television in general, to generate a broader understanding of the reception of television in

a postwar American context. For example, scholars such as Lynn Spigel and Cecelia Tichi have focused on the commercial and cultural rhetoric surrounding the installation of the television set into domestic spaces, while others have concentrated their work on discussions of the domestic sphere within televisual texts of the period. Through this work we have begun to understand how television texts and the medium's marketing drew on middle-class myths and desires for the hearth. I am not the only scholar interested in music who has been influenced by such analytical and methodological decisions. Contemporary writers such as Simon Frith, Holly Kruse, and Marsha Siefert have centered their analyses on the question of marketing these technologies for particular forms of in-home consumption, sometimes directly invoking the concept of the hearth. And Keir Keightley has asked comparable questions regarding the development of record and hi-fi culture in North America in a postwar environment. See Spigel (1992), Tichi (1991), Haralovich (1993), Lipsitz (1993), Frith (1988a), Kruse (1993), Siefert (1994), and Keightley (1996).

Despite these advances, one problem involved in these studies is their persistent focus on the domestic sphere. This consistent focus unveils numerous issues regarding cultural pleasures, but it runs a considerable risk of ignoring other possible social and cultural uses of media. Anna McCarthy points out in her work on the consumption of television in public spaces (1995) that all too often the study of early American television has been focused on specific postwar trends: "the housing boom, suburbanization, growing consumption, increased leisure time, and an 'affluent' working class." According to McCarthy, "This image of early TV viewership is unquestionably the most prevalent one in popular memory, perhaps leading to the impression that the middle-class suburban living room was the only social space where TV was viewed." I would add that the same could be said regarding any examination of the popular music record. Indeed, one of the reasons that I avoid a direct examination of the domestic sphere in this study is to provide models through which other social and cultural issues involving the recorded music and sound object can be framed.

3. My use of the term "assemblage" draws directly from Guattari's interest in what he calls "aesthetic machinery." Guattari conceives of aesthetic machinery as machines of the virtual that "have an important role to play . . . as a paradigm of reference in new social and analytic possibilities (psychoanalytic in the broadest sense)" (1995, 89). These are particularly odd machines: not only are they diagnostic but they provide fantastic premonitions, potentials for day-to-day experiences and social formations: "Strange contraptions, you will tell me, these machines of virtuality, these blocks of mutant percepts and affects, half-object half-subject of the possible. They are not easily found at the usual marketplace for subjectivity and maybe even less at that for art; yet they haunt everything concerned with creation, the desire for becoming-other, as well as mental disorder or the passion for power. Let us try, for the moment, to give an outline of them starting with some of their aesthetic principal characteristics. The assemblages of aesthetic desire and operators of virtual ecology are not entities which

can easily be circumscribed within the logic of discursive sets. They have neither inside nor outside. They are limitless interfaces which secrete interiority and exteriority and constitute themselves at the root of every system of discursivity. They are becomings" (92).

4. I am drawing on Raymond Williams's discussion of "culture" (1981) as both a decided problem and interest for sociology: "The history and usage of [culture] can be studied in Kroeber and Kluckholn and Williams. Beginning as a noun of *process*—the culture (cultivation) of crops or (rearing and breeding) of animals, and by extension the culture (active cultivation) of the human mind—it became in the late eighteenth century, especially in German and English, a noun *configuration* or *generalization* of the 'spirit' which informed the 'whole way of life' of a distinct people" (10–12).

5. This is a simple distillation of Peter Wollen's statement about the rise in critical popularity of *Singin' in the Rain*, a rise correlated directly to the public's access to the film: "In the 1962 *Sight and Sound* poll only one critic named *Singin' in the Rain* in his 'Top Ten List.'" In 1972, there were five. In 1982, seventeen listed *Singin' in the Rain* and it now came fourth overall, running immediately behind Fellini's *8½*, Eisenstein's *Battleship Potemkin* and Hitchcock's *Vertigo*. What caused this steady ascent? First, it should be noted that during the 70s MGM released *That's Entertainment*, a compendium of clips from MGM musicals which highlighted *Singin' in the Rain* more than any other film except perhaps *The Band Wagon*, and then re-released *Singin' in the Rain* itself. Also, as the veteran editor of *Sight and Sound*, Penelope Houston, observed in her introduction to the 1982 lists, *Singin' in the Rain* had also begun to be revived on television. Availability of films is the first necessary condition for their artistic evaluation" (Wollen 1992, 52).

6. For example, it is common knowledge that Edison's phonograph was produced not simply to record music. While Edison believed that the phonograph could certainly record music, he also believed that his invention contained a heterogeneity of technological and cultural potentials. In her history of turn-of-the-century technologies (1988), Carolyn Marvin points out that Edison believed the phonograph held significant social value as a business tool to record dictations as well as having a more "uplifted" potential for preserving the voices and speeches of great men.

7. For an interesting and concise account of how music and the rational sciences' perception of time developed throughout the Middle Ages and Renaissance Europe, see Crosby (1997).

8. One of the most common critiques of this position, a position that I feel this study anticipates, is that we are entering a "post-record" era, an era where CDs, tapes, and records are being outmoded by a file-sharing economy of MP3s. Yet this cultural economy of information exchange is only possible because of the high volume and speed of recent hard-drive technologies. Hard drives, we should not forget, are simply high-volume record and playback devices. In other words, they are only another permutation of the recording object.

9. Indeed, one need only think of Cecil Beaton's costuming, Pan Hermes's

choreography, and the re-enlisting of several actors from the original Broadway show, including Stanley Holloway and Rex Harrison, to understand the popular text's intertextual complexity.

10. I want to reiterate that the debate about whether or not popular music scholarship should have a primary focus on the study of recordings (or any primary focus for that matter) is not one that I feel this book can successfully close down or finalize. Rather, again, throughout this book I am working with the assumption that the need to recognize the materiality of the musical recording for a mature popular music scholarship is a given.

11. In this sense, the term "cinematic" is used as it relates to the French term *cinématique,* the geometry of motion. To be sure, the issue of sound's motility is a vital one to understanding stereo.

1. Buried under the Fecundity of His Own Creations

1. "Exhumed" may actually be the best word for how these compilations are formed. Pressed and distributed through Crypt Records, perhaps the label's most fabled offering is a set of recordings, with each volume titled *Back from the Grave.* Specializing in recordings of "garage" rock from forgotten bands who never achieved any form of national or international recognition, the series continues with the recent release of volume 8, a double-LP set.

2. Of course, there are exceptions. In their essay "Cycles in Symbol Production," Richard Peterson and David Berger mention that the music industry viewed the conclusion to the AFM's protests and strikes by 1948 as one of the keys to "making possible the uninterrupted production of records" in the immediate postwar period. Furthermore, Peterson and Berger use 1948 as the base year for their study on market concentration and homogeneity of cultural products in the music industry. But most often media historians have positioned the strikes as minor events that had an effect in the development of American broadcasting. For example, though John Kittross and Christopher Sterling's history of United States broadcasting systems, *Stay Tuned,* and Erik Barnouw's three-volume set on the same subject only briefly mention the first recording ban, both refrain from mentioning the second ban (1948) altogether. And Lawrence Lichty's and Malachi Topping's wonderful collection of essays, *American Broadcasting,* does not refer to either strike. In many ways this should come as no surprise. Generally, the study of organized labor in American mass media has been one of the more underresearched topics in American media studies. This is partially because the American mass media systems are so often associated with the desires and activities of private enterprise. As a result, much of the scholarship surrounding the subject has engaged in understanding the business, rather than the labors, of mass media. See Barnouw (1968), Lichty and Malachi (1975), Peterson and Berger (1990), and Sterling and Kittross (1990).

3. Marsha Siefert (1994) argues that the American record industry during the

1920s recognized this fact and marketed its wares to middle-class audiences in search of an in-home, uplifted form of entertainment.

4. Aside from a few popular accounts, we have few academic accounts of the history of the jukebox as a means of musical exhibition. See Seagrave (2002) for an account of the jukebox industry that gives media scholars a firm basis to work with in order to construct numerous accounts regarding this complex machinery.

5. According to the testimony of then-FCC Commissioner Lawrence Fly, "The *musicians* [who filed these suits] urged that if a record was made for use only on home phonographs and so labeled, it could not be used for broadcasting. This contention prevailed in the Supreme Court of Pennsylvania. I cite the case *here* [sic] *Waring v. WDAS Broadcasting Station, Inc.* (194 Atl. 631). However, the United States Circuit Court of Appeals for the Second Circuit subsequently decided otherwise and certiorari was denied *RCA Manufacturing Company v. Whiteman* (114 F. 2d 86, 311 U.S. 712)." See A Resolution Authorizing an Investigation (1943).

6. Brian Priestley suggests in the liner notes of *Slim Gaillard—Laughing in Rhythm* (1994) that "Federation Blues," officially unreleased until 1994, may have been withheld for over fory-three years because Norgan (the label for which the song was initially recorded) feared that it mocked the AFM and specifically names union officials.

7. The use of shellac and its eventual replacement by man-made polymers is certainly one of the more overlooked material changes in the production of musical recordings. Shellac is a purified form of lac layered for varnishes and discs that can be etched for musical recordings. Lac itself is a natural substance that is deposited onto the twigs of trees in southern Asia by the female lac insect. Throughout the war, the availability of lac diminished as much of this region became unavailable for lac harvesting. The development of petroleum-based polymers would beget the basis for the high-fidelity, long play record. As a result, many of the problems involved in the production of shellac (i.e., any factor that could impede the harvesting of lac) could be bypassed for a more rational and predictable manufacturing process.

8. Media catalogues are, by their very nature, predictable sets of commodities. While they rarely gain the financial glories of a set of modern-day hits, their importance in American media history, as anyone who has ever followed a media text as a "re-run" knows, is undeniable. Still, as far as academic work goes, these commodities remain relatively unexplored.

9. One of the more often cited anecdotes with regard to the 1942–44 ban concerns how the ban may have accelerated the popularity of wordless vocal arrangements in pop music. According to Joseph Lanza, "The wordless chorus got a boost following James C. Petrillo's notorious American Federation of Musicians recording strike of the early 1940s. He permitted no orchestras to play, forcing choirs to replace instruments. Since vocalists were excluded from the union, they attained prominence over instrumental bands [for recording sessions]—

especially since they worked for less money. Although this may have been disastrous to big bands (which were doomed to extinction by the end of the war, anyway), the AFM strike enhanced the art of background vocals by giving many previously unheard singers exposure that they would not have gotten otherwise (1994, 115).

10. Whereas a portion of this chapter is concerned with the manner in which recorded music technologies are designed to repeat use-times, I do not want to suggest that recordings reify our experience of time. The aesthetic experience of recordings is anything but uniform. Simon Frith, in summing up Jonathan Kramer's work on music and time, has written that part of the pleasure of experiencing popular music (or all music for that matter) is that music offers "us an experience of *time passing*." Certainly, as Frith points out, confronting time, particularly our experience of time, has been a large priority for many twentieth-century composers. "Music," as Frith understands the power of its employment, construction, and reception, "enables us to experience time aesthetically, intellectually, *and* physically in new ways" (149). For a lengthier, more complete explanation of this argument, see Frith (1996).

11. Here the examples are, to say the least, numerous. Ted Turner's acquisition of MGM's film archives, for instance, has provided his media empire with enough product to continually program several television channels. Certainly one of the driving forces behind the slew of recent mergers of media industries is the desire to unify the stockpiled works with intricate means of distribution and promotion.

12. Although many record producers are given a one-time fee or are employed through a salary to a studio for their services, many big-name producers are involved in the practice of "taking points." Similar to receiving royalties, "points" are a percentage of profits resulting from record sales. Put simply, the practice of "taking points" is an economic incentive to produce a hit record. Keith Negus explains that, "in the UK, producers are contracted by record companies for specific projects. Depending on their past work and reputation, a producer can receive between one and four royalty percentage points on the sales of recordings. This percentage will be paid out of the artist's royalty earnings. In most cases involving newly-signed artists the record company will have negotiated a 'total talent royalty' which will be paid in a contract. A new act is likely to receive 12 per cent, so if they use a producer who charges two royalty points, the act will receive 10 points. Thus, if it is a five piece group, the producer's royalties on sales of an album will be equal to each band member" (Negus 1992, 83).

13. I must admit that as I write this I am thinking of the practices of the many record producers who have created large profits from pay-per-performance recordings. These stories loom large in the history of rock, rhythm and blues, reggae, jazz, and other forms of popular music. Unfortunately, many of the producers who have greatly benefited from these recording practices have achieved fame under the banner of socially progressive entrepreneurship. Their status might change swiftly if one took a more critical look at their financial practices.

14. Austin (1980) mentions that the radio industry was left relatively un-
harmed by the strike but she offers no substantial explanation why the industry
thrived. See pp. 45–46. Nevertheless, historians of American broadcasting usually agree that the boom in the industry occurred for a number of reasons, many
of which were a direct result of government policies regarding radio advertising
during the war. For a brief summary of some of these policies and their results,
see Sterling and Kittross (1990).

2. Counterreform and Resignation

1. March 21, 1973, is, according to Bob Woodward and Carl Bernstein, the
date of "the crucial meeting between Dean and the President. Discussion focuses
on ways to insure the continued silence of the burglars and those involved in
the cover-up. 'Hush money' and offers of executive clemency discussed. Later
that day, Howard Hunt's lawyer [attorney for the Watergate burglars] receives
$75,000." See Woodward and Bernstein (1976).

2. According to Russell Sanjek, "when sales were finally tabulated, 1947
proved to have exceeded 1921, the industry's previous best effort. It was a $214.4-
million year at retail; 3.4 million record players of all kinds were produced. The
Big Four issued 300 million popular and classical records, and possibly another
75 million were released by the rest of the industry" (1988, 229).

3. I am using "strategy" as a direct invocation of Michel de Certeau's use of
the term in *The Practice of Everyday Life*. For de Certeau, strategy is a particular
mode of social production that operates in relation to tactical terms of production: "Although they remain dependent upon the possibilities offered by circumstances, these tranverse *tactics* do not obey the law of the place, for they are
not defined or identified by it. In this respect, they are not any more localizable
than the technocratic (and scriptural) *strategies* that seek to create places in con-
formity with abstract models. But what distinguishes them at the same time
concerns the *types of operations* and roles of spaces: strategies are able to produce,
tabulate, and impose these spaces, when those operations take place, whereas
tactics can only use, manipulate, and divert these spaces" (1988, 29–30).

4. The practice of bootlegging as a "black market" industry is, perhaps, one
of the most understudied arenas of recorded music. Nevertheless, its importance
as a factor in legitimizing the products of major recording industries and the
process of recording in the United States should not be ignored. I mention this
simply because we need to remember that the recording industry, no matter how
much any scholar may try to represent it as unified, entails many splinters and
warring interests. For example, the citations mentioned below may only appear
as footnotes to a larger contest, but in fact *Variety* of April 7, 1948, reports that, at
the time, there were "dozens" of independent pressing plants that would print as
many as 40,000 copies of hit songs, label them, and sell them on the side to jukebox companies and small independent stores, no questions asked. "Of course,"
the article continues, "the bootlegged disks look the same as those produced

from the real owners of a master, and to avoid suspicion the thieves concentrate only on hits." For citations in *Variety* that simply mention bootlegging as a response to the AFM strike, see "Indie Cos.' 'Silent' Partners" (1947); "Major Diskers Crack Down" (1948); Woods (1948).

5. According to William Lafferty, the AFM was the leading "talent and craft" union that sought to profit from Hollywood's use of its film libraries on television. Lafferty writes, "Over the next five years, the Screen Actors Guild, the Screen Directors Guild, and the Writers Guild of America followed the musician's lead, demanding in new contracts with the major studios additional payments to their memberships on the television release of films made after August 1, 1948. If a studio failed to negotiate, the guilds could strike the studio, an economically disastrous possibility for an industry just recovering from major postwar labor disputes. The studios, though, had no incentive to negotiate with the unions for the release of pre-1948 films, as the late 1940s and early 1950s saw Hollywood begin to explore avenues by which the film industry could exploit their libraries through alternatives to television release, including pay-television schemes and theater television" (1990; 235–56; 237).

6. According to the *FCC Annual Reports* in the seven-year period from 1946 to 1952, the number of on-air AM stations grew from 961 to 2,355 while on-air FM stations ballooned from 55 to 629 (Sterling and Kittross 1990).

7. Those interested in the history of FM radio in the United States might wonder why contracts between the networks and the AFM were key for AM-FM duplication when most FM stations were nonaffiliated independents. During a congressional testimony Petrillo responded to the question on whether these independent stations had been squeezed by stating, "I can get a better deal out of the networks. They got money. These FM people got no money." Most certainly, within this discussion lies a question concerning the networks' desires and plans to own and operate these stations. ("Not Much Chance of Petrillo Pulling Musicians" 1948, 27, 30).

8. One of the more egregious examples of this reportedly occurred in Philadelphia, where anonymous independent companies cut masters with amateur string bands such as Mummer outfits, a local form of music typically played in nonprofessional situations. These companies "risked nothing except the future wrath of the [AFM] for violating the disk bans—and with non-union musicians." ("$100 Guarantee for Disking" 1948, 43).

9. On June 21, 1948, *Variety* reported that "various recording companies in New York have within the past week received concrete evidence of the dissatisfaction of some members of the [AFM] with the recording ban ordered by that body. Manufacturers have received letters from musicians who state their name and number of the AFM local of which they are members, pointing out that the men are ready and willing to record at any time in violation of the AFM's ban, and if the companies in question contemplate any recording they wish to be considered for jobs." The article goes on to note that while similar types of let-

ters had been received before, never had they included the names and numbers of their locals that would spotlight one's AFM membership. ("Musicians Say They're Willing" 1948, 1).

10. The need for adequate public relations was, by all indications, a point of much contention for the AFM that can be traced throughout many issues of *International Musician*. But during the second strike the debate was manifest in *Variety*. For instance, a June issue of *Variety* noted that "it's obvious from now on the treatment of Petrillo by the press will be a serious item on the agenda of the executive board and the prez itself," as the annual AFM convention featured a newly hired national PR director, as well as promises of affiliate access to this new department and its talents. ("AFM Taking Its Public Relations Seriously" 1948, 42). Two weeks after this announcement *Variety* carried an article recognizing that New York's AFM Local 802, in conjunction with New York City's Department of Hospitals, had launched an experimental music therapy program using monies allocated from the Transcription and Recordings Fund. ("Slice of 802's Record Fund to Finance N.Y. Musical Therapy Test" 1948, 1).

11. For a good example of correspondence between British Musician Unions and the AFM concerning why the AFM was concerned with the use of foreign broadcasts, see "Why Foreign Broadcasts Must Be Regulated" (1946, 1).

12. It is too much of a reduction to view the British strike as a sign of solidarity, no matter how forcefully the claim was made by the British Musicians Union. At the time of this pronouncement, most industry observers were of the opinion that the British Musicians Union ban was imposed for financial reasons: "Britain is and has been dollar-hungry. It's pointed out that when a band makes a background for use by a U.S. performer, or records with a U.S. singer in London, the monetary return is only to the musician working on the recording. Royalties accruing from sales, which are much larger, remain in the U.S. and no dollars go to England. On the other hand, if British vocalists and musicians cut disks for circulation in the U.S. via the London label, a subsidiary of British Decca, or via release by Victor, Columbia, M-G-M, etc., all the coin involved, except publisher royalties to the U.S. firm owning the U.S. rights, go to Britain." And, as the article noted, a good number of hit discs in the United States involved English backgrounds. ("Crackdown on British Recording" 1948, 39).

13. It should not be assumed that recording companies were willing to make this compromise simply out of generosity. Statements made about the recording industry's indifference to the Recording Fund's existence in *Variety* notwithstanding, little is known about what record companies actually thought about the first fund. For example, while *Variety* notes that one of the ostensive reasons for making a compromise with the AFM is the supposed agreeability between both parties with regard to the fund, the same article indicates that significant lobbying by the recording industry, radio, and television by Representative Fred Hartley (co-author of the Taft-Hartley Act) had also occurred. According to the article, Hartley claimed that numerous companies had brought to his attention

that Taft-Hartley had actually caused significant damage to the industry through the marked rise of "illegitimate" and foreign recording industries. ("End-of-Summer Disk Truce" 1948, 35, 41).

3. Which Voice Best Becomes the Property?

1. Indeed, it is unclear what the *inter* or *space* between the texts exactly is. This perhaps is the germ for future debate and discussions by popular music and cultural theorists. Given the need for subjects who pass from space to space for the intertext to have any cultural relevancy I would suggest that the *inter* is processional in nature. That is, there is no cultural terrain per se so much as there are *cultural passages.* In this sense, I am invoking the active connotations of passage and emphasizing its processional elements. Thus the passage of one subject from space to space may involve any number of cultural differences, some of which may be manifest in any number of experiential modes (i.e., scientific, ritual, litigious, etc.). In the case of the intertext, we need to note that these passages are all too often created by market forces. In fact, in some manner the passageways *are essential* to accessing and negotiating the marketable goods, i.e., they too, are part of the market. This is nothing more than a casual proposition, but I do think that it points to potential for specific cultural activities involving any number of texts and textual formations.

2. Feuer's particular example is *Pennies from Heaven.* The film musical from 1982 draws directly from earlier musical performances through a variety of means, one of which involves the film's lead characters lip-synching to recordings of vintage musical performances.

3. This particular concept is taken from *Difference and Repetition,* where Deleuze argues that repeated events should not be viewed as expressions of similarity in either the Platonic or Aristotelian sense, but rather as articulations of difference. For a much more involved yet concise account of Deleuze's metaphysics, see Bogue (1989) and Hardt (1993).

4. According to the same article, Samuel Goldwyn "expressed himself a bit dubious" that the figure of $340,000 was accurate. This owed in part to the telecasting rights CBS procured, for which Goldwyn had also purportedly put in a bid at "the value of $1,000,000" before he had left for Europe. ("Inside Stuff-Legit" 1956, 88).

5. Goddard Lieberson's desire to establish and maintain listening norms and standards extended even to the privacy of in-home listening activities. Simon Frith (1996) points out that in Glenn Gould's famous essay "The Prospects of Recording," Lieberson is noted as having a sense of reservation concerning the implications of in-home mixing and equalizing systems. Frith's observations are insightful in pointing to Lieberson's desire for a passive positioning of the listener. According to Lieberson, "the listener should leave his phonograph alone; if he wants to get into the picture, let him play the piano. I would like to see a standard set with phonographs whereby even the volume could not be changed.

Then you would finally have what the artist wanted. If you carried the opposite to its ultimate *[sic]*, you would end up with a printed piece of music to be played mechanically, with instructions to the customer to set his own tempo and dynamics; then everybody would be his own Beethoven interpreter." See Gould (1966).

6. We should continually remind ourselves that our cassettes and long-play records could very well be composed of great speeches or simply personal narratives. There is no a priori reason why popular music, let alone popular songs, has become the dominant aesthetic experience of the audio record. I would suggest that this simple reminder will help us better separate the issues of the record and the popular song, as well as making their interdependence that much more salient. This kind of separation will only allow us to gain a better understanding of why and how music is experienced in the present and the relative past.

7. I view the "lyrical" as a category that effectively eradicates the distinction between the words sung and the music. Despite this categorization, I view the lyric as the site where music and word intersect and coexist, thus the term's basis in a musical instrument, lyre. As a result, lyrical expression, particularly as it is based in poetic forms of language, is grounded in the belief that it is a more direct form of emotional expression. In this sense, logocentric modes of expression are mediated and mediate the melocentric mode in a manner that affects the articulation of both meaning and emotion. Thus, through the power of the lyrical, a word can become inflected, its meaning temporarily transformed.

8. I am tempted to agree with Altman. It is true that this change did involve a fundamental rearrangement of the terms of musical production. But this focus limits our understanding of music in general by limiting our perception of why and how music is generated. Given Altman's preoccupation with family units and memories of the hearth, the piano, and the collective performance, we might want to investigate how music operated to affectively unify this specific (or any) social organization. Thus playing a love song or a song of collective joy from one's favorite musical may actually have the function of bringing forth specific affective moments to re-enforce the affiliations of the group. It would seem to me that the ownership and playback of recorded musical fares may have continued the same tradition, albeit with a particularly different accent. This, I would offer, could provide a productive site for investigation and theorization and one that may shed light on how many social organizations use music in any number of settings.

4. *Listening to My* My Fair Lady

1. This form of comparative listening might actually have much in common with genetic forms of literary criticism that search through drafts in order to find the origins of a work. According to Laurent Jenny (1996) "Genetic criticism is searching for a phenomenon that is in effect unobservable, unobjectifiable: the origin of a literary work. Its object of inquiry is essentially unstable, or rather its

object of study is the very instability of the 'pre-text' (*l'avant-texte*), where explicit projects, unconscious choices, and the play between what is possible and what is dangerous are intertwined to the point of nonsense." To be sure, listeners who prize "complete" catalogues of an artist's oeuvre often search out bootlegs (both official and unofficial), b-sides, and other versions of songs that are not deemed legitimate for release on an artist's album. In other cases, when a group or artist attains a specific level of popularity their reserve catalogue of rarities and unreleased versions often finds its way into "official" and "legitimate" releases because the desire to hear this back-catalogue is too significant to ignore. It is the wish to reach "back" into an artist's recorded past in search of his or her "roots" that drives many fans to engage in what many consider to be absurd, almost quixotic quests.

2. Of course, not all mechanical reproductions are equal. The logic of mechanical rights demands that record companies and artists who depend on the exploitation of their mechanical rights actively discourage the purchase and production of "bootlegs." These illicit recordings offer no direct return in the form of royalties and saturate the market with an artist's material, thus, in the mind of the industry, limiting the demand for its "legitimate" recordings.

5. A Tale of Two Ears

1. I want to acknowledge that I am alluding to and directly drawing on Jonathan Crary's work on the development of visual techniques throughout the nineteenth century (Crary 1995). Crary argues that "some of the most pervasive means of producing 'realistic' effects in mass visual culture, such as the stereoscope, were in fact based on a radical abstraction and reconstruction of what 're-alism' means in the nineteenth century" (9). Crary is also interested in how the observer was reasserted as a primary force in visual culture in the nineteenth century. Rather than accepting the widespread "suppression of subjectivity" throughout the seventeenth and eighteenth centuries, the nineteenth century involved concepts of vision where the observer, rather than the artist, is placed in a productive role.

2. Typically, when one mentions vertical integration in United States media histories, one is invoking the pre-Paramount-decision Hollywood studio system, whereby the channels of production, distribution, and exhibition were controlled by the studio. After the 1948 decision, the studios decided to sell their theaters in accordance with the antitrust decision. To be sure, the exhibition of records happens at a number of sites, sites where the record label typically has limited control. How the record reaches the public entails a three-step industrial process. This includes the record's production, its distribution through one-stops, rack jobbers, and promotional men, and its eventual placement in retail spaces. Although this process is well understood, compared to detailed studies of the studio system, little is known regarding the details of exactly how these systems have operated now and in the past. While the paucity of work in this area owes

in some measure to evidence of corruption in the distribution of records (see, for example, Dannen 1991), little scholarship has addressed even the most prominent and "above-board" methods of distribution, such as record clubs. Many of these record clubs have existed and continue to exist as direct-to-consumer clearinghouses for a label's product. A historical investigation into attempts to control the entire process of production, distribution, and solicitation of product would reveal useful insights into how the major labels view their audiences and how they could introduce their recordings on a recurring basis.

3. This research was mainly forwarded by Alan Blumlein, whose cutting technique became the basis for the vaunted "45-45" standard for stereo discs. See Chanan (1994).

4. I have argued elsewhere (Anderson 1997) that this sort of desire had an interesting history in early American cinema.

5. Edison reportedly believed that his invention, consisting of three differing tracks recorded through three separate horns, would be helpful in recording "three-part singing or music." Yet Reid's article argues that, although "orchestral stereophony as such was not among [Edison's] objectives," this was probably because "the recording process before electronic amplification was too insensitive to pick up 'room sound.'" Indeed, while the multiplex graphaphone promised a greater intensity with regard to volume and increased tonal range, the belief that Edison foresaw stereo is, at best, nothing more than conjecture.

6. I am interested in the idea of the concrete detail as a "narratively empty" category. Indeed, the thought that the recording entails a relationship with concrete details is particularly important to understanding why so many high-fidelity narratives are constituted around a rhetoric of scientifically disinterested, objective technologies. Barthes, in *The Rustle of Language* (1989), explains the figure of the concrete detail semiotically as it "is constituted by the *direct* collusion of a referent and a signifier; the signified is expelled from the sign, and with it, of course, the possibility of developing a *form of the signified*, i.e. narrative structure itself." High fidelity's stake in rhetorically defining its techniques as outside the province of narrative structures is one that aims to permit its products to define themselves as objective frameworks rather than biased registers.

7. I do not intend to explain or even list the varieties of realism. I hope the reader understands that all theories and methods of realistic rendering require a definition of the "real." It is on each so-called real that every method of realism is based. Thus Marxist critics have typically argued that the "real" in capitalist societies is a system of economic injustice that is hidden under the veils of numerous ideological justifications. Yet, even so, the call for the revelation of the "real" has tended, among Marxists critics, to typically split into two aesthetic camps. These two forms advocate socialist realism, best discerned in the writings of George Lukacs, and other, more avant-garde forms that emphasize techniques of distantiation to create a dialectical theater that would expose the social and economic bases of capitalism. It is true that many critics would deny that the latter has little to do with realism, but nevertheless its techniques have the intent

of revealing a "realer reality," a reality that is hidden and continues to be hidden with reference to day-to-day existence.

8. The issue of the recorded event is always an issue of temporal seizure and eventual encounter. Briefly, the recording and playback of any recording is a particular temporal arrangement that is always in a dialogue with a specific idea of what can occur in an "actual" performance. Each dialogue is particular to the aesthetic and ideological components involved, and each discussion may produce specific musical and audio decisions. These may result in a variety of products, from couching a "live recording" with a musical aspect that was actually unperformed at the moment of the event to simply retreating to a studio to produce records that have no desire to refer to any one event. For example, in rock genres of popular music the key to producing even the most elaborately assembled record is to make it sound as if it is happening in "real" time. Thus the nonlinear, "cut-and-paste" systems of in-studio, multitrack rock productions aim to create records that, no matter how edited and inclusive of numerous performances, sound like singular "performances that *actually happened*" (Gracyk 1996, 40). Certainly, the operative words are "actually happened." The idea that a recording should have the feel of a captured rather than staged event may be one of many aesthetic aims of rock as a genre. But this aesthetic desire exists among other forms of music that are recorded, to be sure.

9. One of the reasons that I am interested in Gracyk's assertions about rock music is his interest in rock's past as a receptacle that contains a detailed aesthetic component centered on the recording and recording processes. Indeed, Gracyk maintains that rock music is invested in investigating and upholding a tremendous aesthetic investment in the recording process. This is most evident "in the realm of ontology, in *what* a musical work *is* in rock music as opposed to what it is, for instance in jazz or country or folk. . . . In rock the musical work is less typically a song than an arrangement of recorded sounds" (40). As controversial as this may be, I would like to suggest that much of the writing concerned with rock music history supports this assertion, if only indirectly. That is, we tend to think of rock's aesthetic past in terms of a lineage of specific sounds (e.g., the "Memphis" sound, the "California" sound, the "Steve Lillywhite" or "Don Gehman" drum sound, Tom Scholtz's guitar distortion, the difference between a Les Paul and a Stratocaster and the musical genres that use them, etc.) and recorded objects such as "great" albums and singles. It is a point that I feel is of significant importance, one that can help us better define and methodologically develop future investigations of popular music and sound.

10. While national and international charts may confirm rock's dominance as a genre, they give only a partial picture. Although popular music histories consist primarily of accounts of artists and genres, there is a lack of long-term historical investigations that research the development of local music scenes and reception. Robert Pruter's work on Chicago soul production (1991) stands out as one of the few quality academic accounts of a local music history. One encouraging development in recent years has been the publication of a number of

sociological investigations of local scenes, such as Barry Shanks's documentation of the rock scene in Austin, Texas (1994) and Ruth Finnegan's work on the popular music scene in Milton Keynes, UK (1989). Also hopeful is Robert Gordon's less academic and more popular history of Memphis's popular music past from the postwar period to the present (1995). The trait that brings these works together is that each author traces out a long-term, complex counterculture of odd alliances and local strategies, whereas studies seem to isolate coterminous trends in popular music, whether they be national or international.

11. By no means do I wish to obscure the importance of understanding high fidelity's masculine appeal, for it is of great importance to understanding the technology's cultural appeal in a postwar, North American context. In the United States, returning veterans, who had been exposed to the great technologies of the war and were now attending American universities on the GI Bill, were influential in drawing attention to the place of science in culture. These movements would assist in generating a widespread amateur interest in high fidelity unseen before or since. This was specifically the case for many middle- and upper-middle-class men in the 1950s and 1960s who, as Keir Keightley has effectively argued (1996), embraced an interest in all things hi-fi, including electronic paraphernalia such as Heathkits and transistor boards. According to Keightley, this new interest in technology along with record collecting existed as a combined "means of escaping [the] feminine mass mediocrity" known as television (154). In order to preserve a sense of masculine self and individual identity in the wake of television, much of the high fidelity vs. television debate centered on the typical gendering of tastes along the binaristic equation of "masculine = individual-artistic-expression = high" against "feminine = mass-entertainment = low" (156). And, to be sure, one could add the binarism of "hard sciences = engineering = masculine" vs. "domestic sciences = homekeeping = feminine" to the equation as well.

12. These interests could be found in a number of organizations ranging from book and record clubs, film houses, and clubs specializing in foreign cinema and revivals to as well as more television programming such as live, dramatic genres typified by *Kraft Theater* and *Playhouse 90* and the "post–quiz show scandal" production of documentaries such as *See It Now*.

13. The following passage from Jim Dorling's review of Varèse's reissue of Command Records important 1959 release, "Persuasive Percussion," furnishes an adequate depiction of some of the more interesting contradictions of lounge revivalism. It is clear that as it separates itself from a rock aesthetic of producing and appreciating "serious artistic statements," Lounge revivalists have quite a bit in common with those more "rock"-influenced subcultures that traditionally honor "ardent honesty," "integrity," and self-enfranchisement: "Lounge revivalists expend a lot of effort juggling two contradictory beliefs: that conspicuous consumption leads to a healthy economy and plentiful sex, and if you know where to shop you can live it up on a shoestring. In last summer's issue of the zine *Organ & Bongos*, a D. Hume reports getting into 'The 2nd Annual Tiki Mug

Party' for a dollar instead of six by bringing his own mug, and a lounge singer, Joey Altruda, dubs the sunken living room of his rented apartment 'The Ski Lodge.' Sometimes the make-believe affluence is funny, possibly even subversive, but just as often it seems to be a cover for frustrated desires to be rich.

In the 50s, men blamed marriage for their inability to move up the economic ladder; in the 90s, lounge revivalists are single and can't muster the commitment to blame corporate greed for their misfortune. What they attack instead, in zines, books, and liner notes, is political correctness. "'There is the movement of p.c.: Second hand smoke causes cancer, people drink too much, eat too much fat. And this is a reaction to all that,' says bachelor-pad guru Irwin Chusid in the *Austin American-Statesman*. 'We're going to drink and light up. Maybe we'll drink too much coffee, drink martinis. Instead of jeans and flannels, we're gonna be fashionable. We're gonna do our hair instead of looking like a slob'" (Dorling 1997, 36–37).

14. I would like to draw from a technical definition of noise here: "Noise can be defined as any unwanted sound which is not related to the wanted sound (if it is related, it is called distortion), and this definition suffices for most uses; but in electronics, noise is specifically defined as a more or less wideband addition to a signal by any electronic or mechanical component" (White 1987, 220).

15. I am not arguing that the collective appreciation of the audience in concert halls does not occur. To be sure, while the concert hall does allow for moments of collective appreciation to be vocalized, these moments are allowed only at specific moments. In most cases these include the beginning and end of the performance and/or the conclusion of a specific musical selection. Unlike the music hall, where critical and comical commentary by a mass audience can take place at any moment during performances, the concert hall is managed in such a manner that this type of activity is quickly and quietly hushed. The concert hall houses collected individuals who work to ensure that any individual's ability to hear is pronounced throughout the space. The management of the music hall, on the other hand, engenders and allows that the presence of a collected audience is felt throughout by the audience and performers alike at the expense of an "individual's" appreciation of the performance only.

16. According to Ross, "Production as nightmare: the repressed world of labor has, it seems, reached a qualitatively new level of invisibility in [a number of postwar, French] novels. Like the new Citroen at the *Salon de l'automobile* analyzed by Barthes in *Mythologies* whose fetishized perfection is attributed to its erasure of any noticeable joints or riveting-together of panels—its seemlessness, in short—tangible signs of fabrication or effort constitute the obscene in this object world" (147). Lynn Spigel makes a similar argument, asserting that postwar America attempted to live in a vision of a bourgeois "Antiseptic Electrical Space" that assisted in the creation of a suburban space that would house the "young, upwardly mobile middle class family": "Although [this] was never totally successful, the antiseptic model of space was the reigning aesthetic at the heart of the postwar suburb. Not coincidentally, it had also been central to utopian ideals

for electronic communications since the mid-1800s. As James Carey and John Quirk have shown, American intellectuals of the nineteenth century foresaw an *'electrical revolution'* in which the grime and *noise* of industrialization would be purified through electrical power. Through their ability to merge remote spaces, electrical communications like the telegraph would add to such a sanitized environment by allowing people to occupy faraway places while remaining in familiar and safe locales" (Spigel 1992, 100; emphasis added). To be sure, the rise of FM, high-fidelity sound reproduction, and "good music" programming during the fifteen-year period immediately following World War II occurred in conjunction with the rise of the suburban middle class who would help forge a middlebrow appreciation for the longhair culture that included broadcasting.

17. According to Corbett, "Various scholars have recently charted the construction of the concept of music as an autonomous sphere of creation. The lineage that produced this conception, persistent in Western musicology, emanates from a precapitalist period in which music making was divided between those musicians outside the aristocratic system (ritual) and those fully under the ownership of the courts, whose production was dictated by them. Subsequently, money entered the scene, serving as a wedge that separated art from its social production. Standardization and widespread dissemination of music notation, coupled with new laws governing copyrights, enabled a valorization of the absolute value of music itself, apart from any material considerations. Musicology, as it now exists, remains a classical mode of analysis bound up in the defense of this independence, in the assertion of music as access to the 'absolute,' as timeless and apolitical. The situation of 'art music' within the academic institution has served to reinforce this supposed autonomy—simultaneously allowing for the individualization and transcendence of music theory. Unencumbered by the social, political, or technological, Western art-music is seen to exist in a vacuous, theoretical space—the contemplative ether of the 'great works'" (40–41).

18. It is tempting to overemphasize the relatively short history of audiophilic technologies and their association with classic pieces from the Western musical canon. To be sure, canonization can and does occur in every genre of popular music. One need look no further than the rise of a "rock" canon of so-called essential recordings to understand this. In fact, though it is true that "classical" music did view classical music audiences as its initial targets, one might argue that substantially more profits and impact have issued from the sale of the "classic" pop catalogue on the compact disc format. One commonly cited statistic regarding the music industry's 1996 fiscal year is the fact that the Beatles moved more units in 1996 than they had in any other previous year and were the best-selling artists for the entire industry during the same period. This success is no doubt attributed to the much-hyped release of the Beatles' three two-disc anthologies. Still, it would be safe to say that these were not the only factors involved in this success. I would argue that the processes of critical and commercial canonization, processes too difficult to explain here, have kept these properties as strong and as flexible as ever.

19. Although I do not examine this material change in this book, I would suggest that it does deserve considerable research and examination. While vinyl is an artificial polymer based on petroleum products, shellac is a natural substance that is created by the female lac insect of Southeast Asia. The insect secretes the lac onto the trees it inhabits and the resin is then harvested. During World War II these supplies were cut off from the Allies. It is not clear precisely when vinylite began to be used for recordings. According to Russel Sanjek, vinylite had been developed by wartime, though virgin quantities were never available since the substance was being rationed for "waterproofing raincoats and other materials." As Sanjek points out, "The transcription companies made do with stock on hand. Because Vinylite was 95 percent salvageable, customers had to return one Vinylite disk for each new one" (Sanjek 1988, 220).

In another account, Michael Chanan notes that the idea of making records from plastic had existed from at least 1909, when Edison had attempted to coat cylinders with plastic with the assistance of Jonas Aylesworth. RCA experimented with using thermo-plastic to cover metal transcriptions in the 1930s, but it was CBS's research during wartime that, according to Chanan, allowed an entire record to be produced out of plastics. Vinylite's postwar appearance as the common substance in the production of LP and 7-inch records in the United States subsequently became a sign of the country's economic dominance and ultramodern condition during this period. Chanan writes, "The result improved considerably on the long-play transcription discs of ten years earlier. Vinyl enabled the size of the groove to be dramatically reduced, with a reduction in surface noise coming from an improved signal-to-noise ratio and at the same time an enhancement in the recorded signal, thus allowing more music to be recorded on a disc the same size as before but revolving more slowly and producing a better sound" (1995, 93).

20. The American discovery of a quality magnetic taping process was one of the many consequences of the Allies' defeat of the Axis forces. The player and recorder was developed by Germany's Allgemeinische Elektrische Gesellschaft and the plastic tape by a subsidiary of Siemens, BASF, in the 1930s. According to Russel Sanjek, magnetic tape appeared to many Americans as an almost immediate postwar technological spoil: "[Magnetic tape recording and reproducing systems were] first revealed to American civilians by the head of the Russians' Radio Berlin in September 1945. He showed a group of visiting radio executives a bulky captured German Magnetophone, whose fourteen-inch reels reproduced symphonic works on magnetic tape with such fidelity of sound they could not be distinguished from the real thing. They were far superior to any commercial disk or the best electrical transcription known in the United States" (1995, 221). No doubt the combination of the machine's excellence and the sudden and exciting nature of the find must have engendered the material of and processes surrounding magnetic tape with a specific aura of conquest, progress, and liberation for those who were interested in recorded sound and who had participated in wartime efforts.

21. Debates concerning authenticity are some of the more difficult, divisive discussions in popular music today. These debates address technological components, but they also embrace legal issues and ongoing deliberations regarding subcultural musical expression and appropriation, particularly those concerned with race. While my work underscores technological questions of authenticity, it is unclear to me whether one can separate a good portion of this period's obsession with recordings as "authentic representations" from other cultural affairs. This matter would probably involve another large-scale study.

22. Though it varies from person to person, this is generally thought to be those frequencies between 20Hz and 15KHz.

23. Questions of spectatorship are wide and varied throughout film studies; I will certainly not try to document them in this chapter. For an interesting account of these debates, see Judith Mayne, *Cinema and Spectatorship* (1993).

24. One of the historical associations between film and high-fidelity sound is that between the somewhat coterminous rise of widescreen/3-D projection techniques and stereophonic sound. This is especially true when one compares some of the techniques of stereophony and stereoscopic film. Despite their etymological roots and popular perception as palpably exploitative technologies whose fame reached its greatest peaks in the 1950s, the two are involved with widely dissimilar aesthetic agenda and economic scenarios. As William Paul points out, "By its institutionalization [as an institutionally embraced technique between 1952 and 1954] 3-D offered a challenge to the dominance of the 'classical' style, an adjective David Bordwell justifies using for Hollywood cinema because the word suggests '. . . notions of decorum, proportion, formal harmony, respect for tradition, mimesis, self-effacing craftsmanship, and cool control of the perceiver's response . . .'.

In fact, 3-D might represent something of an atavism, a return to what Tom Gunning and Andre Gaudreault have designated the 'cinema of attractions' for films of the primitive period, films in which fascination of the image as image supersedes the demands of the narrative. Gunning has described the 'cinema of attractions' as promoting 'exhibitionist confrontation rather than diegetic absorption,' an opposition, my argument will make clear, that is equally relevant to the contrast between 3-D and the classical style" (1993, 321–22).

Alongside Paul's aesthetic points is a reference to the economic and industrial condition of post–Paramount-decision Hollywood that is essential to most narratives that account for the 1950s rise of widescreen technologies. For Paul, it is these two positions, an aesthetic framework of agendas and oppositions and an industrial crisis, that are the primary forces behind the rise of a mainstream acceptance of 3-D, stereoscopic cinema. One of the main points of this section, and my study in general, is that the changing conditions in musical production and recording had encountered a new set of never-before-encountered industrial positions and aesthetic possibilities. I would argue that this moment of technological encounter was much like that of visual culture's encounter with motion picture technologies in the late nineteenth century. As such, this period in music industry history exists as a site for rapid industrial change and stylistic experimentation. To compare the two is to compare a well-established style and mode of production with an industry that had neither when it came to utilizing its newfound technologies. Thus the story of stereophonic techniques becomes a story of aesthetic debate about new aesthetic possibilities, rather than, as is the case with Hollywood's postwar interest in an aberrational film style, a narrative of aesthetic trial and the subsequent subordinance of such experimentation.

25. Though by no means is the following list of books, chapters, and essay collections close to being comprehensive, it does point to an active and intelligent interest in film sound aesthetics: Belton and Weis (1985); Bordwell et al. (1985); Altman (1992); Chion (1994); Lastra (1995).

26. The temptation to examine this record as a general advertisement for new aesthetic materials is great. Not only are RCA Victor and Breck tied up in pushing products of modern beauty (stereo and improved hair care merchandise) but the Alcoa Company is mentioned on the record cover for providing the golden aluminum foil on which the record jacket is printed. "As bright and new as 'Living Stereo,'" claims the Alcoa Wrap plug in the bottom right-hand corner of the cover. In fact, although it was not the rule, this sort of record as tie-in was not uncommon. In an interview with record collector and pop-culture fan Candi Strecker, she presents a "commercial/functional" record produced by Columbia's Special Products division in conjunction with Gold Bond Ceiling and titled *Sound Off . . . Softly*. Describing the record, Strecker says, "It features the usual suspects (such as Ray Conniff, Andre Kostelanetz and Percy Faith), but I bought it for the packaging concept. The cover shows a woman putting a record on a turntable; it's photographed from below so that half of the photo is the acoustical tiled ceiling. Also, it's an 'infinite recursion' photo: the woman is holding the album cover which shows her holding the album cover, *ad infinitum*" (Juno and Vale 1994, 90–91).

27. As far as I know, there has never been any published scholarship detailing the evolution and purpose of commercially produced demonstration discs, largely for reasons of the minor position these records hold in the history of recorded music. For the most part, demonstration records do not pretend to exert even the slightest artistic impression. Rather than being conceived and executed by a singular artistic unit, the demonstration record typically represents a label's vision, a vision typically conceived as a commercial rather than a solely aesthetic expression. Therefore, these products are considered to hold little aesthetic merit or worth beyond their novelty. Yet it strikes me that these records are nothing more than aesthetic expressions: each demonstrates a "novel" sensation, an improvement that the listener can, on comparison to older reproduction methods, immediately appreciate. As such, demonstration records italicize aesthetic methods and possibilities, rather than subordinating these techniques to service music or musical performances as a form of spatial relief.

It is clear that by 1959 the stereo demonstration had become something of a routine in both the industrial and artistic sense. For example, it was common for the stereo demonstration record to include not only musical but also sonic curiosities involving elements of travel, science, and art. As variety became a catchword to sell the new medium, this trope soon appeared as simply an element of the genre. Perhaps this is best confirmed by the emergence of records such as RCA Victor's *Bob and Ray Throw a Stereo Spectacular* (Goulding and Elliot 1958). With a great assortment of stereo samplers to draw from, the well-known national radio comedy duo were able to find the conventional elements of the genre such as an opening thunderclap and still create a parody that mixed "riotous comedy, terrifyingly realistic sounds, and brilliant musical content" (Smith 1959, 41, 45). Indeed, after the stereo demonstration record had lost its industrial utility, many in-studio comedy records adopted the presentation of sonic varieties as a formal necessity. I grant this is a large leap to make, but as the comedy record begins to gain an industrial foothold throughout the 1960s and 1970s, artists such as Spike Jones, Stan Freberg, Peter Sellers, and Vaughn Meader, and comedy troops such as the Firesign Theater, National Lampoon, and Monty Python's Flying Circus gain widespread success as their records become more elaborate audio productions in terms of aesthetics and engineering.

28. Martin Bookspan's critique is aimed at RCA Victor's rerelease of a 1954 recording of Charles Munch conducting the Boston Symphony in a performance of Berlioz' *Symphonie Fantastique* (RCA Victor LM 1900). Although Bookspan admits that Munch's version is good, he points out that it was recorded "on the stage" rather than from the seats of the hall and "some of [Munch's] incredible vitality and spontaneity [are] a bit vitiated": "However, there is not another recording of the *Fantastic* that can touch this one of kinetic energy and drive. RCA Victor's recorded sound is close-to and clear, but there's not much richness or warmth to it, even in the stereo [modified] version. The RCA engineers have learned a good deal about recording in Boston's Symphony Hall since November, 1954. They now rip up the seats from the main auditorium floor and seat the orchestra right in the middle of the hall, rather than on the stage, much as the English Decca engineers have been doing in London's Kingsway Hall for years. Clearly, RCA Victor now has a moral obligation to Munch and the Boston Symphony Orchestra to sit them down in the middle of Symphony Hall as soon as possible and have them re-record the *Fantastic Symphony* in a performance truly representative of everybody concerned at their best" (34).

29. The phrase "easy listening"—a term that in the United States serves as a rather loose designator for a genre of typically pre-rock instrumental music—is most often avoided by mainstream popular music critics for a number of reasons. The most obvious is that the term has been used to categorize a large portion of the very music that so many rock, jazz, and classical music critics have spent much of their time ignoring, assaulting, or both. Joseph Lanza points out that the phrase has "uncertain origins" and that, although it gained popularity in the mid-1970s when many so-called beautiful music stations began to refer to "easy listening," the expression was "already being used as a Top 40 chart hit category in *Billboard* magazine to designate light instrumentals and vocals—anything from

Paul Mauriat's 'Love Is Blue' to the Lettermen's 'Our Winter Love' (Lanza 2004, 128–29). Yet the term, despite its use as a generic label, might be better read as an indication of a wish for a specific type of modern listening experience. As I indicate in this chapter, "easy listening" was a boon granted the general public by the advances of science and technical artistry. Thus we need to further investigate how listeners and producers believed that the listening process would be "eased" if we wish to understand this historical period of musical production and reception.

6. Space, the Pliable Frontier

1. Reverb's excessive ubiquity in popular music during this period is perhaps best confirmed in Stan Freberg's satiric remake of Elvis Presley's "Heartbreak Hotel" record. Best known for his 1961 comedy record, *Stan Freberg Presents the United States of America*, Freberg enjoyed something of a successful recording career throughout the late 1950s as he mocked artists such as Lawrence Welk and ridiculed musical fads and genres such as calypso and "Christmas music." The Tommy Durden/Mae Boren Axton song was released by RCA in January 1956 and became Presley's first national hit. Freberg's parody of Presley's hit was produced only a few weeks after the original "Heartbreak Hotel" reached number one on the charts. Its comedic punchline was organized around Presley's sound, rather than a clever reworking of the lyrics or musical arrangement. While Presley's voice on his record is saturated in reverb, Freberg's version plays up the melodramatic aspect of the effect by simply adding even more reverb and echo to the vocals. The disc's timely satire acts as a humorous unveiling of early rock and roll's already-generic reliance on studio tricks. See Demento (1995), 4–5.

2. Of course the "so-called 'exotic' sound" could be directly traced to Denny's 1957 release of *Exotica*, an LP which included his most famous song, "Quiet Village," and featured "bird calls, jungle sounds and little-known percussion instruments behind [a more standard quartet of] piano, vibes, bass and drums" (Vale and Juno 1993, 142). Selling close to 400,000 copies, *Exotica* propelled Denny to a thirty-seven-LP career (not including reissues) and by 1959 he claimed *Billboard*'s "most promising group of the year" as voted nationally by professional disc jockeys.

3. It would be hard to deny that the sound of the Aluminum Dome was a celebrated attraction for record buyers. Promoting their recordings of Arthur Lyman's *Taboo* and *Bwana'a*, a High Fidelity Recordings advertisement mentioned that they were recorded in the dome ("Now! The Most," p. 79). It was not uncommon to find the structure prominently mentioned on those records recorded within it. Take, for example, Rick Ward's liner notes for *Hawaiian Village Nights* (1958), a stereophonic record featuring the famous Hawaiian vocalist Alfred Apaka. Ward writes, "The recording herein was made in the unique Kaiser Aluminum Dome at the Hawaiian Village Hotel, Waikiki. The first structure

of its kind ever built, the Dome is constructed of diamond-shaped aluminum panels and geometrically arranged and bolted together, requiring no interior support." Of the two pictures that appear on the back of the LP, one is a photo of a large crowd prominently seated in the dome, with the dome's ceiling covering half of the frame.

4. It should be noted that Jones's attention to detail was not simply an effect of high-fidelity technologies. While it is the case that the general public memory of Jones is that of an odd comedic figure, his work as a detail-obsessed musician and record producer has only begun to gain a measure of the critical attention commensurate with the commercial popularity it once commanded. A popular musician with an immense popularity throughout the 1950s, Jones was renowned as a stern perfectionist, which endured him to other "straight" musicians of all varieties. As Cub Koda writes in the liner notes to 1994's *The Spike Jones Anthology,* "Though he often downplayed his musical versatility and achievements (all part of the master plan of selling the idea to the general public), the fact remains that Spike was a strict bandleader and taskmaster, expecting that his musicians were precision-tight, adept in a variety of musical styles from Dixieland to classical, and displaying a level of musicianship several notches higher than most big bands of the day who played so-called 'straight' music" (3–4). This combination of public appeal and musicianship meant that when Jones's group dismantled a composition, the composer could claim a "badge of honor" because his or her work had truly tasted success (see in liner notes, Demento 1995, 3–4).

5. In 1990 the Smithsonian Institution accepted Martha and Emory Cook's donation of the *Cook Laboratories* and *Sounds of Our Times* catalogues, including control of their master tapes and papers. Both record companies produced close to 140 titles from 1952 to 1966 and included European and American concert music, popular music from the Caribbean and the United States, and records including mechanical and natural sounds.

6. Bennett also cites the American example of the Chicago Midway, the popular fair zone of the 1893 Columbia Exposition, as spatial margin where the stress between knowledge and spectacle was particularly noticeable. Of course, this specific tradition in America includes the curiosities of Barnum and Ripley as well as the "showman scientists" Edison and Marconi. In each case palpable tensions are produced. But it is precisely this tension that acts as a margin, an edge that simultaneously cuts through and connects the "objective aims" of science with huckster elements typically associated with the entertainment industry (Bennet 1995, 5).

7. Cook's belief in the duty of a recording engineer is perhaps best evidenced in a *High Fidelity* interview with John M. Conly, wherein he goes to great lengths in distinguishing his job from that of the interpretive artist: "I have a theory that most recording engineers are frustrated musicians. They want to put themselves into the records they make, from behind a forest of microphones and a 17-channel mixer, to 'create' something they can later identify and say 'This is me!'

"It is better to resign yourself to having missed the boat. You're not an artist; you're a craftsman, a documentor, and that's all. The channel should add nothing to the content" (Conly 1954, 49).

8. According to Jacobs's article, Moses Asch took a unique interest in the production and distribution of "specialty" records that found a middlebrow acceptance, thereby distinguishing these objects from novelty and gimmick records. Asch asserted that the "people who buy these records of sounds are individuals that read books. They are mostly professional people, in the upper-middle class, and home-owners." Explaining how he decided whether or not a record would become pressed, Asch noted that "we don't issue a record because it's odd. It has to make sense. Then people will be interested. Folkways is a documentor. We believe that sound has more truth than sight. But our records aren't test records. They are records that people buy for either their work or a hobby." Thus the label issued recordings such as frog and railroad sounds, as well as aural representations of unique spaces such as New York City and South American jungles. In fact, according to Asch, Folkways' recording of the South American jungle was so accurate that at least one professor from the Museum of Natural History, listening repeatedly to the recording before a trip to Peru, claimed, on his arrival, an uncanny feeling of homecoming (Jacobs 1958).

9. The category of attractions draws directly from Tom Gunning's and Andre Gaudreault's development of the term "cinema of attractions" as an analytical category through which early film history can be researched and understood (Gunning 1990). In one sense, this category operates by giving prenarrative cinema a variety of historical frameworks that do not restrict us to a teleological understanding of film as inherently disposed to narrative structure. In fact, as an operating category, early cinema is then framed as a specific assemblage of heterogeneic possibilities. As possibilities, these aesthetic and industrial modes of film have gone through historical moments of closure and employment. I would hope that historical visions of popular music and sound recordings could involve a similar tension between the "musical" demands and the desire for audio spectaculars. To be sure, these categories are not completely stable: the definitions of spectacular and musical sounds are social and vary between genres, audiences, and historical periods.

Indeed, Gunning's emphasis on the aesthetic display rather than the storytelling process is not made to establish a system of strict binarisms. Rather, his point is "not that there are no narrative films before the nickelodeon era but rather that attractions most frequently provide the dominant for film during this period and often jockey for prominence until 1908 or so (and even occasionally later). The desire to display may interact with the desire to tell a story, and part of the challenge of early film analysis lies in tracing the interaction of attractions and narrative organization" (Gunning 1993, 4). This is also a challenge for scholars who are interested in the development of recording aesthetics. These histories need to move to a variety of directions that involve a critical focus on the cultural and material processes that have a purchase on the recorded object.

10. The clearest expression of these negotiations in popular music recordings arrives at the moment when the recording producer and engineer are chosen. In the case of major label artists, this choice is often made through a bargaining process. As in all bargaining scenarios, positions of power and economic imperatives play the dominant roles in determining who can be considered. Thus artists are often required to work with specific producers by recording labels who are searching for a specific "hit sound." The idea of a "hit sound" should not be simply cast aside as pop artifice. The very fact that a specific form of artifice can be identified as "popular" or the sonic signature of a particular producer begs a number of social, industrial, and aesthetic questions. Indeed, the idea of a signature sound, whether it be Rudy Van Gelder's Blue Note "reverb" or a Steve Albini drum kit, comes close to articulating a nascent form of auteur theory for recorded sound. As a specific analytic challenge, closely analyzing an exceptional producer's aesthetic output vis-à-vis the generic output of his day could provide us with a better understanding of recording conventions. More importantly, this type of work could provide scholars with a new set of analytical questions about recorded music production in general.

11. The equalizing unit is a device designed to split up, amplify, or diminish specific portions of the sonic spectrum.

12. The most recent line of thought that I am invoking is the resurgent interest in Bataille's measure and activities in the Surrealist project, particularly his term *informe*. This term is best articulated by Rosalind Krauss: "For Bataille, *informe* was the category that would allow all categories to be unthought. His entry for it in the serialized "Dictionary" that was published in *Documents* likened it to *crachat*, "spittle," noxious.

"Bataille's measure and activities in the Surrealist project differed markedly from the dominant vision of the Surrealist project that focuses on Breton's search for a higher order of experience through shocking scenarios and an embrace of Freudian insights. Unlike Breton, Bataille placed his attention on a Surrealist project that would dissolve the categories that organize our perception of base materials. In contradistinction to Breton, Bataille's interest in base materials is meant to constrain. Allergic to the notion of definitions, then, Bataille does not give *informe* meaning; rather, he posits for it a job: to undo formal categories, to deny that each thing has its 'proper' form, to imagine meaning as gone shapeless, as though it were a spider or an earthworm crushed underfoot. This notion of the *informe* does not propose a higher, more transcendent meaning through a dialectical movement of thought. The boundaries of terms are not imagined by Bataille as transcended, but merely as transgressed or broken, producing formlessness through deliquescence, putrification, decay" (Krauss 1985, 64–65).

It is not clear to me if Bataille's notion of the *informe* can be applied to all audio maneuvers that somehow reconfigure the sonic categories and definitions. Yet I wish to invoke this association if only to frame the *operative* portion of both the *informe* and high-fidelity processes. In this sense, I want to, à la Krauss's and Yve-Alain Bois's recent work on the *informe* and modern visual culture (1997), highlight audio processes and find those moments where slippages between audio categories take place. While these slippages may include moments of audio transformations, negotiations in generic expectations, or reconsiderations of what is signal and noise (music and cacophony), I believe that this will always be most profitable at sites of material mediation. To be sure, this can happen at the level of architecture, instrumentation, and performance, but the recording, the site where biases find their most immediate (and influential) effects, also necessitates a subtle and historically configured consideration. Without it any number of sonic decisions and musical possibilities can remain unnoticed, cloaked under a naive realism that obscures recording conventions and the prejudices that they underline and support.

13. In my eyes, there is no better prescription for this problem than more historical research into how the many players and producers of this period begin to envision what a recording can be. Again, as I argued at the beginning of this chapter and throughout this study, sound-recording technologies are contained and enabled by a heterogeneity of social and technical frames. This is as true for musicians and engineers as it is for audiences and archivists, and in each debate these differences are rendered through aesthetic and archival means. The research possibilities are abundant and could include studies of genre, auteur, and label-recording aesthetics.

14. As an aside, I think it is interesting to note that for some writers it was precisely the hypersensational aspect of stereo that distinguished it from other forms of mass media as the ideal site for concert music. Even the excitement of a live television broadcast or the finest motion picture rendition of a symphony orchestra could not compare to a good stereo system, since, in the opinion of one writer, both media, through the use of visual techniques, tended to distract the listener from the music ("Eye and Ear Story" 1960, 41).

15. I simply want to note that, as a term, "hyperreality" is something of a postmodern juggernaut. As such, the use of the term had something of a critical trendiness throughout the 1980s and 1990s that all too often placed a shorthand understanding of something to be "more-than-real" rather than focusing on the particular processes that are specific to each simulation. I am not here to criticize the notion of hyperreality by demanding that scholars provide better accounts of the actual, the "real." Rather, I would only point out that while invoking the postmodern theory of thinkers such as Baudrillard or Eco to explain the simulations and hyperreal phenomena we encounter is useful, it is no substitute for uncovering and discerning the detailed processes of each particular curiosity. In my own work, particularly this chapter, I have found both Eco's and Baudrillard's thoughts on the hyperreal and simulation extraordinarily helpful. See Baudrillard (1983) and Eco (1986).

16. To be sure, perhaps the most astute criticism regarding the modern listener

comes from Adorno on just this fact. For Adorno, the machinery that makes the mass distribution of products for consumption rather than actual aesthetic pleasures has created a form of music that emphasizes musical tricks, most prominently the figure of the leitmotif, that act as sensual fetishes and a form of listening that is "regressive": "The counterpart to the fetishism of music is a regression of listening. This does not mean a relapse of the individual listener into an earlier phase of his own development, nor a decline in the collective general level, since the millions who are reached musically for the first time by today's mass communications cannot be compared with the audience of the past. Rather, it is contemporary listening which has regressed, arrested at the infantile stage. Not only do the listening subjects lose, along with freedom of choice and responsibility, the capacity for conscious perception of music, which was from time immemorial confined to a narrow group, but they stubbornly reject the possibility of such perception. They fluctuate between comprehensive forgetting and sudden dives into recognition. They listen atomistically and dissociate what they hear, but precisely in this dissociation they develop certain capacities which accord less with the concepts of traditional esthetics than with those of football or motoring" (1982, 286).

While Adorno's critique may feel a tad overly strident to the modern listener, it is interesting that the high-fidelity movement developed within it a similar critique of the casual listener. The solution, as well as the root of each criticism, varied significantly. For Adorno, music has not simply been affected by its mass distribution but substantially changed to accompany the desires of an audience where "deconcentration" is the main perceptual activity when it comes to mass music (288). Adorno's solution, of course, is to hope for a progressive art that leaves behind the road of repetition and similarity and into a new plain of possibilities that force the listener to develop a more mature form of attention. For Adorno, it is in the discordant work of Webern, Mahler, and Schoenberg where form is given "to that anxiety, that terror, that insight into the catastrophic situation" that can only be avoided by regressing, the very act that the music will not allow the listener to perform (298–99).

17. Again, I am drawing on the work of Jonathan Crary, particularly his interest in the stereoscope as a nineteenth-century optical technology. As Crary argues, "The stereoscope as a means of representation was inherently *obscene*, in the most literal sense. It shattered the *scenic* relationship between viewer and object that was intrinsic to the fundamentally theatrical setup of the camera obscura. The very functioning of the stereoscope depended, as indicated above, on the visual priority of the object closest to the viewer and on the absence of any mediation between eye and image. It was a fulfillment of what Walter Benjamin saw as central in the visual culture of modernity: "Day by day the need becomes greater to take possession of the object—from the closest proximity—in an image and the reproduction of the image" (Crary 1995, 127).

WORKS CITED

Publications

"1,700 Songs Submitted to One Firm, Indicating Hectic Disking Pre-Ban." 1947. *Variety*, November 12, 1, 62.

"$100 Guarantee for Disking by 45-Piece Units?" 1948. *Variety*, March 10, 43.

Adorno, Theodor. 1982. "On the Fetish-Character in Music and the Regression of Listening." In *The Essential Frankfurt School Reader*, ed. A. Arato and E. Gebhardt, 270–99. New York: Continuum Publishing.

———. 1990. "Opera and the Long-Playing Record." *October*, 63–66.

———. 1994. "The Curves of the Needle." In *The Weimar Republic Sourcebook*, ed. E. Dimenberg, A. Kaes, and M. Jay, 605–7. Berkeley: University of California Press.

"AFM in Burn at British Musicians." 1948. *Variety*, June 16, 35.

"AFM Taking its Public Relations Seriously as Leyshon Goes into Action." 1948. *Variety*, June 16, 42.

"A.F. of L. Convention Unanimously Endorses Federation's Record Fight: The A.F. of L. Convention at Toronto, Canada, on October 8, 1942, Passed the Following Resolution which was Recommended by Their Executive Council." 1942. *International Musician*, October, 1.

"A.F. of M. Prohibits Making Recordings: President Petrillo Sets July 31st as Dead-line for Members to Make Recordings and Transcriptions." 1942. *International Musician*, July, 1.

"Album Reviews." 1956. *Variety*, July 11, 42.

Alden, Robert. 1964. "Dozen for a Filmed 'Fair Lady.'" *New York Times*, October 25, 1964, 23–24.

"All-Industry Group Set for Publicity Tilt vs. Petrillo; Burnett, Kaye Named." 1947. *Variety*, December 31, 21.

Alpert, Hollis. 1964. "SR Goes to the Movies: No Argument with Success." *Saturday Review*, November 14, 40–41.

Altman, Rick. 1987. *The American Film Musical*. Bloomington: Indiana University Press.

———. 1992. "Afterword: A Baker's Dozen of New Terms for Sound Analysis." In *Sound Theory, Sound Practice*, ed. Rick Altman, 249–53. New York: Routledge.

———. ed. 1992. *Sound Theory, Sound Practice*. New York, Routledge.

"America's Fastest Selling Records Breaking Big in All Markets." 1956. *Billboard*, April 29, 51.

"America's Hottest Band with the Hits from *My Fair Lady*." 1956. *Billboard*, May 5, 31.

"And Now, Stereo." 1957. *Time*, July 8, 48.

Anderson, Tim (1997). "Reforming 'Jackass Music': The Problematic Aesthetics of Early American Film Music Accompaniment." *Cinema Journal* 37, no. 1: 3–22.

Archer, Eugene. 1964. "Audrey the Fair Scales the Summit." *New York Times*, X9.

"As the Editors See It: The Second Wave of Stereo." 1958. *High Fidelity*, September, 39.

Attali, Jacques. 1985. *Noise: The Political Economy of Music*. Minneapolis: University of Minnesota Press.

Austin, Mary. 1978. "Petrillo's War." *Journal of Popular Culture* 12, no. 1: 11–18.

———. 1980. *The American Federation of Musician's Recording Ban, 1942–1944, and its Effect on Radio Broadcasts in the United States*. Denton: North Texas State University.

"Balderdash for People with Two Ears." 1959. *High Fidelity*, June, 41.

Ball, J. 1960. "The Witch Doctor in Your Living Room." *HiFi & Stereo Review*, March, 63–65.

Bangs, Lester. 1988. *Psychotic Reactions and Carburetor Dung*. New York: Vintage Books.

Barnouw, Erik. 1968. *The Golden Web: A History of American Broadcasting in the United States*. New York: Oxford University Press.

Barthes, Roland. 1972. *Mythologies*. New York: Hill and Wang.

———. 1975. *S/Z: An Essay*. New York: Hill and Wang.

———. 1989. *The Rustle of Language*. Berkeley: University of California Press.

Baudrillard, Jean. 1983. *Simulations*. New York: Semiotext(e).

Bazin, Andre. 1967. *What Is Cinema?* Berkeley: University of California Press.

Beautiful Hair Breck Introduces the RCA-Victor New Golden Age of Sound Album. 1959. New York: RCA-Victor.

Belton, John, and Elisabeth Weis, eds. 1985. *Film Sound: Theory and Practice*. New York: Columbia University Press.

Benjamin, Walter. 1968. "Art in the Age of Mechanical Reproduction." In *Illuminations*. New York: Schocken Books.

———. 1968. *Illuminations*. New York: Schocken Books.

Bennett, Tony. 1995. *The Birth of the Museum*. New York: Routledge.

"Bet on Roulette's 'Fair Ladies'." 1964. *Billboard*, October 31, 14.

Blacking, John. 1977. "Some Problems of Theory and Method in the Study of Musical Change." *Yearbook of the International Folk Music Council* 9: 1–26.

Bodec, B. 1948. "Disk Jockey Due for Sustained Run as Commercial Force in Local Radio." *Variety*, January 7, 92.

Bogue, Ronald. 1989. *Deleuze and Guattari*. New York: Routledge.

Bookspan, Martin. 1959. "Rates the Basic Repertoire: Berlioz' Fantastic Symphony." *HiFi Review*, October, 33–34.

Bordwell, David. 1985. *Narration and the Fiction Film*. Madison: University of Wisconsin Press.

Bordwell, David, Janet Staiger, and Kristin Thompson. 1985. *The Classical Hollywood Cinema: Film Style and Mode of Production to 1960*. New York: Columbia University Press.

Bourdieu, Pierre. 1984. *Distinction: A Social Critique of the Judgment of Taste*. Cambridge, Mass.: Harvard University Press.

"British Musicians Back A.F. of M. Recording Ban." 1943. *The International Musician*, March, 1.

Burstein, Howard. 1957. "Going Stereo." *High Fidelity*, November, 53–55, 156–58, 160.

———. 1960. "How to Explain Stereo to Your Friends." *High Fidelity*, January, 52–54, 123.

Cage, John. 1991. "For More New Sounds." In *John Cage: An Anthology*, ed. R. Kostelanetz, 64–66. New York: Da Capo.

Campbell, John W. 1953. "Hearing Is Believing?" *High Fidelity*, July–August, 27–28, 96, 98, 102.

Canby, Edward Tatnall. 1958. *High Fidelity and the Music Lover*. New York: Harper and Brothers.

———. 1961. "Stereo for the Man Who Hates Stereo." *High Fidelity*, September, 48–50, 134.

———. 1963. "Taping FM Stereo." *High Fidelity*, August, 45–47, 110.

"Capitol Stereo Records Capture the Full Spectrum of Sound." 1958. *High Fidelity*, October, 71.

Cerf, Bennet. 1956. "Trade Winds." *Saturday Review*, May 5, 5.

Chanan, Michael. 1994. *Musica Practica: The Social Practice of Western Music from Gregorian Chant to Postmodernism*. New York: Verso.

———. 1995. *Repeated Takes: A Short History of Recording and Its Effects on Music*. New York: Verso.

"Charges Petrillo Attacks Freedom: Arnold Tells Senators Musician's Head Uses Coercion on Industry and Individuals." 1942. *New York Times*, September 22, 1942, 24.

Chernoff, John M. 1979. *African Rhythm and African Sensibility: Aesthetics and Social Action in African Musical Idioms*. Chicago: University of Chicago Press.

"[Chicago] Indie Diskers Scurry after Talent to Head Disk Ban." 1947. *Variety*, November 5, 24.

Chicago Recorded Music Workgroup. 1993. "What Are We Listening To? What Are We Talking About? Recorded Sound as an Object of Interdisciplinary Study." *Stanford Humanities Review* 3, no. 2: 171–74.

Chion, Michel. 1994. *Audio-Vision: Sound on Screen*. New York: Columbia University Press.

"Cinema: Still the Fairest One of All." 1964. *Time,* October 30, 106.

Cohen, A. B. 1954. "Reflections on Having Two Ears." *High Fidelity,* August, 28–31, 78, 80, 83.

"Col's 'Fair Lady' Set in Hot Col Getaway with 100,000 Advance." 1956. *Variety,* April 4, 43.

Conly, John M. 1954. "Adventurers in Sound: Brahms, Thunderheads, and Cachalot Courtship." *High Fidelity,* October, 49–51, 128, 130, 132.

Cook, Emory. 1952. "Binaural Disks." *High Fidelity,* November–December, 33–35.

Corbett, John. 1994. *Extended Play: Sounding Off from John Cage to Dr. Funkenstein.* Durham, N.C.: Duke University Press.

"Crackdown on British Recording May Veer Yanks More to Mexico." 1948. *Variety,* September 1, 39.

Crary, Jonathan. 1995. *Techniques of the Observer: On Vision and Modernity in the Nineteenth Century.* Cambridge, Mass.: MIT Press.

Crosby, Alfred W. 1997. *The Measure of Reality: Quantification and Western Society, 1250–1600.* New York: Cambridge University Press.

Crowther, Bosley. 1964. "Welcoming Two Fair Ladies." *New York Times,* October 25, 1964, X, 9X.

Cunningham, J. C., and R. O. Jordan. 1956. *Sound in the Round: An Astounding Introduction to Stereophonic Recording.* Wilmette, Ill.: Concertapes.

Dannen, Frederic. 1991. *Hit Men: Power Brokers and Fast Money inside the Music Business.* New York: Vintage Books.

de Certeau, Michel. 1988. *The Practice of Everyday Life.* Berkeley: University of California Press.

"Decca Plans Flock of British Discs." 1948. *Variety,* August 11, 42.

Demento, Dr. 1995. *Dr. Demento 25th Anniversary Collection: More of the Greatest Novelty Records of All Time.* Los Angeles, Rhino Records.

"Designed for Music in the Modern Manner." 1959. *High Fidelity,* January, 40–44.

"Disk Biz 20% over Prewar: Upped Costs Cut Slump-Jump Net." 1948. *Variety,* August 18, 83.

"Disk Business in 3 Words: Original Cast Albums." 1962. *Variety,* January 10, 187.

"Diskeries Putting Showtime Albums into Assorted Grooves—Jazz, Pop, Etc." 1956. *Variety,* December 12, 55.

"Disk-Film Tie-Ups Promote Mutual, Hefty, Dog-Day Hypo." 1956. *Billboard,* August 18, 38, 40.

"Disk Firms Steam as Artists Seek to Fatten Up on Waxers for AFM Ban." 1947. *Variety,* November 5, 1.

"Disk Yen for Legit Scores Started with 'Fair Lady,' Livingston & Evans." 1958. *Variety,* February 5, 57.

"Diskers Mull Assn. to Hammer Buying Theme." 1947. *Variety,* November 26, 46.

"Diskers' Petrillo 'Insurance'—Talent Gambling to Protect B.O." 1947. *Variety,* November 26, 1.

Doane, Mary Ann. 1985. "The Voice in the Cinema: The Articulation of Body and Space." In *Film Sound: Theory and Practice*, ed. J. Belton and E. Weis, 162–76. New York: Columbia University Press.

Dorling, Jim. 1997. "Single-Minded: Enoch Light, Persuasive Percussion (Varese Vintage)." *Chicago Reader*. Chicago: 36–37.

"Double Scoop! Two Sensational Discs for Summer Sales!" 1956. *Billboard*, June 23, 31.

Eco, Umberto. 1986. *Travels in Hyper Reality*. New York: Harcourt Brace.

"Eddie Corners the Hit Market Singing." 1956. *Billboard*, May 26, 49.

Eddy, Chuck. 1991. *Stairway to Hell : The 500 Best Heavy Metal Albums in the Universe*. New York: Harmony Books.

Editorial. 1942. *Chicago Daily Tribune*, August, 5, 1942, 14.

"Editorial Comment: Lest Ivory Tower Tempt." 1947. *International Musician*, February, 13.

Ehrenstein, David. 2000. DVD liner notes to *Pygmalion*. Criterion.

Eisenberg, Evan. 1988. *The Recording Angel: The Experience of Music from Aristotle to Zappa*. New York: Penguin.

Eisenman, D. P. 1963. "Room Acoustics for Stereo." *High Fidelity*, February, 50–53, 125.

Elsaesser, Thomas. 1981. "Vincente Minnelli." In *Genre: The Musical*, ed. R. Altman, 8–27. Boston: Routledge and Kegan Paul.

"End-of-Summer Disk Truce: Petrillo Meets with Recorders." 1948. *Variety*, July 14, 35, 41.

Ennis, Phillip. 1992. *The Seventh Stream: The Emergence of Rocknroll in American Popular Music*. Hanover, N.H.: Wesleyan University Press.

"The Excitement Is about to Begin." 1964. *Billboard*, September 26, 17.

"Eye and Ear Story." 1960. *High Fidelity*, October, 41.

"'Fair Lady' a Palpable Hit, 16 Records in the Making." 1956. *Billboard*, March 24, 19.

"'Fair Lady' Album Off to Hot Start." 1956. *Billboard*, April 7, 22.

"'Fair Lady' in Stereo Come London Preem." 1957. *Variety*, April 23, 47.

"'Fair Lady' Score Nixed in N.Z. Till Show Bows." 1958. *Variety*, April 23, 47.

"'Fair Lady' Tops 300,000 in Store Sales; Club Extra." 1956. *Variety*, July 25, 107.

Faith, Percy. 1956. *Percy Faith Plays Music from the Broadway Production My Fair Lady*. Columbia Records.

Fantel, Hans. 1959. "Private and Panoramic: Modern Headsets 'Personalize' Listening in Full Stereo Dimensions." *HiFi Review*, August, 36–37.

———. 1959. "Satellites for Stereo." *HiFi Review*, December, 58–62.

———. 1960. "Enhance Your Mono with Pseudo-Stereo: New Gadgets Simulate Stereo from a Single-Channel Source." *HiFi Review*, January, 46–48.

Feld, Steven. 1982. *Sound and Sentiment: Birds, Weeping, Poetics, and Sound in Kaluli Expression*. Philadelphia: University of Pennsylvania Press.

———. 1994. "Communication, Music, and Speech about Music." In *Music Grooves*, ed. S. Feld and C. Keil, 77–95. Chicago: University of Chicago Press.

Feld, Steven, and Charles Keil, eds. 1994. *Music Grooves.* Chicago: University of Chicago Press.

Ferrell, Oliver P. 1958. "The Flip Side." *HiFi Review,* October, 55–56.

———. 1959. "The Flip Side." *HiFi Review,* September, 116.

———. 1960. "The Flip Side." *HiFi and Stereo Review,* April, 98.

Feuer, Jane. 1993. *The Hollywood Musical.* Bloomington: Indiana University Press.

"Film Reviews: My Fair Lady." 1964. *Variety,* October 28, 6.

Finnegan, Ruth. 1989. *The Hidden Musicians.* Cambridge: Cambridge University Press.

"First Plan for the Expenditure of the Recording and Transcription Fund." 1947. *The International Musician,* February, 5.

First Session Pursuant to House Resolution 111. 1947. *Special Subcommittee of the Committee on Education and Labor.* Washington, D.C.: U.S. Government Printing Office.

Fiske, John. 1987. *Television Culture.* New York: Routledge.

"For the Information of the Members." 1947. *The International Musician,* November, 5.

Fowler, Charles. 1953. "Hi-Fi for Two Ears." *High Fidelity,* January–February, 46–48, 108–9.

Freas, R. 1960. "The Coming Breakthrough in Tape: An Exclusive Interview with Dr. Peter Goldmark on the Home Music System of 1970." *High Fidelity,* March, 46–47, 122.

Frey, Sidney. 1960. *Sound Effects, Volume 1.* New York: Audio Fidelity.

———. 1960. *Sound Effects, Volume 2.* New York: Audio Fidelity.

Frith, Simon. 1981. *Sound Effects: Youth, Leisure, and the Politics of Rock'n'Roll.* New York: Pantheon.

———. 1988a. *Music for Pleasure: Essays in the Sociology of Pop.* New York: Pantheon.

———. 1988b. "Picking Up the Pieces." In *Facing the Music.* New York: Pantheon.

———. ed. 1989. *World Music, Politics, and Social Change.* Manchester: Manchester University Press.

———. 1993. "Music and Morality." In *Music and Copyright.* Edinburgh: Edinburgh University Press.

———. 1996. *Performing Rites: On the Value of Popular Music.* Cambridge, Mass.: Harvard University Press.

Gaillard, Slim. 1994. *Slim Gaillard—Laughing in Rhythm: The Best of the Verve Years.* New York. Polygram Records.

Gaines, Jane M. 1991. *Contested Culture: The Image, the Voice, and the Law.* Chapel Hill: University of North Carolina Press.

Ganzert, Charles F. 1992. "Platter Chatter and the Pancake Impresarios: The Re-invention of Radio in the Age of Television, 1946–1959." Ph.D. diss., Ohio University.

Garner, L. E. 1958. "Adding Channel Two." *High Fidelity,* November, 47–49, 146, 148–51.

Gehman, J. M. 1942. "Letter to the Editor: Curb for Labor Dictators." *New York Times,* August 12, 1942, 18.

Gelatt, Roland. 1977. *The Fabulous Phonograph, 1877–1977.* New York: Macmillan.

Giles, Dennis. 1981. "Show-Making." In *Genre: The Musical,* ed. R. Altman, 14–25. Boston: Routledge and Kegan Paul.

Goodwin, Andrew. 1992. *Dancing in the Distraction Factory: Music, Television, and Popular Culture.* Minneapolis: University of Minnesota Press.

"Gordon MacRae's 'Fair Lady' Medley Unfair to Show, Levin Squawks." 1956. *Variety,* August 8, 1, 49.

Gordon, Robert. 1995. *It Came from Memphis.* Boston: Faber and Faber.

Gorman, R. 1960. "The Sound of Ambiophony." *High Fidelity,* December, 42–44, 125–26.

Gould, Glenn. 1966. "The Prospects of Recording." *High Fidelity,* April, 46–63.

———. 1987. *The Glenn Gould Reader.* London: Faber.

Goulding, Ray, and Bob Elliot. 1958. *Bob and Ray Throw a Stereo Spectacular.* New York, RCA Victor.

Gracyk, Theodore. 1996. *Rhythm and Noise: An Aesthetics of Rock.* Durham, N.C.: Duke University Press.

Grevatt, R. 1956. "Spinner of Records Also Spirals Sales on Sponsors' Goods: Many Factors Point to Disk Jockey Rise as a Top Mover of Products." *Billboard,* November 10, 1.

Grimes, W. 1994. "In 'My Fair Lady,' Audrey Hepburn Is Singing at Last." *New York Times,* August 15, 1994, 9, 12.

Gross, M. 1964. "It Looks Loverly for 'Fair Lady' Again." *Billboard,* September 5, 1.

Guattari, Félix. 1995. *Chaosmosis: An Ethico-Aesthetic Paradigm.* Bloomington: Indiana University Press.

Gunning, Tom. 1990. "The Cinema of Attractions: Early Cinema, Its Spectator, and the Avant Garde." In *Early Cinema: Space Frame Narrative,* ed. T. Elsaesser, 56–62. London: BFI.

———. 1993. "'Now You See It, Now You Don't': The Temporality of the Cinema of Attractions." *Velvet Light Trap* 32: 3–12.

———. 1995. "'Animated Pictures,' Tales of Cinema's Forgotten Future." *Michigan Quarterly Review* 34, no. 4: 465–85.

Handzo, Stephen. 1985. "Appendix: A Narrative Glossary of Film Sound Technology." In *Film Sound: Theory and Practice,* ed. J. Belton and E. Weis, 383–426. New York: Columbia University Press.

Haralovich, Mary Beth. 1993. "Sit-Coms and Suburbs: Positioning the 1950s Homemaker." In *Private Screenings: Television and the Female Consumer,* ed. L. Spigel and D. Mann, 111–41. Minneapolis: University of Minnesota Press.

Hardt, Michael. 1993. *Gilles Deleuze: An Apprenticeship in Philosophy.* Minneapolis: University of Minnesota Press.

Hartung, Phillip T. 1964. "The Screen: Mirror, Mirror on the Wall." *Commonweal,* November 13, 238–39.

"Hear Everything There Is to Hear with Knapp Total Sound." 1958. *High Fidelity,* October, 91.

Heidegger, Martin. 1977. *The Question concerning Technology and Other Essays.* New York: Harper and Row.

"High Fidelity Ill Defined." 1963. *High Fidelity,* February, 45.

Hinton, J. 1953. "In One Ear." *High Fidelity,* September–October, 49, 148–49, 153.

Holt, J. Gordon. 1956. "The Haunted Loudspeaker." *High Fidelity,* March, 47.

Hornby, Nick. 1995. *High Fidelity,* New York: Riverhead Books.

"Indie Cos.' 'Silent' Partners—Hit Platters Bootlegged." 1947. *Variety,* December 3, 39.

"Inside Stuff-Legit." 1956. *Variety,* September 19, 88.

"Installation of the Month: Hi-Fi Hideaway." 1961. *HiFi & Stereo Review,* January, 46.

"Is 'My Fair Lady' a Fair or Unfair Game for Parody?" 1957. *Variety,* March 20, 1, 76.

Ivey, William. 1982. "Commercialization and Tradition in the Nashville Sound." In *Folk Music and Modern Sound,* ed. W. Ferris, 129–38. Jackson: University Press of Mississippi.

Jacobs, F. 1958. "Tweet, Klunk, Whoop: A Round-Up of Recorded Noises—Odd and Otherwise." *High Fidelity,* September, 32–35, 64.

Jarrett, Michael. 1998. *Sound Tracks: A Musical ABC.* Vols. 1–3. Philadelphia: Temple University Press.

Jenkins, Henry. 1992. *Textual Poachers: Television Fans and Participatory Culture.* New York: Routledge.

Jenny, Laurent. 1996. "Genetic Criticism and Its Myths." *Yale French Studies* 89: 9–25.

"Jockeys Ride Herd on Disk-Buyers; Poll Shows No. 1 Consumer Influence." 1948. *Variety,* May 19, 1.

Jones, Spike. 1957. *Dinner Music for People Who Aren't Very Hungry: Spike Jones Demonstrates Your Hi-Fi.* Los Angeles: MGM Verve.

———. 1959. *Spike Jones in Hi-Fi.* Los Angeles, Warner Bros. Records.

Jones, Steve. 1992. *Rock Formation: Music, Technology, and Mass Communication.* Newbury Park, Calif.: Sage Publications.

Juno, Andrea, and V. Vale, eds. 1994. *Incredibly Strange Music.* Vol. 2. San Francisco: RE/Search Publications.

Keightley, Keir. 1996. "'Turn It Down!' She Shrieked: Gender, Domestic Space, and High Fidelity, 1948–1959." *Popular Music* 152: 149–77.

Kennedy, Michael. 1980. *The Concise Oxford Dictionary of Music.* New York: Oxford University Press.

Kraft, James P. 1996. *Stage to Studio: Musicians and the Sound Revolution, 1890–1950.* Baltimore: Johns Hopkins University Press.

Krauss, Rosalind E. 1985. "Corpus Delecti." In *L'Amour fou: Photography and Surrealism,* ed. R. E. Krauss, J. Livingston, and D. Ades, 55–112. New York: Abbeville Press.

Krauss, Rosalind E., and Yves Alain Bois. 1997. *Formless: A User's Guide*. Cambridge, Mass.: MIT Press.

Kruse, Holly. 1993. "Early Audio Technology and Domestic Space." *Stanford Humanities Review* 3, no. 2: 1–14.

Kutler, Stanley I., ed. 1997. *Abuse of Power: The New Nixon Tapes*. New York: Free Press.

"'Lady' Disk $$ Astronomical." 1956. *Billboard*, May 26, 12.

Lafferty, William. 1990. "Feature Films on Prime-Time Television." In *Hollywood in the Age of Television*, ed. T. Balio, 235–56. Cambridge, Mass.: Unwyn Hyman.

Lanza, Joseph. 1994. *Elevator Music: A Surreal History of Muzak, Easy-Listening, and Other Moodsong*. Revised and expanded ed. Ann Arbor: University of Michigan Press, 2004.

Las Vegas Grind, Part 1. 1995. Crypt Records.

Las Vegas Grind, Part 2. 1995. Crypt Records.

Lastra, James. 1995. "Standards and Practices: Aesthetic Norm and Technological Innovation in the American Cinema." In *The Studio System*, ed. J. Staiger, 200–225. New Brunswick, N.J.: Rutgers University Press.

Lavely, J. H. 1954. "Collecting Jazz: About Discophiles, Their Records, and Starting a Collection of Their Own." *Playboy*, September, 12.

Lears, Jackson. 1989. "A Matter of Taste: Corporate Cultural Hegemony in a Mass-Consumption Society." In *Recasting America: Culture and Politics in the Age of the Cold War*, ed. L. May, 38–57. Chicago: University of Chicago Press.

Leiter, Robert D. 1953. *The Musicians and Petrillo*. New York: Bookmans Associates.

Lerner, Alan J. 1956. *My Fair Lady: A Musical Play in Two Acts*. New York: Coward-McCann.

———. 1994. *The Street Where I Live*. New York: Da Capo Press.

Lerner, Alan J., and Frederick Loewe. 1959. *My Fair Lady*. New York.

"Lerner-Loewe vs. Jubilee Label on 'Lady' Lampoons." 1957. *Variety*, July 17, 43.

"Let's Talk Stereo." 1958. *High Fidelity*, September, 67.

"Liberace, 'Lady' and Truncated Trot at Aussie Troc." 1958. *Variety*, March 12, 2, 18.

Lichty, Lawrence W., and Malachi C. Topping, eds. 1975. *American Broadcasting: A Source Book on the History of Radio and Television*. New York: Hastings House.

Lipsitz, George. 1993. "The Meaning of Memory: Family, Class, and Ethnicity in Early Network Television Programs." In *Private Screenings: Television and the Female Consumer*, ed. L. Spigel and D. Mann, 71–208. Minneapolis: University of Minnesota Press.

———. 1994. *Rainbow at Midnight: Labor and Culture in the 1940s*. Urbana: University of Illinois Press.

M**r, P. 1963. "Confessions of an Illicit Tape Recordist." *High Fidelity*, August, 38–40, 109, 110.

"M-G-M Makes 1st Disk since AFM Ban." 1948. *Variety*, July 21, 41.

"Major Companies Ditching Many Pre-Ban Masters, Despite Coin Loss." 1948. *Variety*, April 7, 42.

"Major Diskers Crack Down on Coast Bootlegging of Hit Recordings." 1948. *Variety*, April 7, 42.

Malm, Krister, and Roger Wallis. 1984. *Big Sounds from Small Peoples: The Music Industry in Small Countries*. New York: Routledge.

Malone, Bill C. 1985. *Country Music, U.S.A.* Austin: University of Texas Press.

"The Man behind Command." 1962. *High Fidelity*, August, 74–75.

"Many Musicians Offer Bootleg Aid in Recording Ban." 1947. *Variety*, April 7, 47.

Marre, Jeremy, and Hannah Charlton. 1985. *Beats of the Heart: Popular Music of the World*. London: Pluto Press.

Marvin, Carolyn. 1988. *When Old Technologies Were New: Thinking about Electric Communication in the Late Nineteenth Century*. New York: Oxford University Press.

Mayne, Judith. 1993. *Cinema and Spectatorship*. New York: Routledge.

McCarthy, Anna. 1995. "'The Front Row Is Reserved for Scotch Drinkers': Early Television's Tavern Audience." *Cinema Journal* 34, no. 4: 321–55.

Meehan, Eileen. 1991. "'Holy Commodity Fetish Batman!': The Political Economy of a Commercial Intertext." In *The Many Lives of the Batman: Critical Approaches to a Superhero and His Media*, ed. R. Pearson and W. Uricchio, 47–65. New York: Routledge.

"Meetings with Film Industry." 1944. *The International Musician*, May, 1.

"Mercury to Put Accent on Disk Jockey Platters." 1948. *Variety*, July 28, 91.

Metz, Christian. 1985. "Aural Objects." In *Film Sound: Theory and Practice*, ed. E. Weis and J. Belton, 154–61. New York: Columbia University Press.

"Mex Diskers Eye Hop in U.S. Exports; Aussie Tooters Back Petrillo." 1948. *Variety*, January 21, 39.

Meyer, Leonard B. 1996. *Style and Music: Theory, History, and Ideology*. Chicago: University of Chicago Press.

Millard, Andre. 1995. *America on Record: A History of Recorded Sound*. New York: Cambridge University Press.

Miller, Edwin. 1964. "Love Letter to Eliza." *Seventeen*, September, 194–95.

"More Than Just Re-Issues . . . the Arista Masters." 1996. *Pulse*, October, 65.

Morley, David. 1992. *Television, Audiences, and Cultural Studies*. New York: Routledge.

"Movies: Audrey for Julie; Julie for Emily." 1964. *Newsweek*, November 2, 96–97.

"Mr. Petrillo's Hopeless War." 1942. *Nation*, October 3, 291–93.

Mugglestone, Lynda. 1993. "Shaw, Subjective Inequality, and the Social Meanings of Language In Pygmalion." *Review of English Studies New Series* 44 (175): 373–85.

"Music: Noise Merchant." 1961. *Time*, May 19, 87.

"Music on the Air." 1951. *High Fidelity*, Summer, 15–16.

"Music Puzzler: Sheets Off, Disks Big." 1948. *Variety*. March 17, 1.

"Music Swirls around You." 1958. *High Fidelity*. November, 87.

"Music Union Cornered: D of J Suit Seen as K.O. Wallop; Saves $$ for Radio." 1942. *Billboard*, August 1, 1.

"Musicians Say They're Willing to Record Even in the Face of Petrillo Ban." 1948. *Variety*, January 21, 1.

"'My Fair Lady' Authors' Blast Unfair to the Art of Radio Jingles." 1956. *Variety*, October 31, 1, 20.

"'My Fair Lady' Has No Sense of Disk Humor." 1957. *Variety*, May 15, 1, 69.

"'My Fair Lady's' Dream Comes True." 1964. *Look*, February 25, 60–64.

Negus, Keith. 1992. *Producing Pop: Culture and Conflict in the Popular Music Industry*. London: Edward Arnold.

"New Horizons in Sound." 1956. *High Fidelity*, June, inside cover.

"New Music-Record Feature: Chart of Disking Activity Is Unique Pubber Service." 1952. *Billboard*, March 22, 1, 15.

Nixon, Richard. 1990. *RN: The Memoirs of Richard Nixon*. 1978. Repr. New York: Simon and Schuster.

"No Disk Jockey Left Unturned in 'Fair Lady' Tour." 1957. *Variety*, February 27, 43, 50.

"No Parallel in Other Crafts: Royalties on Records Based on Unique Situation." 1945. *International Musician*, April, 1.

"No Pic Deal in Sight for 'Lady,' Sez Lerner." 1956. *Variety*, July 25, 121.

"Norelco Loudspeakers: Attention All Two-Eared Music Lovers." 1958. *High Fidelity*, November, 146.

"Not Much Chance of Petrillo Pulling Musicians, Despite No New Pact; FM Duplication Looks Set to Ride." 1948. *Variety*, January 28, 27, 30.

"Noted with Interest: Stereo." 1957. *High Fidelity*, December, 16.

"Obituary: James Caesar Petrillo." 1984. *Time*, November 5, 80.

"Omaha AFM Bans Guest Maestros from Disk Shows." 1948. *Variety*, February 4, 46.

Osborne, C. L. 1962. "As High Fidelity Sees It: Opera's Stereo Spectaculars." *High Fidelity*, November, 43.

"O'Seas Pubs Nix Airing of 'Fair Lady' on AFN but Album Sells Hot." 1956. *Variety*, December 19, 51.

Oulahan, Richard. 1964. "Movie Review: It Wasn't Only 'Iggins What Done Me Wrong." *Life*, November 20, 10.

Padway, Joseph. 1947. "The Supreme Court's Limited Decision on the Lea Act." *International Musician*, July, 5.

Paley, William S. 1979. *As It Happened: A Memoir*. New York: Doubleday.

Paul, William. 1993. "The Aesthetics of Emergence." *Film History* 5, 321–55.

Peary, Danny. 1981. *Cult Movies: The Classics, the Sleepers, the Weird, and the Wonderful*. New York: Dell.

"Peggy Lee Nixes British Backings." 1948. *Variety*, June 23, 35.

Peterson, Richard, and David Berger. 1990. "Cycles in Symbol Production: The Case of Popular Music." In *On Record: Rock, Pop, and the Written Word*, ed. S. Frith and A. Goodwin, 140–59. New York: Pantheon.

"Petrillo as a Case Study." 1942. *New York Times*, August 5, 1942, 18.

"Petrillo Cartoons." 1944. *International Musician*, February, 17.

Petrillo, James C. 1944a. "For the First Time the Federation Succeeds in Procuring a Written Contract with Film Industry." *International Musician,* 1.

———. 1944b. "Synopsis of Entire Recording Controversy." *International Musician,* 1.

"Petrillo Opens AFM Convention under Pall of Gloom; Foresees Rough Union Road; Continues Ban." 1948. *Variety,* June 9, 39, 44.

"Polydor 'Ideal Cast' Tag for 'MFL' LP Irks Philips." 1962. *Variety,* May 2, 65.

"Pop Music's Global Vistas." 1956. *Billboard,* June 23, 1.

"Pre-Disk Ban Hustle Setting Up Current Headache for Recorders." 1948. *Variety,* March 28, 42.

"Profit Pick of the Month! 4 Hits from Broadway's Biggest Show." 1956. *Billboard,* May 26, 22.

Pruter, Robert. 1991. *Chicago Soul.* Chicago: University of Illinois Press.

"Public Continues Old-Song Happy as A.K. Tunes Pile Up the Clover." 1948. *Variety,* February 4, 1, 44.

"Pubs Sing 'Wrong Recording Blues' When Surprise Hit Tunes Pop Up." 1948. *Variety,* April 14, 1, 53.

"Radio's Petrillo-less Format: Webs Prepare If Musicians Vamp." 1947. *Variety,* December 17, 1.

Read, Oliver, and Walter L. Welch. 1977. *From Tin Foil to Stereo: The Evolution of the Phonograph.* Indianapolis, Ind.: Howard Sams.

"Records: Woofers and Tweeters." 1959. *Newsweek,* August 17, 78, 80.

Reid, Herbert. 1959. "Stereo in the Gay Nineties: Edison's Three-Channel Cylinder System Stirred No Bustle." *High Fidelity,* 61 (November 1959).

"Release Protest Highlights Growth of Disk-Pic Tie Ups; Shapiro-Bernstein, Vol. Pic Beef Gets Immediate Action from RCA." 1956. *Billboard,* March 24, 19.

A Resolution Authorizing an Investigation of the Action of the American Federation of Musicians in Denying Its Members the Right to Play or Contract for Recordings for Other Forms of Mechanical Reproduction of Music. 1943. *Subcommittee of the Committee on Interstate Commerce.* Washington, D.C.: U.S. Government Printing Office.

Rosen, G. 1948. "Radio-Television 'Sister Act': Map Duplication of Top Programming." *Variety,* February 11, 1, 55.

Ross, Kristin. 1995. *Fast Cars, Clean Bodies: Decolonization of the Reordering of French Culture.* Cambridge, Mass.: MIT Press.

Rubin, Joyce Shelley. 1992. *The Making of Middlebrow Culture.* Chapel Hill: University of North Carolina Press.

Salzman, Eric. 1959. "Towards the Stereophonic Orchestra." *High Fidelity,* October, 48–51, 160, 162–64.

Sanjek, Russell. 1983. *From Print to Plastic: Publishing and Promoting America's Popular Music (1900–1980).* Brooklyn: Institute for Studies in American Music, Conservatory of Music, Brooklyn College of the City University of New York.

———. 1988. *American Popular Music and Its Business: The First Four Hundred Years,* Volume 3, From 1900–1984. New York: Oxford University Press.

Schmich, Mary. 1989. "Taped Tunes Put Musicians on Picket Lines in Vegas." *Chicago Tribune*. August 21, 5.

Seagrave, Kerry. 2002. *Jukeboxes: An American Social History*. Jefferson, N.C., McFarland.

"See $5,000,000 as Jackpot on 'Lady' Labels." 1956. *Variety*, May 23, 1.

Seltzer, George. 1989. *Music Matters: The Performer and the American Federation of Musicians*. Metuchen, N.J.: Scarecrow Press.

"Serve Platter, Sans Gimmick." 1952. *Billboard*, June 7, 16.

Shank, Barry. 1994. *Dissonant Identities: The Rock 'n' Roll Scene in Austin, Texas*. Hanover, N.H.: Wesleyan University Press.

Shaw, Bernard. 1963. *Pygmalion*. Baltimore: Penguin Books.

"Sheet Slump Blamed on Gimmick Disks, Floods." 1952. *Billboard*, May 31, 18.

Siefert, Marsha. 1994. "The Audience at Home: The Early Recording Industry and the Marketing of Musical Taste." In *Audiencemaking: How the Media Create the Audience*, ed. J. S. Ettema and D. C. Whitney, 186–214. Thousand Oaks, Calif.: Sage Publications.

Silverberg, R. 1961. "The Return of the Vanished Mono." *High Fidelity*, December, 50–52, 119–21.

Sinclair, Charles. 1962. "The Fine Art of Stereomanship." *HiFi & Stereo Review*, May, 43–46.

"'Singling Out' the Showtunes." 1956. *Variety*, December 5, 57, 64.

"Slice of 802's Record Fund to Finance N.Y. Musical Therapy Test." 1948. *Variety*, June 30, 1.

Slobin, Mark. 1993. *Subcultural Sounds: Micromusics of the West*. Hanover, N.H.: Wesleyan University Press.

"The Smash Hits from 'My Fair Lady' Are on Columbia!" 1956. *Billboard*, May 19, 27.

Smith, Bernard B. 1945. "Is There a Case for Petrillo?" *New Republic*, January 15, 76–79.

Smith, J. 1959. "Sampling the Samplers in Stereo." *High Fidelity*, April, 41, 45.

Smith, Jeff. 1998. *The Sounds of Commerce*. New York: Columbia University Press.

Snyder, Terry, and the All Stars. 1959. *Persuasive Percussion*. Command Records.

Solomon, Seymour. 1959. "The Search for a Third Dimension." *High Fidelity*, February, 37–40, 130, 132.

Spector, Phil. 1991. *Back to Mono*. Abkco.

Spigel, Lynn. 1992. *Make Room for TV: Television and the Family Ideal in Postwar America*. Chicago: University of Chicago Press.

"Spike Jones in Stereo." 1960. *High Fidelity*, April, 94.

Stam, Robert, Robert Burgoyne, et al. 1992. *New Vocabularies in Film Semiotics: Structuralism, Post-Structuralism, and Beyond*. New York: Routledge.

Stanley, R. 1961. "EMI's Aussie Cast 'Sound of Music.'" *Variety*, December 6, 51.

Steding, A. 1964. "Headphones Up to Date." *High Fidelity*, April, 52–55.

Sterling, Christoper H. 1975. "WTMJ-FM: A Case in the Development of FM Broadcasting." In *American Broadcasting: A Source Book on the History of Radio* and *Television*, ed. L. W. Lichty and M. C. Topping, 32–139. New York: Hastings House.

Sterling, Christoper H., and John M. Kittross. 1990. *Stay Tuned: A Concise History of American Broadcasting*. Belmont, Calif.: Wadsworth.

Stockfelt, Ola. 1993. "Adequate Modes of Listening." *Stanford Humanities Review* 2, no. 3: 153–69.

Stokowski, Leopold. 1943. *Music for All of Us*. New York: Simon and Schuster.

Stringham, John E. 1946. *Listening to Music Creatively*. New York: Prentrice-Hall.

"Studios' Music Soundtrack Pix Still Nixed in AFM-Web TV Pact." 1948. *Variety*, March 24, 31.

"Suggest Pooling of Disk Sales Data." 1948. *Variety*, June 16, 42.

Tardy, David. 1959. *A Guide to Stereo Sound*. Chicago: Popular Mechanics Press.

Taylor, Timothy. 2001. *Strange Sounds: Music, Technology, and Culture*. New York: Routledge.

Teaford, Lee. 1948. "Why the Record Ban." *International Magazine*, January, 3.

Theberge, Paul. 1997. *Any Sound You Can Imagine: Making Music/Consuming Technology*. Hanover, N.H.: Wesleyan University Press.

"Threatened with Suit, MacRae Drops 'Fair Lady' from His Las Vegas Act." 1956. *Variety*, August 15, 55.

Tichi, Cecelia. 1991. *Electronic Hearth: Creating an American Television Culture*. New York: Oxford University Press.

Tosches, Nick. 1992. *Dino: Living High in the Dirty Business of Dreams*. New York: Doubleday.

"Truth Crushed to Earth." 1944. *International Musician*, December, 12.

Vale, V., and Andrea Juno, eds. 1993. *Incredibly Strange Music*. Vol. 1. San Francisco: RE/Search Publications.

Villiers de L'Isle-Adam, Auguste. 1982. *Tomorrow's Eve*. Urbana: University of Illinois Press.

Ward, Ed, Geoffrey Stokes, and Ken Tucker. 1986. *Rock of Ages: The Rolling Stone History of Rock and Roll*. Englewood Cliffs, N.J.: Rolling Stone Press.

Watergate: Chronology of a Crisis. 1975. Washington, D.C.: Congressional Quarterly.

Weiss, Allen S. 1995. *Phantasmic Radio*. Durham, N.C.: Duke University Press.

"WFMT Broadcasted from the Show." 1957. *WFMT Radio Station Fine Arts Guide*, September, 67.

White, Glenn. 1987. *The Audio Dictionary*. Seattle: University of Washington Press.

White, Llewellyn, and Commision on Freedom of the Press. 1947. *The American Radio: A Report on the Broadcasting Industry in the United States from the Commission on Freedom of the Press*. Chicago: University of Chicago Press.

"Why Foreign Broadcasts Must Be Regulated." 1946. *International Musician*, March, 1.

Williams, Alan. 1981. "The Musical Film and Recorded Popular Music." In *Genre: The Musical*, ed. R. Altman, 147–48. Boston: Routledge and Kegan Paul.

Williams, Raymond. 1981. *The Sociology of Culture*. Chicago: University of Chicago Press.

Wojcik, Rick. 1994. "Putting the 'Easy' in Easy Listening: Veiled Female Nudity and The Tiajuana Brass." Unpublished conference paper.

Wolff, Christian. 1993. "New and Electronic Music." In *Writings about John Cage,* ed. R. Kostelanetz, 85–92. Ann Arbor: University of Michigan Press.

Wollen, Peter. 1992. *Singin' in the Rain.* London: BFI.

Woods, B. 1948. "Disk Ban May Strangle Development of New Talent, Injure All Show Biz." *Variety,* January 7, 195.

Woodward, Bob, and Carl Bernstein. 1976. *The Final Days.* New York: Simon and Schuster.

Wormer, Otto R. 1962. "Letters: The First-Balcony Ideal." *High Fidelity,* April, 14.

Zhito, L. 1956. "Hollywood Tuner Up to Send Box Office a Musical Whirl; Ditties in Dramas for Disk Jockey Plugs." *Variety,* January 14, 1, 15.

Films

American Graffiti. 1973. Directed by George Lucas. MGM/Universal Pictures.

Batman. 1989. Directed by Tim Burton. Warner Brothers.

Breakfast at Tiffanys. 1961. Directed by Blake Edwards. Paramount Pictures.

Bugsy. 1991. Directed by Barry Levinson. TriStar Pictures.

Casino. 1995. Directed by Martin Scorsese. Universal Pictures.

Dick. 1999. Directed by Andrew Fleming. Columbia Pictures.

Fantasia. 1940. Directed by James Algar et al. RKO Radio Pictures.

Funny Face. 1957. Directed by Stanley Donen. Paramount Pictures.

Go, Johnny, Go! 1958. Directed by Paul Landres. Valiant Pictures.

Hawaiian Village Nights. 1958. Directed by Alfred Apaka. ABC-Paramount.

The King and I. 1956. Directed by Walter Lang. Twentieth Century-Fox.

Lady Be Good. 1941. Directed by Norman Z. McLeod. MGM.

Leaving Las Vegas. 1995. Directed by Mike Figgis. United Artists.

Mister Rock and Roll. 1957. Directed by Charles S. Dubin. Paramount Pictures.

My Fair Lady. 1964. Directed by George Cukor. FoxVideo.

Nixon. 1995. Directed by Oliver Stone. Buena Vista Pictures.

Pygmalion. 1938. Directed by Anthony Asquith and Leslie Howard. Loews.

Spartacus. 1960. Directed by Stanley Kubrick. Universal Pictures.

Summer Stock. 1950. Directed by Charles Walters. MGM.

Vertigo. 1958. Directed by Alfred Hitchcock. Paramount Pictures.

West Side Story. 1961. Directed by Robert Wise and Jerome Robbins. United Artists.

INDEX

Adorno, Theodor, 134, 214–15n16,
Alpert, Hollis, 51, 53
Altman, Rick, xli–xlii, 61–62, 75–76,
  199n8, 208n25
American Federation of Musicians
  (AFM), 3–47, 112, 192n1,
  193n6, 193–94n9, 195–96nn4–5,
  196–197nn7–11, 197–98n13
Anderson, Tim, xl, 201n4
Andrews, Julie, xxxviii–xxxix, 54–56,
  69, 91, 98–99
Arnold, Thurman, 15–16
Asch, Moses, 167, 212n8
Attali, Jacques, xxvii, xxxv, xxxvii,
  20–21, 112
Austin, Mary, 8, 13, 18, 24, 32, 195n14

Barthes, Roland, 62–63, 82–83, 123,
  132, 201n6, 204n16
Bataille, Georges, 213–14n12
Baudrillard, Jean, 214n15
Bazin, Jacques, 123
Benjamin, Walter, xxxvii, 105–6,
  115–16, 128
Bennett, Tony, 166, 211n6
Berger, David, xxx, 67, 192n2
Billboard: record sales chart,
  xvii–xviii
Blacking, John, 107
"Bob and Ray," 164, 208–9n27

Bogue, Ronald, 63, 198n3, 218
bootlegging: practice of, 37–38, 96,
  195–96n4, 199–200n1
Bordwell, David, 142, 207–8n24, 208n25
British musicians, 17, 43; unions, 44,
  197n12
Burello, Tony, xiii–xv

Cage, John, 109–10, 159
Campbell, John W., 136–38
Canby, Edward Tantall, 130–31, 138,
  155
Chanan, Michael, xxvii–xxviii, xl, 18,
  131–32, 135–36, 143, 156–57, 189n1,
  201n3, 206n19
Charlton, Hannah, xli
Chernoff, John, xl
Chicago Federation of Musicians
  (CFM), 12, 47
Chicago Recorded Music Group,
  xli–xlii, 84
Chion, Michel, xlii–xliii, 208n25
cinematic sound, xlii–xliii, 114, 121,
  192n11
Command Records, 125, 162–63,
  203n13
Como, Perry, xvi
concert hall aesthetic, 108, 110, 119–22,
  129–33, 143–44, 148–50, 153, 159,
  169, 177, 181, 204n15

Cook, Emory, 140, 165–67, 211n5
Corbett, John, xxiv–xxv, 84, 133, 205n17
Crary, Jonathan, 200n1, 215n17

Dannen, Frederic, 68, 71, 200–01n2
Davis, Elmer, 15
Decca Records, 19, 43, 66, 92, 197n12, 209
de Certeau, Michel, 195n3
Deleuze, Gilles, 63, 198n3
Demento, Dr., xiii–xiv, 210n1, 211n4
Denny, Martin, xxii, 125, 161–62, 210n2
dialogism, 60
disc jockey (DJ), xvi, xxxi, xxxvi, 40–41, 46, 68, 79, 93—94
d'Isle-Adam, Villiers, 64
Doane, Mary Ann, 115, 264
dubbing: practice of, xxxix, 19–20, 23, 52, 54–56, 79, 100, 110, 124, 136

Edison, Thomas: experiments in stereo sound, 122, 137, 201n5; phonography, 191n6, 206n19
Elsaesser, Thomas, 73–74, 77
Ennis, Phillip, xxxi, xxxiii
Esquivel, Juan Garcia, xxii, 125, 172–74

Faith, Percy, 87–90
Famous Music, xvi
Fantasia, 117, 119–22
fantasound, 120–22
Fantel, Hans, 141–42, 152, 154
Feld, Steven, xl, 158
Ferrell, Oliver P., 148, 154
Feuer, Jane, 62, 72–73, 198n2
Finnegan, Ruth, 202–3n10
Fiske, John, 60
Fly, Lawrence, 15, 23, 193n5
Freberg, Stan, 209n27, 210n1
Frey, Sidney, 167–70, 177
Frith, Simon, xxvii, xxix, xxxi–xxxiv, xli, 79–81, 85, 124, 133, 190n2, 194n10, 198n5,

Gaines, Jane, 84
Ganzert, Charles, 127
Gelatt, Roland, 189n1
Giles, Dennis, 73
Goldmark, Peter, 149
Goodwin, Andrew, 60
Gordon, Robert, 202–3n10
Gould, Glenn, xliii, 52, 128–29, 134, 136, 198–99n5
Gracyk, Theodore, xxvii, 123–24, 135–36, 202nn8–9
Guattari, Félix, xxi, 190–91n3
Gunning, Tom, x, 114, 207n24, 212–13n9

Haralovich, Mary Beth, 190n2
Harrison, Rex, 52–54, 69, 91, 192n9
Heidegger, Martin, 22–23
Hepburn, Audrey, xxxviii–xxxix, 51–52, 54–56, 89, 99–100
high fidelity, xxiii, xxx–xxxi, xlii–xliv, 105–50, 151–78, 201n6, 203n11
Holloway, Stanley, 53, 69, 91, 192n9
Hornby, Nick, v
Horrible Records, xiv–xv

Incredibly Strange Music, xxiii
intertextuality, xxxix, 51, 56, 58–62, 66, 94, 183, 192n9, 198n1
Ivey, William, 107–8

Jarret, Michael, 152
Jenkins, Henry, 60
Jones, Spike, 164–65, 209n27, 211n4
Jones, Steve, xxvii, xli, 169

Kaye, Sammy, 87–90
Keightley, Keir, xxxi, 129, 183, 190, 203n11
Keil, Charles, xl
Kittross, John, 32, 34, 40, 67, 192n2, 195n14, 196n6
Kraft, James, 8–9, 112, 203n12
Krauss, Rosalind, 213–14n11

Tim J. Anderson is assistant professor of communication at Denison University.